Feb. 19, 2006

Dear Christopher —

We thought you would enjoy

reading this on your birthday ski trip.

Happy Birthday

Auntie Ellen and Uncle Ride

SKI TO DIE

The Bill Johnson Story

JENNIFER WOODLIEF

books

For further information, contact the publisher at

Emmis Books
1700 Madison Road
Cincinnati, OH 45206

www.emmisbooks.com

Library of Congress Cataloging-in-Publication Data

Woodlief, Jennifer.
  Ski to die : the Bill Johnson story / by Jennifer Woodlief.
      p. cm.
  ISBN-13: 978-1-57860-248-3
  ISBN-10: 1-57860-248-3
  1. Johnson, Bill, 1960 Mar. 30- 2. Skiers--United States--Biography.
3. Downhill ski racing. I. Title.
  GV854.2.J64W66 2005
  796.93'092--dc22

                      2005016718

EDITED BY JACK HEFFRON
DUST JACKET DESIGNED BY ANDREA KUPPER & STEPHEN SULLIVAN
INTERIOR DESIGNED BY STEPHEN SULLIVAN
COVER PHOTO BY KATHY SULLIVAN/MOUNTAIN PHOTOGRAPHY

TO MILES,
WHO BELIEVES IN HAPPILY EVER AFTER

*　　*　　*　　*　　★

ACKNOWLEDGMENTS

First and foremost, I would like Bill himself to know how grateful I am for all of his help—his memory loss was a problem at times, but he always tried his hardest. Bill's family has been invaluable in my research of the book—a special thanks to Vicki who patiently and graciously endured my almost daily e-mails over the course of the past year checking and re-checking facts and timetables. I admire and appreciate your strength in going back to a time you had long put behind you.

The book would not be nearly the complete story it is without the full cooperation of Gina, who opened her home and her heart to me in re-living some of the most painful memories possible. The willingness of all of Bill's former teammates, whether friends of his or not, to step up and share both the positive and the dark times in Bill's life have made this a better book. To Blake Lewis, Jo Jo Weber, Andy Luhn, Barry Thys, Mark Herhusky, Doug Lewis, Erik Steinberg, and John Creel—thank you for everything. At the start of this project I could not have imagined how many deep feelings, and tears, Bill's story would elicit in the people I spoke with during the process.

To my agent Justin Manask, I deeply appreciate your giving me the shot. I also owe a great deal to my agent, Ron Formica, and my editor, Jack Heffron, who both excel at what they do.

Finally, thanks to my family: my husband, who—while doubling as a fact checker, an editor, and a therapist—all along believed in me as well as this book, and my children, who, while very young, in their own way supported their mom in writing a book about "the best skier in the world."

CHAPTER ONE

"It's a fictitious club we just made up, the guy who does my skis and me. Ski to Die is basically…we put our life on the line every time we go out on the course. We're out there to win or die."

– BILL JOHNSON, 1984

He was dancing around, singing "I Feel Good" in the start area. He told some of the other racers he was selling his Olympic racing bibs on eBay to raise money for his comeback, but most of them thought he was kidding. It turns out he wasn't.

The race starter, Kent Taylor, joked with him that if he crashed and burned on the course his bibs would be worth a lot more. Bill Johnson laughed. He was skiing in Montana in the Doug Smith Memorial Downhill Race, first run in 1948 in honor of a young local racer who was shot down in World War II, and he did feel good.

In the Big Mountain lodge just before the race, signing autographs and posing for pictures, Bill seemed happier than he had in a long time. Relaxed and confident, he teased the other skiers and coaches almost until it was his turn to line up. He would not crash and burn on the mountain that day. That day he would finish 14th, in a field of 92. But his comeback would end, nearly where it began, on that same mountain, just shy of two months later.

At the age of 40, Bill had already experienced among the highest highs and the lowest lows anyone could expect from life. At the time of the Doug Smith downhill, run on January 24, 2001, Bill told reporters he was attempting an Olympic comeback 11 years after he had stopped skiing competitively—17 years after he won gold—because he was "bored, broke, and wanted to have some fun." The reality was that he felt he was out of other options.

Phil Mahre, upon winning Olympic gold in the slalom in Sarajevo in 1984, said, "It's wrong to say this is the best day of my life. If it is, what am I going to do with the rest of my life?" It is a bit extreme, perhaps, for an athlete to be so self-possessed after an Olympic victory, but in a way it was a warning Bill should have heeded.

The consequence to Bill of being the best in the world was that he never really recovered from it. After his 15 minutes of fame ended, his 16th minute got off-track. Since the '84 Olympics, his life had largely been a series of missteps and false starts. He wanted to recapture the moment when he knew he could beat the world. He wanted, despite the risks, to return to a time when he was a winner.

Other sports legends have tried a comeback long after their retirement—Bjorn Borg, Mark Spitz—with the difference being that the biggest potential injury facing those athletes was a bruised ego. There was never really any danger involved, not like in downhill racing. In this sport, Bill and his coach, John Creel, knew that the athletes ski close to the edge, risking their lives every time they race. And Bill's style had always been to go as fast as he could in the dangerous sections. "Where everyone else slows down," Creel says, "he speeds up."

At the Doug Smith race, there were maybe a hundred people in the start area on the top of the mountain—other racers and coaches, as well as Kent Taylor, the ski techs, the slip crew, the Chief of Course, and the Chief of Race. Bill's presence generated excitement and a certain amount of awe, in part because of his goal to make the team for the 2002 Salt Lake City Olympics. The reaction was mixed, but most of it was positive—racers and coaches wishing him well. A few people thought it was a shame, sensing that beneath the jokes about selling his Olympic memorabilia Bill had real money trouble. And some of the younger racers felt Bill didn't belong there with them, that he had already done it and he wasn't one of them now.

All the skiers waiting for their number to be called were stretching—jumping up and down, getting their muscles ready to relax. The numbers were called out in advance, five at a time, and at that point—with less than five minutes to go (50 seconds between racers, assuming no one crashed or skied off course), most of the racers stopped making eye contact with anyone. Bill, cocky as he ever was, kept joking around, even as Creel helped him click into his bindings and cleared them of snow.

Ski races are timed by a wand with an electric eye at the racer's boot level. The racer's reaction time to the start is irrelevant—the skier actually has five seconds before or after the start to trip the wand. The start is now almost always signaled by a series of automated beeps, with a long beep for the "go" signal. In 2001, however, at this race, the signal to start was a voice countdown. Once Bill planted his poles in the snow, the start area became very quiet. Taylor had his eyes on the wand. Bill gazed straight down the course.

Taylor called "Racer ready, 5,4,3,2,1, go," and Bill propelled himself out of the starting gate and full speed into his comeback.

CHAPTER TWO

"Everyone else is here to fight for second place."
– BILL JOHNSON, 1984

As sports predictions go, Bill's should rank right up there with Babe Ruth calling his shot in the 1932 World Series, underdog Cassius Clay bragging prior to his 1964 bout with Sonny Liston, Joe Namath guaranteeing victory over the heavily favored Baltimore Colts in 1969.

Bill's was bolder in a way—Clay and Namath theoretically had a 50-50 chance of being right. They were either going to win or they were going to lose. Bill's claim not only required him to stay on the course and finish without crashing (hardly a given for any downhill racer), but also to finish first in a field of the 61 best skiers in the world.

Somehow, though, his prediction doesn't seem to be included on that list. It should be, and maybe it still will be; maybe history will be kind to Bill Johnson. Maybe the effect of a week's worth of taunts such as "I don't even know why everyone else is here," and "They might as well hand the gold medal to me" will soften with time. The country's tolerance for bad boys seems to have expanded over the years, but 1984 wasn't the time for such arrogance and the Olympic Games weren't the place.

On February 16th, 1984, Bill was the quintessential nobody from nowhere. He wasn't supposed to win. He certainly wasn't expected to win. In its Winter Olympic Preview issue, for example, *Sports Illustrated* didn't list Bill as a favorite for a medal of any color (instead citing Franz Klammer, Erwin Resch, and Peter Mueller).

Sports Illustrated did mention him as a "dark horse" and a "long-shot daredevil," and the fact that he even got that much recognition was due to a spectacular win at the World Cup on the Lauberhorn in Wengen, Switzerland, the previous month. With that win, Bill became the first American to win a

World Cup downhill. During the run, near the bottom, Bill's left ski caught an edge, and his skis splayed wide apart. He pulled them back together, but they split again, and when he dragged them together that time, one ski knocked the other ski out. His right ski flew up in the air, and on one ski, he fell over backward.

Billy Kidd, silver medalist in the slalom at the 1964 Innsbruck Games, announcing the Wengen World Cup for CBS, called the race like this: "The time, the fastest so far—but—Johnson is losing it. He's almost lost it right there. He's off the course, he's on the course again. Johnson's all over this hill…. I don't believe it. He pushes right to the absolute limit." Bill not only managed to finish the run, but win the race as well. John Tesh, announcing the race live with Kidd, got so excited that he jumped up and swung his arm, knocking Kidd off his chair. Kidd referred to the race as "one of the most incredible series of recoveries I've ever seen in ski racing."

For Bill to win with such an out-of-control performance made it easy for the press and other racers to view his victory as a fluke. Winning that way also made it easy for Bill, heading into the Sarajevo Olympics, to believe he could do anything.

Sarajevo was an odd locale for the Games, in that no Yugoslavian athlete had ever won a medal in the Winter Olympics. Jure Franko would snap the streak in 1984 by winning the silver medal in the giant slalom for his home country. Quaint by today's standards, the 1984 Games gathered 1,437 athletes from 49 countries (in Salt Lake City in 2002, over 2,400 athletes competed from 77 countries). Conscious, perhaps, of being the first Socialist country to host a fully attended Olympics, the locals went out of their way to accommodate the athletes, as well as the press and the tourists attending the Games. Service people took Berlitz classes to improve their English language skills. Taxi drivers returned tips. One morning, an American reporter from Detroit hailed what he thought was a taxi and rode for hours trying to reach Mt. Bjelasnica, only to find out that the downhill race had been postponed and that the man who had spent the day driving him wasn't a cabbie at all, just a citizen trying to help.

The Olympic downhill was originally scheduled for February 9th, the day after a record 124 American athletes in tan sheepskin jackets and cowboy hats marched into the Opening Ceremonies (behind a banner declaring "SAD," the Serbo-Croatian acronym for U.S.A.). But poor weather conditions on Mt. Bjelasnica—fog, high winds, and a snowstorm that dumped two feet of new snow—resulted in continual delays, which in turn, in terms of the skiing competition, resulted in a bored and restless press corps looking for stories.

There was plenty to report from the skating arena—these were the Olympics of Scott Hamilton, Katarina Witt, Jayne Torvill and Christopher Dean—but little to say about another postponement on the slopes. Bill, the kid who had always chosen negative attention over no attention at all, was quick to step in with a guarantee of victory. Despite the painstaking efforts of the Yugoslav army to clear the slopes, the race was ultimately not run until a full week later, by which time Bill had made himself the focus of the world media, receiving much more coverage than he normally would have and more pre-race exposure than he probably deserved.

The impact of the "vagaries of weather" on Mt. Bjelasnica was mentioned in *Sports Illustrated*'s Olympic Preview issue, and that turned out to be right. The weather, and the ensuing week's worth of delays, played a major role in the race. Just a week before the opening ceremonies, the whole city of Sarajevo was melting. Olympic officials desperate for snow got their wish—in the form of 80-mph winds and a four-day blizzard.

In a sport as psychological as it is physical, Bill had the edge in staying, or least appearing, calm throughout the cancellations and postponements. According to Erik Steinberg, the U.S. men's assistant downhill coach, "the Europeans were freaking out, going home [to train, and then return]. Bill was cooling his heels in the Olympic Village, chewing Copenhagen and playing pinball." When Bill passed the Austrians in the Olympic Village, he would laugh and toss out a "Hi guys! It's still snowing up there." Team trainer Topper Hagerman, who calls the whole Olympic experience a "sweet spot in time," had Bill playing basketball in the afternoons. "I would try to get him to go up on the mountain to make some turns, would say, 'Let's just go up for an hour,'" Steinberg says. "But Bill asked, 'Is it still windy up there? I'm happy down here.'"

Happy Bill was, in his way, which was sort of a slacker-cool way, and handsome, in a distinctively American way, with tousled blond hair and ice-blue eyes. The way he carried himself, he seemed taller than 5'9" When he was in shape, which he was in February of 1984, he weighed 170 pounds. He had the ideal physique for a racer—narrow shoulders and strong thighs. His classic, strong features and smirky smile made him, if not exactly a poster boy for the U.S. Ski Team, at least a favorite of cameramen from around the world.

The U.S. Ski Team was allowed to send four downhill racers to Sarajevo, but surprisingly sent only two. Bill Marolt, then the team's alpine director, set a policy that to go to the Olympics, a racer had to be able to win. Under the Ski Team definition, that meant that a skier had to have finished a race at least once in the top 15 in the world or twice in the top 20. Bill had obviously qualified with his win in Wengen the month before. The only other U.S. downhiller to qualify (by way of two top-20 finishes) was Doug Lewis, a wide-eyed 20-year-old from Salisbury, Vermont, who, as Doug puts it, had been "thrown together" with Bill since he was 17 years old. The two were roommates and teammates, but never really friends. Bill was, as Doug politely says, "a tough guy to get along with."

The press seemed to have a lot of fun, in Sarajevo and beyond, poking at the two Olympians' vastly different personalities. The *Denver Post*, for example, ran a story about "Brash Billy v. Delightful Doug," complete with various team-player quotes from Doug and anti-team, lone-wolf remarks from Bill.

Although Bill didn't have much respect for the concept of team in ski racing ("They call it the U.S. Ski Team because you travel together. You ski alone."), he thought enough of Doug's talent to treat him with a bit more respect than he did some of the other American downhillers. In the athlete's village, Bill and Doug hung out together by default while they waited for their race, often playing video games, including a simulation of the American hockey team beating the Russians, then Finland, for the gold medal in the 1980 Games.

They also endured together the pressure from the European teams, although Doug referred to it as more "Austria v. Bill." The rivalry was, at the time, right on the edge of good fun and ugliness. There was some sending drinks back and forth, but, according to Doug, "[The tension] was there. Phil Mahre, who would go on to win the gold in the slalom three days after the downhill race (thereby becoming the *second* American man to win gold in an alpine skiing event), recalls that due to Bill's challenging words to the press, the Austrians were "all out for blood."

Bill, outwardly at least, turned the repeated delays into a positive. Blake Lewis, Bill's Atomic service rep and undoubtedly the best ski waxer/technician in the business at the time, began calling them "fire drills." Sometimes the racers waited in the start house at the top of the mountain for hours, ready to go, until officials called off the race. Bill took the delays as part of an outdoor sport, but he did complain, as he did throughout his skiing career, about being cold. Blake admits that no one but the Norwegian racers liked standing out in the snow. "It's horrible," he says. "The suits aren't very warm."

It was in the Olympic Village that Bill and Doug saw their Olympic race suits, made by Descente, for the first time. The suits were skintight, made of a polyester-based mixture, which, by FIS (Federation Internationale de Ski, the International Ski Federation) regulations, allowed 50 liters of air per second per square meter to pass through the material. The suits would otherwise be too slippery, and therefore much too dangerous if a racer fell. All the Olympic Descente suits had the same design, with different colored candy stripes for each country. Apparently drawing the short straw, America got hot pink. Bill, upon seeing his suit, immediately declared, "Wow. I'll look like a fool in this."

A day or two before the downhill race, two sportswriters, Tom Callahan from *Time* magazine and David Kindred from the *Atlanta Journal-Constitution*, got a preview of Bill in that suit. They rode up on the chairlift, without skis, to the top of the Olympic downhill course, which started on the top floor of a ski lodge/restaurant, and walked right into the start house. (They ended up having to borrow skis to ski down to the next level—it was scary, they say, and took them a long time.) The writers knew that they weren't supposed to be up there, but nobody was keeping them out. It was snowing softly, puffy cottonballs landing on their eyelashes. They looked at the hole in the bottom of the start house, a chute with glass windows, and thought that throwing yourself off of it would be like falling off the world.

When Callahan and Kindred walked into the little hut on top of the mountain they found Bill lying there, just waiting, loose. His skis were leaning on the wall. He did not act surprised at seeing reporters wander in. "Most of those [racers] looked like they were wearing ascots," Callahan says. "There was a bearing about those guys that Bill definitely didn't have. But we didn't know then that he was James Dean. He was affable. I felt like he was trying to be cute for us. There was nothing mean-spirited about him."

At the time, Doug might have disagreed about the mean-spirited part.

On the Ski Team, Bill would do anything to get an edge, to put someone off their game, even with teammates—who were, after all, also his competitors. Bill would try to gain the advantage in any relationship, but it was more conspicuous in a team setting. On the road, for example, the night before a race Bill's teammates would get their skis ready to go—strap them up, put the poles on them, and lean them against the wall—when they went to bed. In the morning, they would find the strap off, the skis across the room, and the poles missing, courtesy of Bill. Nothing was sabotaged, just out of place. For the most part, Bill's teammates shook off that type of stuff.

Every now and then, however, Bill went too far. One incident that Doug will certainly never forget, and probably never forgive, occurred a day before the Olympic downhill. They were riding up the mountain on the chairlift when Bill turned to Doug and said, "You know what? You don't belong here. You should be back in the states running NorAms [a circuit of ski races in America and Canada]." Of course Doug belonged there, and he went on to finish 24th in the Olympic downhill at only 20 years old. It is unclear what impulse prompted Bill's comment, but it was the kind of thing that would lead Doug to say, decades later, "He could be the sweetest guy—polite, turn it on. But underneath it all…."

The American downhill team, such as it was, did manage to have some good times together. One of the nights prior to the downhill, when Bill and Doug might have wanted to have been, say, resting up for the biggest race of their lives, they decided to bypass the not-insubstantial Olympic security—video cameras and Uzis—to steal an Olympic flag. They teamed up to take a flag not for Bill, but for Doug, who wanted one. "Who better to help me?" Doug says. "He had fun corrupting me." They borrowed the Ski Team Subaru on some pretense or other, and drove around until they finally selected a flag located on a relatively remote stretch of road. They parked at the side of the street, with Bill remaining in the car as the lookout/getaway driver. Bill yelled to Doug when it was clear, and Doug scampered up the flagpole. He couldn't easily extricate the flag, and in the process of trying, a cop drove by. Bill yelled for Doug to grab the flag, and Doug reached for it and rode it to the ground, ripping it free as he fell. Meanwhile, the police officer either didn't see or didn't care what the Americans were up to, and he drove on by. With Bill revving the engine, Doug jumped in and they sped away. They kept the flag hidden in the team car for three days afterward "just in case."

Bill Marolt (perhaps unaware of the flag-stealing) now claims to have liked and respected Bill, despite having tossed him off the Ski Team for a year in 1981. "He was a bit of a rebel," he says. "Sometimes it served him well and sometimes it was a problem." Others, including Bill, remember the relationship differently, and even Steinberg, a big Marolt supporter, says that Marolt "never cottoned to Bill all that much." Steinberg recalls the Ski Team's position on Bill at the time as "'Erik, he's your problem. Just keep him out of jail and get him on the podium. The rest we don't want to know about.'" Blake Lewis astutely observed, "Bill Marolt was afraid to be embarrassed by Bill."

The fact that Bill made good on his boasts probably helped ("If you're going to do that, you'd better walk the walk," as Steinberg says), but Marolt must have been made at least a little uncomfortable by Bill's pre-race performance in Sarajevo. Some of Bill's responses to the media were calm enough — "My chances are very good. This is my kind of course." A day or two into the delays, Bill claimed to be "skiing better than anyone right now." When a reporter asked him if he was going to win the race, his response was, "Oh, yeah," followed by his classic uh-huh uh-huh laugh. And mixed in were those other, bolder comments, with which he practically dared the public to hate his guts. Steinberg called him the perfect American bad boy.

Some of Bill's remarks danced the line between confident and arrogant: "There's no doubt that I am going to win;" "This is my gold medal;" "Top three? I'll finish in the top one;" "Nothing can stop me." Others were outright cocky: "I don't know why the other guys bothered to show up;" "They're just postponing the inevitable." And at least one was nothing short of unsportsmanlike: "You ought to be asking the Austrians how they feel. I enjoy sticking it to them. They're rattling at the knees."

Then there was Bill's candid admission during his ABC up-close-and-personal segment that he had been arrested as a teenager for stealing a car (later leading to at least one European headline about the car thief stealing gold). The press also made the inevitable comparisons between Bill and the protagonist of the 1969 film *Downhill Racer*, in which Robert Redford played a self-satisfied loner railing against ski team authority. After Bill finished his first training run, an Austrian TV news team asked if he knew the film, and he replied, "I've seen it many times, and that's exactly the way it'll happen now. You can start writing your story. This course was designed for me."

Actually, there was some merit to Bill claiming that the course was designed for him. The Bjelasnica downhill course, especially at the bottom, was full of straight, flat sections. Bill was known as a glider, meaning that in a low tuck he could cover relatively flat sections of a mountain at extraordinary speed.

There were two elements to Bill's fast glide—holding a tight tuck and riding a loose ski. The key to a tuck is to be as compact and oval as possible to reduce drag. Bill's body seemed to tuck effortlessly—his armpits lined up with his knees, his elbows in, his back rounded, his head down.

In wind test results from the Calspan wind tunnel in Buffalo, New York, Bill was told he had 5 percent more speed in his natural tuck than any skier who'd ever been tested. When Bill folded his body into a tuck, he fell naturally into what Steinberg calls "a perfect egg."

"Aerodynamically," Steinberg says, "he was a freakin' bullet."

Bill believed that aerodynamics played more of a role in a downhill race than technique, claiming that while he only got into that perfect tuck position for 10 to 15 seconds on every course, for those few seconds he was gaining speed and momentum for the rest of the run. And Bill extended those moments as long as he could, holding his tuck on straight-aways and in midair, pulling against a desire to lift his head up an extra millimeter or two. "A skier can only see out of about 20 to 30 percent of his eyeball in a tuck," Steinberg says. "Holding that position is a bitch."

The other part of Bill's particular gliding style was to allow his skis to find their own line, or path, down the mountain. He rode as flat as possible, his skis floating across the snow. Most other racers drove their edges and carved clean, powerful turns. When Bill raced, his skis looked almost unstable as they wandered about the course.

Another aspect of Bill's success was Blake Lewis, the man responsible for designing and preparing his skis—the infamous Atomic red sleds. Those skis—and Blake himself, who sat next to Bill at his post-medal press conference, answering questions about the skis—have been widely praised as helping Bill win the race. In Sarajevo, there was a lot of talk, and controversy, about Bill's high-speed skis. Certainly the ski community agrees that they were the fastest skis in the world. Not the brand, or the style, or the model, but that specific, one-of-a-kind, individual pair of skis.

"The red sleds were magic," Doug Lewis says, laughing. "Different grinds, different materials, the moon was up when they were made, someone did a voodoo dance over them…."

Years later, in a low moment, Bill would attempt to sell those skis on eBay.

Blake, who sums up his relationship with Bill with a cryptic, "We had our moments," started with Atomic in Austria as a part-time winter job that ended up lasting ten years. He worked as an apprentice to the head of Atomic, training on the technical aspects of stone-grinding and waxing. He learned about using softer waxes for warm weather and wet snow, harder waxes for the bitter cold. He tested compounds, waxes, and grinds, honed edges for turns, and smoothed bases for maximum speed on the flat runs. He prepared some waxes to condition the base of the ski, others for use as a top coat. He also learned to prepare for dramatic changes in temperature and weather conditions.

When Blake joined the U.S. Ski Team as part of "race services" in 1982, he introduced the team to Atomic skis. His title was "Service Rep," the only service guy for as many as 3 to 8 skiers. He was in the factory when skis were designed for a particular skier—individual conditions, bases, flexes, pressure distribution— "soup to nuts," as he says. A world-class skier at that time usually had 12 to 14 pairs of skis a year custom-designed for him. In Bill's case one pair was slightly better, meaning slightly faster, than the rest.

The press reported that Blake slept with Bill's skis the night before the Olympic downhill, and although that had been the case at races in the past, in Sarajevo Blake locked the skis in a bomb-proof room to which Blake had the only set of keys. Blake had been at races where other ski reps destroyed things. "There was definitely a threat of sabotage," he says. In a sport where a few hundredths of a second often determines the winner, Blake was questioned constantly about the skis—what kind of wax he used, what kind of base, what the secret stuff was. "I was never evasive but never direct," he says. "I took a chance with the wax. Everyone had access to it, but no one wanted to take a chance on it. It was very fast."

U.S. downhill coach Theo Nadig and Tom Kelly, the slalom coach responsible for Phil and Steve Mahre ("the twins," as he refers to them), checked out the Olympic course the previous summer, long before Bill had been named to the Olympic team. Even then, Nadig, who had come to the U.S. team from Switzerland, told Kelly that the course was perfect for Bill, and that was while they were walking it on grass. With snow on the slope, especially all the new-fallen soft snow, the course was an exact match for Bill's tuck-and-glide approach. And, as Kelly says, "The mountain even had his name on it—Bill-as-nica."

In the training runs, Bill finished impressively—a seventh place, two firsts, and two seconds. He was always fastest on the long glide at the bottom, once by as much as .86 seconds. In the first training run, the only one in which there was not freshly fallen snow on the course, Bill used his race skis and finished seventh. He was .62 seconds behind Peter Mueller of Switzerland, but even on that run Bill was .41 seconds faster than Mueller on the bottom section of the course. Afterward, Nadig told Bill that if he skied like that, he wouldn't be Olympic champion. "That," Nadig says, "made him mad." It perhaps motivated him as well: following that little pep talk Bill won the next two runs.

During the second training run (which Bill won), ABC announcers Frank Gifford and Bob Beattie were clearly impressed with Bill's performance, and perhaps with his composure most of all. Gifford commented, "He's a cool one, he really is," and later, describing the run, said, "He stays so low and he's so smooth." Bob Beattie responded, "He doesn't try to fight these turns—if it means his skis going a little bit wide, he lets his skis flow. Look how low he is here." Gifford added, "He's either really cool, Bob, or he's one of the great athletes I've ever seen. Nothing *ever* seems to shake him."

Looking back now on his interviews with Bill in Sarajevo, Gifford recalls him as "a loosey-goosey kind of a guy, almost a flake, and so laid-back." In terms of Bill taunting his opponents, Gifford says, "You could argue that he was ahead of his time. It happens all the time now, but it didn't go over well then. It just wasn't done in that proper world. There were not a whole lot of characters. There were real gracious guys and then there was Billy Johnson."

To explain her brother's behavior at the Olympics, Bill's sister Vicki says, "When you raise yourself, you don't teach yourself manners." Indeed, Bill's mom DB (short for Dale Baby, a nickname given to her by an old boyfriend) was unfazed by her son's behavior. The day after Bill's victory, she told the *Sandy Post*, a local Oregon newspaper, "If he's been brash, good for him."

When Bill won his gold medal, no one from his family was there to see it. Long-time friend and teammate Jo Jo Weber once said of Bill's childhood, "Some people grow up on the wrong side of the tracks. With Billy, the train went right through his living room." As a teenager in Oregon, Bill lived first with one parent, then the other—and even with his older brother at one point—as a prolonged separation eventually became a divorce. According to his sisters, Bill was basically on his own after about the age of nine.

Chris England, who skied with Bill in high school, wasn't surprised to hear Bill taunting the competition. "People that have that kind of success," he says, "they brag like that, but they brag inside, they keep it inside. There is a filter in there. Bill doesn't have that filter."

For the most part, the other members of the U.S. Ski Team seemed unaffected by all the commotion surrounding Bill. Debbie Armstrong, who skied the giant slalom on the U.S. team, says, "It was some game Bill was playing for the entertainment of others. It didn't perk the entertainment interest [of the women's team]."

Alan Lauba, Bill's teammate on the U.S. Ski Team and later a grooms-man in his wedding, believes that Bill purposely used intimidation. "If he got the other competitors mad, riled up, then they couldn't perform," Lauba says. Billy Kidd claims Bill was playing with the minds of the Austrians. He was a street-smart kid and intuitively knew his prediction would just add to the pressure they were feeling." Blake Lewis is definitive when he says, "It was by design. It was a way to tick people off, to make them think harder about it. He knew he irked a lot of those guys."

Phil Mahre agrees: "Bill played it to the hilt, went out on a limb. Everyone wasn't thinking about their own game. The Europeans didn't like it, especially the Austrians. It was a slap in their faces."

Austrian skiing legend Franz Klammer, reflecting on the experience two decades later, may or may not speak for his teammates when he says, "Billy bumping himself up, he had all the right to do it. We knew he's cocky. We were not insulted. We all knew he could win."

While it is pretty clear that Bill was deliberating trying to bait his oppo-nents, Bill's sister Kathryn (who cringed a bit at her brother's brashness) likely comes closest to his real motivation. She believes that consciously or unconsciously, Bill was giving himself an added incentive to win. And what-ever the cause or the reasons behind it, that is clearly what Bill accomplished by placing his arrogance on display. He put extra pressure on himself.

As Klammer says, "If you say you are going to win, you have to do it." Steve Podborski, a downhill racer on the Canadian team, feels that Bill's attitude "made him go faster rather than slowed everybody else down." He says that Bill was trying to ensure victory by leaving himself "no graceful exit, no way out."

Continuing a theme that would carry throughout his skiing career, ultimately with tragic results, Bill told a local Oregon paper three months after the race, "Was I surprised? Not really. I knew at the starting gate I was going to win it. I was going to win it or die."

Klammer, the 1976 gold medalist, was one of Bill's main rivals on the circuit but performed poorly in training. His best finish in the training runs was a tie for 11th, and in one of them he crashed and broke his skis. Following Bill's World Cup win in Wengen, Klammer had supposedly referred to him as a "*nasenbohrer*" — a term that means a novice but is literally translated as "nosepicker" — and much was made of this rivalry at the Sarajevo Games.

For the record, Klammer denies verbalizing this infamous insult ("I didn't bring it up, it was not actually my invention"), placing the blame on Austrian teammate Erwin Resch. He does, however, admit that he, along with the rest of the Austrian team, was *thinking* it.

The Austrians and the Swiss, however, recovered from the shock of Bill's win in 1984, and they genuinely congratulated each other at the finish lines of races from that point forward. In December 2003 at Klammer's 50th birthday party, the Austrian "nemesis" presented Bill personally with a generous grant from his foundation to help with living expenses and medical bills.

Klammer now says, "Billy was fast, and he thought he could do it. The real advantage he had? Confidence. He was always convinced he could do it. It brought him up to the top tier. That's what it's all about in racing, that's what you have to have." Then again there is a glimpse of the old rivalry in his matter-of-fact comments about Bill's win being course-specific: "He showed up as a glider. He couldn't really make turns. [The Austrian team] didn't find the right equipment for that course. It suited him very well. Not too difficult. Any other downhill he could not have won."

Upon hearing these types of comments following the race, Bill's response was always, "If it was so easy, why didn't they win it?"

In the end, Bill's volatile temperament proved to be one that worked well on a mountain but not so successfully anywhere else. "He didn't need to fit in a mold, he didn't need to stay in shape," Blake says. "He said 'I can ski fast or I can't.' The rules didn't apply to Bill. He used other criteria."

Many top athletes, in skiing as well as in other sports, make it their own way, winning with techniques that coaches do not teach, but having his own path didn't stop Bill from pushing and challenging everyone around him. He rarely said thank you, at least not genuinely, and he never said he was sorry, which his teammates say would have helped. Those closest to him seem to know that he was appreciative of their support. "At the time I was one of the best technicians in the world," Blake says. "Bill acknowledged it on some level."

Phil Mahre, whose even-keeled personality seems completely at odds with Bill's nature, graciously refers to him as "an individual, a loner." In saying that Bill wasn't a team player, Phil also makes the point that skiing is not necessarily a team sport. He goes on to say, somewhat understatedly, "I don't think Bill had good people skills. He didn't deal with people one on one very well."

Steinberg, Bill's coach, is more direct: "He didn't play well with others."

Bill had no time for people who didn't share his focus or perspective. And often his point of view did seem to make sense in a quirky sort of way. He didn't agree with his coaches, for example, when they wanted him to watch film of his mistakes so they could point out what he was doing wrong. He believed there were lots of racers skiing better than him at the time, and he would prefer to watch them to see what they were doing *right*.

"He was his own person," Phil says. "He said what he felt and he didn't worry about the consequences." Bill's failure to accept, or seemingly even consider, the consequences of his actions would cause problems for him more than once. It would play out in the future, for example, as an undesirable trait for a husband and father. Later, this characteristic would shape-shift to self-destructiveness, even nihilism.

"You couldn't tell Bill he couldn't do something," Phil says. "He wasn't going to step down. He was very, very strong-willed. He was going to do it his way, and if people didn't like it, that was their problem, not his."

Then there was his raw intelligence, not just street-smart cunning but innate intellect. He was a master at crossword puzzles and chess, a tournament-level bridge player. His sister Vicki recalls that shortly after the Olympics Bill scored a 139 on a home IQ test. If that is true, even give or take a few points, that puts him at an extremely high level of intelligence. (Only about 2 percent of the population scores over a 130, and scores of

140 and above are generally considered to be genius level.) Blake says that Bill was "crazy-intelligent," and Doug comments, "Bill was smart. *Smart.* Unbelievably smart. Weird smart."

Bill's intelligence—or at least his psychological makeup—was obviously an asset to his performance. According to Nadig, Bill trained himself to concentrate totally on what he was doing at the moment he was doing it. Topper, the team trainer, whose emphasis was obviously on conditioning, believes that while Bill had the athletic ability to do anything he wanted, more than that he had "an incredible mental focus." Marolt perhaps sums it up the most concisely: "He was physically strong and mentally strong. And he wanted it."

The desire to win was clearly there, but it was still unlikely that Bill would do it. No American had ever won an Olympic downhill. In fact, no American male had ever won a medal of any color in an Olympic downhill. Since downhill skiing made its debut in the Garmisch-Partenkirchen Olympics in 1936 as part of a combined event, no American male had finished better than fifth. The European dominance of the sport made the idea of an American win akin to the Jamaicans winning the bobsled.

Further, no American male had ever won gold in *any* Olympic alpine event (alpine skiing, as distinguished from cross-country skiing or ski-jumping, has five separate events: downhill, slalom, giant slalom, Super-G, and combined). In 1964, Billy Kidd and Jimmy Heuga finished second and third in the slalom in Innsbruck, and then in 1980 Phil Mahre took silver in the slalom in Lake Placid. Mostly, though, U.S. alpine skiing was noted for a series of disasters. In 1960, Buddy Werner broke his leg in training eight weeks before the Games in Squaw Valley (and later, in 1964, died in an avalanche in Switzerland). In 1968, Moose Barrows broke his back during the downhill race in the Grenoble Olympics. In 1972, Eric Poulsen was sent home from Sapporo after dislocating his wrist and tearing knee ligaments the day before the Olympic competition.

Nevertheless, the U.S. Ski Team believed. Bill might have come out of nowhere as far as the press and the public was concerned, but Ski Team members—coaches and teammates—were absolutely convinced that Bill would win. In early 1984, the Ski Team bulletin stated that U.S. coaches expected Bill to occasionally finish in the top 15. By the time the team arrived in Sarajevo, perspectives had changed.

Marolt says, "I thought he would win. He was training too well, going too fast. If he had his run on that course…." Steinberg was similarly convinced. "Oh, I knew he would win," he says. "I would have bet everything I owned."

Doug Lewis also had no doubt. "I knew he was gonna win. I wish I was a betting man." Reflecting back on that time now, Doug looks in the distance, shakes his head, says it again: "I knew he was gonna win."

Even Topper, who tends to understate things—expressing, for example, Bill's temper in terms of him being "grumpy" – says, "I had a good feeling. He was running well. He was running really well."

And, of course, no one believed more strongly than Bill himself. There is a difference between an athlete thinking he can win and knowing he can do so, and Bill, in almost an eerie way, genuinely, absolutely knew that the gold medal was his. His teammates, his coaches, his trainer, and his ski rep all believed that Bill believed he was going to finish on top. Jo Jo Weber says simply, "Bill never thought he *wasn't* going to win."

Bill would later convey the same certainty to the *Los Angeles Times* that he gave to the local Oregon newspaper, but he suggested a reason of sorts: "I knew I was gonna win. It was just in the cards. " Afterward, Bill also told the press that it had been his destiny to win.

On February 16th, Bill woke up feeling nervous for the first time all week. The day was sunny and cold, with a dense cloud hanging over the summit and the first 100 yards of the course. Blake's preparations matched the conditions perfectly—he had prepared three pairs of skis (for warmer or colder weather), but he had correctly waxed Bill's red sleds for new, medium-cold snow.

Bill was set to race sixth, according to a random draw. In the starting gate, elevation 6800 feet, Topper rubbed Bill down, keeping his lower back and hamstrings loose. There were some nerves, a little tension in the air, but Topper describes Bill as "intense, focused, and ready to ski."

Nadig believed that Bjelasnica was Bill's course, but there was one especially difficult section, about 300 meters long, that concerned him. He was convinced that if Bill didn't make a mistake there, he could win. As a result, he posted all three of his assistant coaches along only that stretch of the course—which the Europeans thought was crazy. The coaches observed the changing conditions there—the ice, the temperature, how the snow was developing—and reported it to the starting area.

Skiing on ice was not Bill's strength. He had learned to ski in the western part of the United States, where the slopes are not as icy as in other parts of the country or the rest of the world. The European teams knew this, and according to Nadig, they responded by pressuring the organizers to ice the course. It is not completely unusual for a course to be iced before a race, but here, Nadig states that it happened solely because no one wanted an American to win. Based on information he learned from his European contacts, Nadig claims that the Sarajevo downhill course was iced only after the Swiss and Austrian teams used their influence to push for it to happen.

As a result of the icy conditions, Bill had to change his line down the mountain. "We found a special line for him," Nadig says. "A completely different line for him."

Up at the starting gate, Bill was talking very little. He says he was thinking only about the first turn. Bill and Blake had their own roles, with Bill confident that Blake had taken care of his equipment so he didn't have to worry about it, and their own routine—talking about girls and baseball and other skiers' quirks, anything but the race at hand. Blake was trying to keep it loose, singing a song. As Bill prepared to leave the gate, Topper simply told him, "Let's get after it."

Out of the start, Bill was pulling hard. Coming out of the first gate, the clouds were moving in and out and it was difficult for him to see. Both Blake and Topper, watching from the top, saw Bill slip out of the starting gate and almost fall. One of his skis slid out, and he caught his ski and his pole. Looking back today, Bill recalls the slight slide at the beginning of the run, saying it happened because, "I ran it with plans to win so I had to risk it all, all the way down."

He brought his skis back together almost instantly and kept going. He wasn't sure if he was going to be able to see the rest of the course, but once he got past that first part the sky was clear the whole way down. At the top of the run, after Blake saw Bill's slip and quick recovery, he headed to the bottom of the mountain. He recalls his trip down as especially quiet. He had turned off his radio, not wanting to hear the reports. Topper, however, was monitoring Bill's progress on his way down, and he knew something special was happening.

Although Bill never excelled at turning, Nadig figured that he could lose time (as much as .8 seconds) on the two sharp turns at the top as well as the midsection turns and still make up enough time on the bottom part of the run to win. Bill looked smooth going through the first turns. Spectators didn't see him carve an edge, just a slide, fast, and then he was past them. Only Peter Mueller was faster in that section, by .17 seconds.

Bill continued to transfer his speed evenly, his skis fluttering across the fresh snow. On the critical midcourse turns he lost a little time—Mueller and Pirmin Zurbriggen from Switzerland and Anton Steiner and Helmut Hoeflehner from Austria were all faster there—but his split at that point was fourth best, only .56 of a second behind Mueller.

On the lower part of the course, a long coast to the finish over a couple of fast jumps, Bill made up all that time and more. He tucked. He glided. He flowed over the jumps with the softest of touches on the landings, seamlessly carrying his speed from the air back to the snow. And he was, predictably, the fastest racer on the bottom section of the course. His average speed for the run was 64.75 mph, and he reached speeds of over 75 mph during the course of the race. He crossed the finish line with a time of 1:45.59.

When his time flashed, Frank Gifford, announcing the race for ABC, cautiously said, "Yes…" and Bob Beattie, referring to Bill having beaten the time of Zurbriggen, who had raced before him, shouted, "Yes, he's done it! He's done it!" Bill still, however, had to wait and watch 55 more skiers race. Ultimately, Bill won the race by .27, an eternity in ski-racing terms. Over twenty years later, Gifford still recalls his reaction: "Stunned."

Peter Mueller took silver for Switzerland, and Anton Steiner represented Austria with the bronze. Zurbriggen finished fourth (and would go on to win the event at the 1988 Olympics). Klammer, who claims not to recall his placement ("I don't remember. Anything out of the top three, I don't care."), ended up 10th.

"Bill won because he wanted to win," Nadig says. "And not because he was specially gifted. He had this ability, this kind of determination." Nadig, who had worked with plenty of Olympic medalists in his native Switzerland before coming to the U.S., had never seen anyone quite like Bill with respect to that quality. "When Bill wanted to do it," Nadig says, "he could do it."

By the time Blake got to the bottom of the mountain, the race was not over but most of the skiers had already raced— "Only the Prince of Mexico or something was left," Blake says—and he knew Bill had won. Bill was in the press area at the finish line. "Bill," Blake says, "was pretty excited."

Bill was quotable as ever, with comments like, "I'm number one, heh-heh-heh." But he dropped the bravado for at least a moment, seeming earnest and proud and ultimately sincere when he told reporters, "It's just my kinda course and this is my kinda day."

At the finish area, Nadig and Topper sat on a hay bale slightly away from the crowd. From there they watched the scene—journalists crowding around Bill and running after him and Bill, triumphant, raising his hands in the air—and Topper turned to Nadig and said, "Theo, we just created a monster."

Pushing his way through this crowd, Blake's priority, given the time that had gone into preparing them, was to safeguard the red sleds and swap them for training skis. (Virtually all of the photos of Bill taken at the finish area are of him posing with a pair of Atomic training skis, not the actual red sleds.) In lieu of congratulations, Blake's first and only comment to Bill at the finish line was, "Gimme the skis."

Within minutes of the end of the race Marolt was giving his own interviews to the press, and Bill couldn't resist taking a jab at him. "Look at him taking all the credit," he said. "I thought it was me in the starting gate." As Blake describes the situation, "The team enjoyed the success, but Bill wasn't a team guy. There was a lot of friction."

If Bill wore his bitterness a bit too openly, he wasn't completely off in his assessment. Marolt, as one might expect, is a consummate politician, but he is first and foremost a cheerleader for the U. S. Ski Team, and he did, in fact, claim a team victory. He didn't take credit for Bill's win for himself, but even now he calls it a "tribute to our entire organization" and ascribes it to Bill having "a cool team around him" who knew how to "manage" him. Given the enormity of the achievement, beating the Europeans in their own backyard, maybe it isn't surprising that Marolt felt there was enough success to share. "With the Europeans, when it came to downhill, that was sacred to them," he says. "And Bill did this thing. It was a huge accomplishment. An awesome accomplishment."

Following the press crush at the finish line, Bill had to report to the drug test required of all athletes who medaled. Concerned about the test, he hadn't chewed tobacco all day (immediately upon passing it, he resumed chewing). In fact, when officials offered Bill some beer to expedite the production of urine for his test, he declined lest alcohol show up in the results and somehow disqualify him.

Officially drug-free, Bill packed up for the two-hour drive back to the Olympic Village and the medal ceremony. He was misty-eyed on the podium, standing above the Austrian and Swiss skiers. He took a deep swallow and mouthed the words while "The Star-Spangled Banner" played.

Current World Cup overall title holder Bode Miller, age six at the time, recalls the image of Bill on the victory stand even more than his winning run. "He was tearing up, all emotional," Miller says. "It was a good visual as a little kid."

The American anthem didn't play many times in 1984. The U.S. won eight medals in Sarajevo, only four of them gold. Of those, five medals (and three of the gold) were won by ski racers. On February 19th, Phil Mahre won gold in the slalom, and his twin brother, Steve, was right behind him for the silver. Debbie Armstrong, at age 20, bet her coach $50 that she would take a medal in the giant slalom, then ended up winning gold. Christin Cooper won silver in the same event. The other medals won by Americans were in figure-skating: Scott Hamilton, despite an ear infection, won gold in front of a decidedly pro-American crowd at the Zetra Ice Arena, Rosalyn Sumners took silver to East Germany's Katarina Witt, and the brother-and-sister team of Kitty and Peter Carruthers took silver in pairs skating behind Elana Valova and Oleg Vasiliev from the U.S.S.R.

After the medal ceremony, Bill, Blake, and Theo Nadig were off to a press conference about the victory, where Blake was asked, "What's the secret?" (answer: "It's sitting right next to me"), and Bill was asked about the importance of his win.

In response to the question of what the gold medal meant to him, Bill's answer was, "Millions, we're talking millions."

It is astounding, really, that the instincts and reaction time critical to Bill on the mountain failed him in the split second when he was asked, minutes after having the gold medal placed around his neck, what it meant to him. To put it in context, he was jubilant and exhausted, and he approached the moment from the perspective of having been dedicated enough, as a teenager, to sleep in his car the night before ski races because he couldn't afford lodging, of having been committed enough to travel to races on his own dime when the U.S. Ski Team kicked him off, sometimes again sleeping in his car in frigid temperatures, once selling his skis in exchange for transportation home. Bill was a working-class kid in a sport long ruled by the rich. That's the viewpoint from which he responded to the question about what the medal meant to him.

The question could have been answered so many different ways—involving the American flag, or his dedication—none of which would have been a lie. Bill's answer could have, and probably should have, been "Everything," because that, really, was the truth. It meant everything to him.

Bill would later claim on *The Tonight Show* that he was quoted out of context, that the question actually had to do with prospective monetary gain. But even Blake—who was sitting right next to Bill at the time and who loves him dearly, who cushions the event in the context of Bill being "in a fog" at the end of a very long day—admits that the reporter just asked Bill a general, soft-ball question.

It is interesting to wonder about how, if at all, Bill's life might have been different if he hadn't come up with the four-word answer he did. Certainly the press thought that even for a bad boy Bill crossed the line with his response—for example, in a 1987 article in *Sports Illustrated*, William Oscar Johnson called Bill's performance off the slopes in Sarajevo "a breathtakingly outrageous combination of loudmouth immodesty and ice-cold commercialism" —and it follows that potential sponsors may have thought so as well, thereby affecting Bill's endorsements (or lack thereof) and his financial future.

Bill essentially called his shot twice in Sarajevo, and by winning the gold medal he was able to fulfill the much harder of the two predictions. His second one, about the financial gain that would result from the win, even in the '80s, a less sophisticated time than now as far as endorsement money, should have been a gimme. But ultimately, Bill's boast about making millions is the one that he did not make good on.

In many ways, if it is possible to compare one man's life to the scope and horror of war, Bill's life would come to mirror that of the city where he won gold. The 1984 Winter Olympics were universally considered a remarkable success—two weeks in an enchanted city that brought the world together at the height of the cold war. Serbs, Muslims, and Croats danced together in a rainbow of colors in the closing ceremonies. Less than a decade later, Sarajevo would be enmeshed in a brutal civil war. The Olympic stadium would be in rubble. Mt. Bjelasnica would become an artillery site.

The city has since been rebuilding, has even attempted a comeback. Sarajevo made an offer to host the Olympic Games again, in 2010. They lost that bid, but they were in the running. The city is recovering, and there is hope for its future.

Decades after Bill's Olympic race, Steinberg, a religious man, would admit that he had always felt that somehow, some way, Bill had sold his soul to win the medal. Later, when Bill's life began to spiral out of control, Steinberg claims not to have been so surprised, feeling that in a way he can't completely articulate, it was all part of the deal. But there, then, Bill didn't see any of what was coming. The night of the race, when Doug Lewis, after a late night out celebrating, came home to the room he shared with Bill, he found, for the first time ever, Bill already back before him and asleep in his bed. The Olympic champion was, for the moment at least, sleeping peacefully.

CHAPTER THREE

"Bill made his own luck."
– DUANE BRIDGE, co-founder
of the Cascade Ski Club

I n 1948, when she was 12, Dale Ethel Morris (now known as DB) moved from Wilmette, Illinois, to Sherman Oaks, California, with her brother and her mom. DB's dad had left the family when she was four and her younger brother, Bill, was two. Looking back at her childhood, DB says she was "an okay student with lots of boyfriends." She had very few female friends. Mostly, she recalls hanging out with boys: "All the boys that surrounded me did things like name their neighborhood baseball team after me—the "Dales!" That always makes me chuckle."

Around the same time that DB moved to Sherman Oaks, Wallace Lee Johnson came there with his family from North Dakota. Wally lived two blocks away from DB. She first met him at a Youth Night meeting at the Sherman Oaks Methodist Church.

"Wally was exciting," DB says. "He was extremely bright, sharp as a whip with a very high IQ, way above all the other boys." Wally also had his own car. Bill Morris, DB's brother, recalls that Wally was a tough macho kid, great with cars and good in sports.

DB married Wally on January 10th, 1954, while she was still in high school, and they moved into an apartment in Van Nuys, California. She was pregnant and not allowed to stay in school, but she finished her classes at night and graduated with her class. DB worked for her mother, who was a milliner, crocheting hats and helping her in the office. Wally went to college at night and worked on the assembly line at General Motors for a couple of years. He also pumped gas and worked as a machinist. Eventually he took a position as a computer analyst for UNIVAC.

Wally Jr. was born in September of 1954, just after DB turned 18. By age 23, she had had all four of her children. After Wally, Bill's sister Kathryn was born, then Vicki, then Bill on March 30th, 1960, in Van Nuys.

Born William Dean Johnson, Bill never had the kind of name that lent itself easily to nicknames. During his ski career he would sometimes be referred to as Brash Billy, Bad Billy, Wild Bill, Bronco Billy, and Billy D., but those nicknames were largely invented by the press and none of them really caught on.

Bill was about three when Wally and DB bought their first house and moved the family to Canoga Park, California. DB claims that Bill was always good-natured when he was a kid, but others recall him differently. Even before Bill started school, other mothers used to call DB to tell her that her four-year-old wouldn't stop screaming obscenities. During their upbringing, Bill and his siblings never heard a raised voice from their parents. In terms of disciplining her children, DB says, "An icy glare would do."

Looking back now, Bill's mom is almost motionless when she talks, not at all animated, allowing the modulation in her often muted voice to make her points. Her movements are controlled and deliberate. She is solid, sturdily built, heavier now than in her youth. Her hair, which she keeps natural, long, has more gray in it than blond these days, but she makes no effort to hide it. She folds her arms together frequently, emphatically. Her blue eyes are at their most piercing when she is angry or feels she has been crossed.

When Bill was six years old, his schoolteachers at Canoga Park Elementary recognized in him what everyone in Bill's life, supporters and critics, would come to agree on—he was too smart and he needed to be challenged. As a result, Bill skipped the second half of first grade and the first half of second grade.

The summer after Bill turned seven, Wally's job at UNIVAC took the family to Boise, Idaho. Skiing was the big sport in the area, and all the Johnson kids received skis for Christmas. Bill got on skis for the first time on a little slope in his backyard.

That winter, Bill brought home first-place trophies in his first season skiing at Bogus Basin resort. Bill's siblings all raced as well, but he seemed to have the most drive. In 1968 Jean-Claude Killy won three gold medals at the Winter Olympics in Grenoble with a form that involved sitting back a bit on his skis. Most racers started to emulate that style, but Bill continued to ski his own way, pushing forward, one arm back. By the end of his first season, Bill was the top racer in the region in the eight-and-under class. Bill's dad later told a reporter that in the late '60s Bill would sometimes win a 30-second race by ten seconds. "Bill always assumed he would win every race he was in," Wally said. "If he came home without a trophy, you couldn't even speak to him."

As an eight-year-old, Bill was kicked out of school for fighting, which in this case meant throwing a punch at the school principal. Bill's school counselor attempted to solve that problem by moving Bill to a school in a tougher neighborhood. DB approved of this solution, saying that within the first week, Bill came home bloodied and never fought again after that. "Well," she adds, "at least not for a long time."

In fact, Bill never stopped fighting, not as a child, not ever. In the decades to follow, Bill's temper and his fists would result in failed business opportunities, the loss of friendships, and several arrests.

Bob Hansen, a counselor at Bill's school in Boise, says that he disciplined Bill not by taking skiing away, but by giving him more. "It helped calm him down," he says. Skiing may have absorbed some of Bill's anger, but it was never able to contain it.

Two years after moving to Idaho, the family again relocated with UNIVAC, this time to Oregon. DB ran a secretarial business in Portland, then later worked as an office manager. Wally and DB bought a little house in Brightwood, on the Salmon River, about a half-mile from the Brightwood store. "We were a bit isolated on the mountain," DB says. "We taught the kids to play games and cards to amuse themselves."

On their own, Bill and his sisters learned to fend for themselves. From age nine, Bill got around the mountain by hitchhiking. At age 11, Vicki did the same thing.

Vicki maintains that her parents got her and her siblings involved in skiing so the kids would all be off on their own every weekend during the season. As their parents' neglect transitioned to abandonment, any semblance of home life basically unraveled for the Johnson children. According to Bill's sisters, Wally and DB had an open marriage, and they discuss instances in which DB would return home and tell her children about her exploits, including hailing down a truck driver/co-worker for dope and sex.

With year-round skiing, Mt. Hood was the ideal place for Bill to train and get out of the house, and he took full advantage it. Even as a child Bill glided over the snow like he had wings on his feet, but his type of talent did not necessarily translate to people expecting that he would one day be the best downhill racer in the world. Tim Patterson, a childhood friend of Bill's brother, Wally, in Boise (who would later handle some of Bill's equipment endorsements), says that unlike the Mahre brothers, who had obvious talent from an early age, Bill's skill wasn't necessarily in his form. He was good, definitely good, but he was a scrappy skier, and no one especially saw greatness in him. Bill himself always thought that he was better than he was. His primary talent was, simply, the ability to win.

Erik Pearson, a classmate of Bill's, first met him when they were about 10 or 11 years old. Bill went with Pearson's family to Bend, Oregon, for a two-day skiing event. Bill was quiet toward Pearson and his parents, but extremely confident in terms of the races. Pearson says that Bill wasn't cocky at that young age but just surprisingly sure of himself, announcing things like "I'm gonna win this. I'm gonna beat everybody." Then he would, in fact, do it. Bill took the championship that weekend, blowing everyone else away. "Every event he competed in, he won hands down," Pearson says. "No contest."

Bill couldn't seem to get enough racing or enough competition. He would compete in Mighty Mite races on Saturday, then race against older, better skiers on Sundays. At age 10, Bill was racing—and winning—against kids in the 13-15 age group. Even then, he was a full-throttle adrenaline junkie. He skied over huge jumps, flew 30 feet in the air and 150 feet down the course. One time Bill broke his arm on a jump. The following week he taped his ski pole to his arm and competed in a ski-jumping event called a *gelandesprung* at Timberline resort. Wally, at age 15, won the event. Bill finished third.

Bill's childhood coaches describe Bill as a talented but troubled kid. When he first moved to Oregon, Bill competed for the Cascade Ski Club's racing team, cofounded by Duane Bridge and Matt Greenslade. Those coaches would later send a telegram to Bill in Sarajevo that read, "Go get 'em, Billy, show 'em the heels of your skis." When Bridge and Greenslade retired in 1997, after heading up the longest-running race program on Mt. Hood, they were the first people to ever receive lifetime ski passes.

Bill's family didn't have a lot of money, but Bridge wanted all the Johnson kids to be able to participate, so he offered to sponsor the four of them for the price of one. They all raced that season for $75.

Bill was a quiet kid, short and small, and no child was more focused on his skiing. As young as age nine, he would wax and prepare his own skis, then put socks on each end so the tips wouldn't rub together.

Foreshadowing Bill's later opinion that a ski race should end in either a win or a crash, Bridge says that Bill won almost every race he stood up in. He didn't get many second or third places. He had an eye for the hill, and he could see how to get down quickly. If Bill hit his own line down the mountain, he usually won. It he missed it, he would usually blow out.

Bridge says there is no doubt that Bill had a genius IQ. In a sad twist given the injury Bill would later suffer, Bridge discusses the incredible memory Bill used to have. Before every race, Bill would start at the bottom of the mountain and work up, memorizing every gate. At that point Bill was racing slalom as well as downhill, with sometimes as many as 50 gates per event. By race time, Bill knew exactly where he was going to be at every point on the course.

Most of Bill's coaches say that Bill was a smart-ass even when he was very young. Bridge seems to say the same thing, but with a more positive spin. "Bill said exactly what he thinks, and he was always thinking," he says. "You couldn't stop him."

Greenslade says that Bill always had a shield up. "He was wondering 'Should I trust these people or not?'" he says.

On the Cascade racing team, Bill was a loner. He wasn't popular with the other racers, and just as in school, he wasn't close to anyone. "He wasn't accepted by the norm," Greenslade says, "but maybe he didn't care." To some degree, Bill seemed to have been separating himself deliberately. He often did things to upset his teammates like mocking them when he was in the starting gate.

While he wasn't friends with any of the other kids, Bill did try to get close to his coaches. "When he was real young he attached himself to you like glue," Bridge says. "He looked up to someone helping him, looking out for him." Bill's Cascade coaches feel that Bill acted out and sought attention because he wasn't getting much at home.

"Quite frankly, he was left to grow up like a weed," Bridge says.

"Those kids went through a hell of a lot," Greenslade says. "Bill's home wasn't a home to come home to."

Bill always tried to do a little better for himself, seeing an opportunity and taking advantage of it. Even as a child he was strong-willed and independent—Greenslade says that was because, "If anybody was going to take care of Billy it had to be Billy." He was very strong physically, he could handle himself, and he certainly wasn't going to back down from anything. "A lot of times somebody would challenge him," Greenslade says, "and you didn't want to do that."

Despite his temper, while Bill was at the Cascade Ski Club he was interested in learning and improving, and he respected his coaches. The admiration went both ways—Bridge is obviously proud of Bill. "He didn't have any money or any backing—he did it on guts and his own luck," he says. "And there wasn't anybody that did it any better."

After only a year with the Cascade team, Bill's parents switched their kids to the Mt. Hood Meadows Race Team because a coach DB and Wally knew from Idaho, Rene Farwig, had moved to town and taken a position there.

Steve Bratt was an instructor at Mt. Hood Meadows then, and later the director of the ski school. When asked about Bill the first word that comes to his mind is incorrigible, and he doesn't say it in an aw-shucks-he-was-such-a-prankster kind of way. Bratt goes on to describe Bill as a rebel who never liked authority. A bit of an outlaw. A good talent if you directed it. A racer who could have been a lot better a lot sooner.

Bratt feels that Bill's "emotional side" prevented him from earlier success. "He was moody," Bratt says. "And when he had a mood, he was kind of impossible. We couldn't deal with it. He didn't look at things the way other people did. He always felt justified doing whatever antisocial behavior he was doing. You were always watching…you always had to keep tabs on the kid. And sometimes you threw your hands up and said, 'Who cares?'"

Although Bratt saw a charming side to Bill as well, and claims, "I couldn't help but like the kid," he says that Bill was raw and completely lacked discipline. Bill's brother Wally agrees with that assessment, saying that since there was no authority figure at home, Bill felt, "So why should anyone else have authority over me?"

Most aspects of Bill's adolescent personality ended up staying with him as an adult. Even back then, as Bratt describes it, Bill had "this sense of rage, fire—an 'I'll-prove-it-to-you' kind of thing. 'I'll show everybody.'" Bratt also noticed that when Bill was determined, he could do most anything. Those traits would weave throughout Bill's life, turning him into the champion he would become as well as causing him, much later in his life, to believe he could do it all again.

Not all of the races Bill competed in with the Mt. Hood Meadows team were local. Unable to afford the hotels where the other racers stayed, Bill often slept in his run-down Pinto in parking lots and ate food he had brought with him. Named "Little Deb" for no apparent reason, the car had a metal pipe fitted over the gear shift in place of the original one, and later, a huge Atomic sticker on the back window. In freezing temperatures, Bill tried to sneak into his teammates' hotel rooms and sleep on the floor, but he was rarely successful. According to Vicki, since Bill wasn't paying, his coaches kicked him out when they caught him curled up on the floor, and Bill was back to his car. Despite the cold nights and the sleeping conditions, Bill kept winning.

By the time he was 13, Bill was racing against the 18-and-older group in the Pacific Northwest Ski Association and routinely beating skiers in their twenties. When he was a teenager, he only increased the risks he took on skis. A skier named Harold Burbank trained with Bill during the day at Mt. Hood Meadows and washed dishes at the lodge restaurant with him at night. Harold vividly remembers watching Bill run a CanAm (now called NorAm) downhill series after it had snowed for four straight days. The course had accumulated over six feet of snow and built up a nasty lip on the headwall of "The Elevator Shaft" section. The Elevator Shaft was so named because over the lip, the mountain fell away at about 45 degrees for at least 250 feet before sloping into a flat at the base. The lip launched racers into the air and down the mountain. Many kids were injured there, some seriously. Bill hit the jump, flew at least 65 feet up into the air, stood straight up to keep his balance, then sailed almost 200 feet to the bottom of the shaft, where he landed cleanly and kept right on going.

Although Bill was succeeding on skis, his anger continued to be a problem for him, even during training. "Sometimes he had a mean spirit to him, and there was a physical aspect to it," Bratt says. "It was really nothing to him to smack some kid in front of him in line."

Bill was thrown off the Mt. Hood Meadows team twice for fighting. The second time he got into a serious fight, an altercation involving a lift operator, he was kicked off for good. In high school at the time, he headed back to coaches Bridge and Greenslade and finished his racing career in Oregon with them.

Bill's fighting escalated when he was a teenager, but early on, both Kathryn and Vicki remember their little brother as a sweet kid.

"Bill was more decent than any of us," Vicki says. "If we got caught, he would put his hand up and take the blame. He was a little tiny tough guy."

Both Bill and Vicki skied for the Mt. Hood Meadows team, and in the last race of the 1973-'74 season, they both won first-place trophies. Bill's had a little boy on it, Vicki's had a girl. Wanting to go out on top, Vicki quit racing that season. Now estranged from much of her family except Bill, and living in Australia, where she owns and runs a wholesale jewelry business, Vicki still has that trophy.

Wally mostly recalls Bill tagging along after him as a kid. They would set poles and run gates together on the mountain, just the two of them. Their dad bought them a stopwatch once, and Wally made the most of it as a training device, running with Bill down to the gas station or the bank and timing the trips.

Bill's kindness as a child was apparent. One time Dave Ligatich, a childhood acquaintance of Bill's, broke his arm while skiing and screamed for help. Bill, riding above him on the chairlift, jumped off the lift to comfort him until rescue workers arrived.

But by Bill's teen years, that side of him became harder to see. He didn't seem to want to associate with anyone, and he never gave anybody the opportunity to like him. He didn't attend school very often, and when he was there, he got in a lot of fights.

Bill's classmate Erik Pearson says that Bill was unreadable. "He was deeply troubled," Pearson says. "Nobody understood him. People were afraid of him—they didn't know what was going on in his head. He was the kind of character that when he got in a fight he might never stop. There was deep-seated hate in the kid."

Bill didn't have any friends in high school, never even hung out with anybody. "I always wondered why he wasn't socially connected to other people," Pearson says. "He didn't do well with the, let's say, letterman-jacket type. He was a Jesse James character."

Lon Welsh, a high school teacher, refers to Bill as the kind of person who can "tell the system where to go and still survive." Bill's classmate Chris England believes that some aspects of Bill's character, while a problem in high school, were qualities that sometimes, in sports, make champions. "He was a loose cannon. He didn't want to follow the rules," he says. "And he was *absolutely* fearless."

Pearson agrees that Bill had no sense of fear. "For other downhill racers fear can be such a distraction that they can't perform," he says. "Bill didn't have that holding him down."

In terms of his athletic ability, Pearson refers to Bill as a superhero. "He was *way* better than the rest of us," Pearson says. "It was extreme talent. He was always the best at anything he did, always the best in his age group and beyond." Bill excelled at both diving and gymnastics, but didn't pursue either one. Oddly, although Bill was a natural athlete, he never touched any of the three big sports, never seemed to want to let himself get involved with a group. Even with the high school ski team, Bill would ski a few events and then be gone, always consciously ostracizing himself.

"People just basically felt that mentally something was wrong with him," Pearson says. "Something with him you had to be careful with, that alerted you that something wasn't right. There was something off with him."

Although Bill was never particularly big physically, he was always exceptionally strong, and what England describes as a "ready-to-punch-your-lights-out-kid." If someone made any kind of snide comment to Bill, rather than say anything back he would simply hit the kid who said it.

One time, in his sophomore year, three football players, all bigger than Bill, were teasing him for being odd, different. They were right in his face, in the middle of a packed hallway between classes. In front of a crowd of about 80 students with their mouths open, Bill took on his tormentors and finished off all three of them. Even then, he wouldn't stop hitting them until he was finally pulled off.

"People stayed away from him after that," Pearson says.

This was around the time Bill's mom and dad were splitting up, and everyone around Bill says that the divorce devastated him. "Bill had all this energy," England says. "He had other frustrations that were playing out in a violent way. His parents' [dynamic] probably had a lot to do with why he hit people."

Just as he had as a young child, Bill turned to skiing. He skipped school virtually as often as he attended, and despite an exceptional ability in both physics and geometry, he seemed to just fit in his classes around his skiing schedule. Skiing, Pearson says, was Bill's "vent out."

Peggy Hart, Bill's U.S. history teacher and guidance counselor, recalls that Bill didn't try all that hard academically, but also says that as bright as he was, he didn't have to. "He was very rarely there. When the snow would fly, he would be off," she says. "He was very, very, very dedicated to skiing. Other parts he was not as concerned about. He was so smart, but school was not important to him. I don't know that that family really put much emphasis on schooling."

During the first week of his junior year at Sandy Union High School (now Sandy High School) in Sandy, Oregon, Bill was suspended for a week. The suspension was the result of an incident witnessed by the principal, in which Bill threw apples at a car and then, as Bill says, "kicked the ass" of the driver when he got out. Bill claims that he was unable to catch up with his classes afterward, and therefore chose to stay out the rest of that year.

Bill's mom refers to his skipping a year of school as "an appropriate choice," noting that Bill "was doing well and always had. He never had to study, and rarely cracked a book open."

According to his sister Kathryn, Bill spent much of his year off tending to a garden—of marijuana—he was growing on the side of his house. He had started smoking pot as an adolescent, first experimentally with his brother Wally, and became a fairly heavy user as a teenager.

In a bizarre twist to Bill's skiing career, that winter, when Bill was 15, an age when serious racers were maybe a year away from consideration for the U.S. Ski Team, he sat out for much of a ski season, with no funds to race except for sponsorships. He did it for his mom. As DB explained on a *This Is Your Life* episode on Bill after his Olympic win, she commended Bill for foregoing a ski season because there wasn't enough money for her to ski as well. "He decided he wouldn't ski because I couldn't," DB says. "He was always very caring that way."

Vicki feels that her mom "did nothing for Bill's success but put a rock in the way." After Bill won the Olympics, both parents tried to assert their role in his victory.

In the final analysis, Bill's mom let him skip a ski season. His dad got him to Lake Placid.

During Bill's senior year, in addition to competing for PNSA, he also skied on his high school team. He formed the high school team, really—there was no team before that—along with England and Pearson. Hart, the coordinator/chaperone of the high school ski team, says that Bill had great timing, great agility. "You could tell he was above and beyond everybody else," she says. Every time Bill skied for the high school team, they won.

England recalls that Bill tried to make time to ski for the high school team when he could, but Bill's nonattendance in school was an issue: "With his family or whatever and racing with PNSA—he was only in school when he wasn't skiing."

England's older sister, Kim, was also a ski racer. Ironically, a quarter-century later, during Bill's comeback, Kim's son would compete against Bill in the downhill race in which he very nearly killed himself.

Bill's failure to attend school wasn't the only issue affecting his ability to race for the team. One time his erratic behavior almost prevented him from competing. "It happened at the bus stop," England says. "The kid Bill hit was not the kind of kid that got in fights. Maybe he looked at Bill wrong or said something. It didn't take much to get Bill going." In response, the vice-principal suspended Bill for the following weekend's race.

The pattern of self-destructiveness Bill evidenced, even as a teen, also resulted in the emergence of another trend—things tended to go Bill's way. In this case, with the team preparing to go to the state championships, Hart sent England to the vice-principal's office to try to convince him to let Bill ski. It worked. Bill competed, and won, that weekend.

Even with missing so much school, Bill still graduated with his class in 1977, just after his 17th birthday. Even now Bill gets agitated when discussing this time in his life, saying, "Anyhow my mom is trying to make it sound okay but it was not. I don't even know if she was at the house at the time."

This era—encompassing Bill's adolescent and teen years—was a particularly chaotic one for the Johnson family. Wally Sr. and DB were engaged in a great deal of drinking, partying, and dalliances with other partners. Vicki calls her dad a good old boy, the kind of guy everybody loved. Kathryn, who loved him fiercely, says her dad never criticized her, ever. True to that persona, none of his children ever heard their father say anything negative about DB, even during their divorce. In contrast, Vicki says that her mom "bad-mouthed [our dad] until the day he died."

There were financial troubles as well. After a few years in Portland, Wally got out of the computer business and started building houses, allegedly in conjunction with some less-than-reputable people. That business went sour for a variety of reasons—some potentially shady business dealings combined with one of Wally's uninsured houses sliding down a hill during a rainstorm.

The recession of the mid-'70s may have played some role in Wally's failed business as well. Bill certainly blamed the economy for his family's financial problems, a topic he supposedly took up with former President Carter when he met him at Crested Butte resort years later.

With Wally out of a job, DB arranged with her brother, Bill Morris, to hire him as a facilities manager at one of Morris's companies, a car radio import business in Los Angeles. The plan was for Wally to go to L.A. by himself to work for a year, at which point the family would join him. Bill was an adolescent at the time.

The job didn't work out. "Wally was an alcoholic—it was news to me, and an embarrassment to me," Morris says. "He was obnoxious, would cause problems. I was mad at Dale for not letting me know." Wally was also suffering from depression at the time, losing almost 40 pounds off his already thin frame while he was in L.A. Fired for having an open container in a company car, Wally came back home after about a year.

At that point, when Bill was 14, his mom, pursuing a job selling t-shirts, left him with his dad and moved to Los Angeles, ultimately returning a year later when a doctor she was involved with put her up in an apartment in Portland. Vicki says that she does not recall her mom ever coming to visit during the year she was gone.

With DB back, Wally moved again to L.A., then returned to Oregon with a girlfriend (Mary Ramirez, whom he later married). They lived on a houseboat in St. Helens, Oregon, and later moved to Scappoose.

The family house in Brightwood was being rented at that time. The doctor DB was dating gave Wally $10,000 on a handshake deal to buy him out of it. Instead, Wally kept the money and the house, but eventually lost both to bad debts.

A long time coming, Bill's parents' divorce was final in 1976.

The timeline is so confusing with DB and Wally going back and forth to Los Angeles and moving around within Oregon that neither of Bill's sisters can completely sort it all out. "It was so long ago," Vicki says. "It's strange looking back at it all…. We were all so fucked up."

Vicki, only a year and a half older than Bill, recalls "living wherever my head fell those years." Kathryn describes the time as follows: "I guess you could say we had an open-door policy. Mom was there, then not, Dad was there, then not. We 'did our own thing' at that time. We were a dysfunctioning dysfunctional family, but didn't know it."

And as the youngest, Bill was hit the hardest. "He had no parents to speak of," Bill's brother Wally says. "They were both into their own lives."

Wally says there was no supervision. Vicki says there was no guidance. Kathryn says they raised themselves.

Looking back now on his parents' role in his upbringing, Bill says only, "They were both absent a lot."

Bill can't or won't psychoanalyze himself on this point, but people close to him later in his life say that he was deeply scarred by his parents' neglect, by the fact that throughout his adolescence and teen years, his mom and dad essentially took turns abandoning him. As a result, he still does not trust easily. Forced to be so independent so young had another consequence throughout Bill's life as well—he was never able to let anyone help him.

Wally Jr., as the oldest, was by default put in the position of overseeing a situation that Vicki describes as "*Lord of the Flies*." Saying that their parents, "had no idea how to take care of kids," and moreover, "wouldn't come home timely," Wally explains that he at least had to make sure Bill didn't burn down the house. Bill's brother was the one the teachers called to the school office if there was a problem with Bill. "I didn't know any different," Wally says. "It was just the way it was."

People outside the family—coaches, teachers—could see that things weren't right. Even Wally's friend Tim Patterson, only a kid himself at the time, was able to recognize that, "No question it was quite a dysfunctional outfit."

For part of his teenage years, Bill lived with his brother Wally and Wally's wife, in a house in the middle of a strawberry field in Boring, Oregon. "He had to find a place to live," Wally says. "He was right in the middle of their divorce. There was no place for him."

Now an accountant living on Bainbridge Island, Washington, Wally ended up on as different a path as two brothers could take. The family resemblance is there, but superficially, Wally doesn't even look like his brother. He looks like an accountant—wire-rimmed glasses, receding hairline, mature. Wally lives in a house that he custom-designed, with plans in the works to renovate it. There is a new walkway leading to the front door made of stones that he meticulously hand-cut. Wally commutes to work five days a week—on the ferry—to his CPA firm. He speaks carefully. Bill's brother is reserved and steady, and he exudes stability.

Some thirty years after he was first put in the role of watching over Bill, Wally would reluctantly find himself in that position again, just for the evening, while visiting him in the hospital after his crash. Bill attempted to open the door to his hospital unit by punching numbers on the keypad, but he didn't know the correct code. Finally, he just waited by the door until somebody opened it and then slipped out. Saying, "It wasn't my job to police him," Wally didn't try to prevent Bill from escaping, but he did go with him. Bill, with Wally following, wandered around the hospital, looking for a way out.

"You know how you carry a baby around and they like to look at things?" Wally asks. "That's how Bill was looking around." Eventually they wound up down in admitting, where Bill located a computer and started hitting the keys. They were discovered fairly quickly.

Bill's hospital records reflect the escape attempt, stating that Bill was "agitated" and "went off unit." The nurse entering the notes described Bill's retrieval this way: "This nurse directed [someone] to go with them and coax patient back. Patient refused. Security notified to assist."

After Bill's parents split up, each of them found another partner. In 1978, when DB was 42, she met Jimmy Cooper, age 24 at the time, at the The Inn Between in Wemme, Oregon. With a bushy, extra-full blond beard running from sideburn to sideburn, he looked like central casting's version of a mountain man. Jimmy was authentic, though, and as laconic as they come. When talking about Jimmy now, DB uses a conversational tick she is probably unaware of, an ironic one given the color of Bill's Olympic medal. She uses the word "golden" to describe anything really good, as in Jimmy is "just wonderful, just golden."

Only a few years older than Bill, Jimmy never stepped in as a father figure. As DB says, their relationship has always been more like "peers, good friends."

As a teenager, Bill lived off and on with his dad and his eventual stepmother, Mary, in St. Helens. Mary says that Bill and his dad were very much alike—competitive, determined, intelligent. Bill, hurt and angry about his parents' divorce, clashed bitterly with Mary at first. "It was a very intense situation," Mary says. "I had to be careful how I approached him." Bill's relationship with Mary progressed to the level of love-hate, and eventually, Bill accepted her.

After Bill graduated from high school, he alternated between living with his brother in Boring and his father and Mary in St. Helens. That fall, when he was 17, Bill got into trouble for something other than fighting.

He worked with his dad in construction in the mornings—in exchange for room and board and $20 a week for 40 hours of work—and trained in the afternoon. In a later interview, Wally said, "Every summer Bill was a problem to me. He was always in trouble."

Apparently that $20 a week wasn't stretching too far, and Bill found a way to supplement it. According to Bill, he was breaking into houses, but he was never caught. He was also stealing cars, with a kid named Doyle Boswell, and selling them for parts. Discussing these events now, Bill remembers—and announces—the name of the person he and Doyle sold the cars to. Then, to protect that person, he slyly adds, "But you have no knowledge of this 'cause I didn't tell you."

Bill's memory of the car thefts seems clear: "I remember a few, the one we were transporting we got chased by the cops that night, and we stayed that night on the top of the mountain which overlooks Brightwood. Then we were in Estacada, the next night looking for another, one to steal, that is. And since the car broke down a lot we got stuck in Estacada and the same cops that chased us the night before recognized the car, and while I was sleeping in the back Doyle got caught looking around and then I was picked up sleeping in the back seat."

Bill was arrested for stealing that car, a 1956 Chevrolet. His dad got him out of jail, but Bill stole another car and got caught again. Then he had a run-in with a cop—an incident in which a security officer threatened to take a beer away from Bill while Bill was behind the wheel. Bill sped away, hitting the accelerator while the officer's head was still inside the car window.

Bill's later comment on facing three felony charges—two for car theft and one for assault on a police officer—was, "I was being a rebel."

At the time of Bill's arrests, his dad had already sent an application on his behalf to Mission Ridge Academy, a ski school in Wenatchee, Washington. Prior to Bill's court hearing, Wally called Richard Knowles, the director of the school, to tell him about Bill's situation. Knowles agreed to take Bill on. Wally brought several letters of recommendation from teachers and ski coaches in support of Bill's admission to Mission Ridge to court and presented them to Judge Frank J. Coumont. The judge was impressed, but wanted to talk to Knowles personally. Knowles recalls it as a one-sided conversation, with the judge discussing Knowles's responsibility to the court and asking whether Bill would be getting off easy if he was sent there.

Knowles assured the judge that Bill would play by the rules or the judge would be the first to know. Apparently satisfied, rather than sentence Bill to jail, or remand him to adult court where he could have faced prison time, Judge Coumont allowed him to go to ski school instead. As portrayed dramatically in the TV movie that would later be made about Bill's life, the judge told Bill something along the lines of, "Go to Wenatchee to school, go skiing, but don't even spit on the sidewalk while you're there."

Doyle, Bill's accomplice, didn't have the option of ski school. A juvenile at the time, he got two years probation for his role in the theft of the '56 Chevy. For various other offenses, he figures that he's served about five years, but he's been in and out of prison, doing time in what prosecutors refer to as an installment plan.

Doyle still lives in Oregon with his dad on a plot of land accessed through a road made of roof tiles. Various vehicles are littered about, including a CTRAN bus and a red and orange helicopter. Outside the house is a multi-story accumulation of dirt, which Doyle proudly confirms is "a dirt pile." It is there, he explains, "in case you need material to build a dam."

He has a full beard and very erect posture, and he dresses all in black, favoring silky, button-up shirts, sort of like a throwback preacher. On the kitchen table, as if preparing for a scrapbooking meeting, he carefully and painstakingly lays out dozens of newspaper articles about Bill, mostly from local papers when Bill was young. He also sets out a wallet-size class photo of Bill. He talks about Bill almost deferentially, describing a time when they were teenagers and lost in the snow together, unable to find their way back to the car. The cold was so extreme that Doyle says he was ready to end the pain quickly by throwing himself over a cliff, but Bill managed to grab him before he could. Bill talked Doyle down and eventually located the car.

Discussing his past, Doyle does not come off as a hardened criminal, but more like that lost little boy in the snow. He is shy, almost embarrassed. He does light up when discussing a car chase with Bill at the wheel, and the description of the car flying in the air sounds vaguely reminiscent of Bill on skis: "He was going 100 [mph] plus, the car [landed] so hard I thought glass was gonna break, it was side to side, on two wheels. I can't believe he didn't wreck."

Having escaped both a car crash and a jail sentence, Bill went off to Mission Ridge in 1977. For the most part, Bill did follow the rules there. As Knowles says, the fact that Bill "knew I would throw his ass in jail" was probably a strong motivator. Oddly, the fears most young men correlate with prison, such as rape or violence, didn't seem to concern Bill. Instead, Bill associated prison with boredom, repeatedly referring to how he "didn't want to sit around in jail counting cockroaches."

While at Mission Ridge, Bill attended four hours of classes at a junior college and four hours of race training daily, except Mondays, which were off days. On weekends, the training tended to go a lot longer than four hours. Bill was also working a shift that started at 5 a.m. as a dishwasher at the Big Boy restaurant. He was at Mission Ridge for two ski seasons, and while he was there, he won the Northwest Cup (a series of races for elite skiers from Oregon, Washington, and Idaho) in both 1978 and 1979.

Knowles says that Bill showed up at the school as "a rough kid with a street mouth." Bill stayed with Knowles for about a month when he first arrived until he found a place to live. Vicki makes it clear that her parents "never taught us a lot of class or tact," and apparently Bill's manners were an issue with Knowles—he says Bill "had to be housebroken" in terms of things like not eating peanut butter and jelly sandwiches on the sofa.

"He was pretty callous when he came in," Knowles says, "and pretty guarded for a young kid." Although Knowles claims that Wally Sr. pretty much only told him what he wanted him to know, Bill's dad, and also his brother, stayed in touch with Knowles throughout Bill's time there. Bill's brother Wally actually traveled with Bill to races during this time, encouraging him and helping him out with his equipment. Knowles says he wonders why he never heard from Bill's mom, but he didn't want to ask and "open a can of worms."

According to Knowles, Bill was not the most popular kid, but he does say that he could be counted on in tough situations—to spell the coaches at the wheel when driving to a race, to pitch in to help when a vehicle was stuck in the snow.

Knowles talks about discipline being the key to handling Bill, and he says he needed to use "tough love" with him. Knowles won't confirm or deny the following story, but as the academy founder, Jon Bowerman, tells it secondhand, one day Bill was having a bad day at practice and said he was going to go in. In response, Knowles told him to stay out and keep training. Bowerman says, "Billy said 'Fuck you, I'm going in,' and Dick [Knowles] punched him, knocked him right out of both bindings." Bill went up the mountain again and ran it right.

Bill wasn't laughing much in those days, but when he did it was with an extremely distinctive and oddly infectious style—sort of forced out like "uh-huh, uh-huh, uh-huh." Almost three decades later, Klev Schoening, one of Bill's teammates at Mission Ridge, remembers that laugh.

Klev was with Bill when he attended a U.S. Ski Team development camp at Snowmass in Aspen, Colorado, during the '78-'79 season. The participants were informed that the fastest skiers would be named to a team that would compete in Europe on the Europa Cup circuit. The race times were shared among the skiers and Bill was one of the fastest there, easily qualifying based on the criteria. At the end of the camp, Ski Team personnel brought everyone together and declared that despite Bill's performance, they had decided to "watch him for another year" rather than include him on the team.

"Upon that announcement," Klev says, "Bill turned into a wild animal. There were people in that room who feared for their safety."

Skiers accept that they are racing against time, but the concept that a skier's success actually relies on political clout, or that of the coach, is something else entirely. The idea that the sport was anything other than objective was totally foreign to Bill. "Other racers would have been discouraged by something that seems bigger than you, not just the clock anymore," Klev says. "But after that whole process, Bill put his shoulder into it."

What the Ski Team did to Bill at that camp brought out what Klev calls his "gritty bulldog determination not to quit" and steeled Bill for that type of rejection in the future. "What set Bill apart from the competition," Klev says, "was that he applied survival skills to a competitive sport."

The only comment Bill has now on the situation is that he "just wasn't getting anywhere" at Mission Ridge. Wally says that it was clear that Bill was the best skier in the northwest and that the ski establishment "really screwed him over." After a pause, Wally adds that just by being the way he was, maybe Bill screwed himself over. Possibly it was a little of both. But it's not clear that with his background, Bill ever really had much of a chance. Looking back on his own childhood, even Wally, age 51 now, says, "It's hard for me to be normal." Bill was younger, needier, more sensitive. No one ever seemed to take responsibility for him.

As he always had, and as he would for most of the rest of his life, Bill made things happen on his own. In an effort to receive more national exposure and assure that the Ski Team couldn't help but "watch" him, Bill decided that he needed to go east.

CHAPTER FOUR

"Gold."

**– BILL JOHNSON, listing his goals
on a U.S. Ski Team form**

It was Bill's idea to attend the Whiteface Alpine Training Center in Lake Placid, New York, for the 1979-'80 season. For Bill and his dad, money was still extremely tight, and the program's willingness to offer Bill a scholarship affected their decision about where Bill should go next. More likely, the appeal of the place was the small matter of the Winter Olympics being held there the following year.

Bill never talked to the coaching staff about his childhood, and Chris Jones, the director/head coach never met his parents, only speaking to Wally Sr. on the phone. Bill was only in the program for a year. Jones says, "He had no plans to be there longer. We served his purpose." In one season, however, Bill managed to make an impact.

"He was a smart-ass," Jones says. "No one really liked him."

On the way to a race at Snow Ridge, in New York, one of the coaches kicked Bill out of his van, announced to the team, 'That guy's just a complete jerk,' and told Bill to find somebody else to ride with. Bill got into a van driven by Teddy Blazer, a coaching intern, and began mouthing off. "Not in my van," Blazer said. He hit the brakes hard, slamming Bill's mouth into the windshield. "From then on," Jones says, "he and Teddy got along great."

The Oneida Silversmith race Bill competed in that day at Snow Ridge was a slalom, not a downhill, but he still won. Twenty-five years later, Bill would return to Snow Ridge for the 50th anniversary of the race and, his memories jumbled after his crash, tell a local TV station, "It's great to be here. Where am I?"

Jones, who describes himself as a strict disciplinarian, says that although

Bill was not lazy, he seemed to need people to push him to meet the team's physical standards. The evaluation of Bill's talent from the Lake Placid coaches, even with the benefit of hindsight, is surprisingly mild. "He was good," Jones says. "Real natural ability as a glider. A-frame stance and good feel for the snow. He was a gifted glider." After a pause, he can't seem to leave the compliment alone and he adds, "But that doesn't necessarily make you a great downhiller."

Jones, perhaps not Bill's biggest fan in those days, is unswerving in his evaluation of Bill's skills when he knew him. "I was not extremely impressed with his skiing. I had other kids that were better," he says. "He was the one that was impressed with his skiing." Asked whether he thought Bill would be a champion, Jones is quick to say, "No. I don't think anyone thought that. He was not an impressive kid. Not a really impressive skier."

Jones is hardly alone in that evaluation among the Lake Placid coaches. Dave Wenn, another coach at the program, was later quoted as saying, "I never saw a more disrespectful, uncoachable know-it-all." He has since backed down from that comment somewhat, saying, "Bill had a work ethic that was hidden in his talent," and, "It's not that I didn't respect his *ability*."

What coach Horst Weber recalls most about Bill was that he questioned everything and wouldn't follow the rules. In terms of Bill's personality, Weber says, "He was brutal. At the dinner table, or it didn't matter where, he was absolutely brutal." As for what it was like to coach Bill at that time, Weber says only, "You could not fool Bill."

About the most positive thing Jones, or anyone from Lake Placid, can say is, "Bill was, and seems to remain, a very interesting individual." But what was perhaps most interesting to Jones, what still seems to sincerely shock him some twenty-five years later, was Bill's confidence level.

"I coached many skiers with more talent than Bill," he says, "but not one who believed in himself as much as Bill did."

Jones ran into Bill in Mammoth, California, in 1982, the season Bill had been excluded from traveling with the U.S. Ski Team. "Well, they've got to take me now," Bill told him. "What are they going to do? I'm the best downhiller in the country."

"And he hadn't done *anything* yet," Jones says. "He really believed in himself."

The other coaches agree that Bill didn't lack self-confidence. But maybe part of what these coaches really saw, and failed to recognize, was a defense mechanism from a young kid, 3,000 miles away from anyone he knew, in a clubby, privileged environment, entrusted to coaches who made fun of him. The program was almost exclusively for younger kids, most of whom attended high school there. The coaches viewed Bill as an outsider from California (even though he was from Oregon and most recently Washington) and a skier who, at age 19 and not on the U.S. Team, was already too old to be trying to do anything in downhill racing.

"The coaches were sitting around laughing among themselves," coach Jeff Byrne says, "asking, 'Why is this guy here?'"

One day during training Bill rode up the triple chair with the other racers and coaches to the second headway of the downhill course, the only place snow had been made at that point. They were preparing to hike up to the third headway to ski down when Bill turned to the coaches and said, "You may laugh at me now, but I'm going to prove myself later. I'm gonna show you guys."

Early on, Bill's skiing career was fueled by the conviction that he had to prove his worth, not to himself, but to all those who had failed to believe in him along the way. With every new setback and each fresh rejection, that feeling only intensified over the years. His resulting attitude—what Jones refers to as "confidence way above his real ability"—undoubtedly made Bill a winner. It was also, perhaps, his undoing.

Later in the season, Bill won the New York State Invitational downhill and then was in the right place at the right time when the U.S. team needed a forerunner—a skier who goes down first to clear and check the course for the racers—for the 1980 Olympic downhill on Whiteface Mountain in Lake Placid. "Getting to be the forerunner—I have to hand it to Billy," Jones says. "He's a pretty shrewd guy. I wouldn't be surprised if coming here, he had that in the back of his mind all along."

Acting as Olympic forerunner was an honorary role only. Still, Bill later claimed that if the officials had timed his run, he would have won the race.

That summer, Andreas Rausch came to the U.S. team from Austria, where as the downhill coach from '76-'80, he had coached many legendary racers, including Franz Klammer. He agreed to coach the American team on one condition: "I will decide who is on the team. Who they race, what they race, all my call." He knew from his experience with the Austrian team that if he picked candidates with "beautiful motoric skills" who knew skiing, they didn't need to know ski racing. Rausch could teach them how to race.

With that in mind, in June of 1980, Rausch selected 35 Ski Team hopefuls to attend what he called a "talent camp" in Mammoth Mountain, California. Bill, at 20 years old, was already considered by Ski Team management to be too old to race. Whereas American racers now excel well into their 30's, the philosophy of the U.S. Team at that time was that if a skier hadn't made the team by his late teens, he wasn't going to. Jo Jo Weber, a downhill racer on the U.S. Team at that time, says that although Bill's age was the least of the coaches' problems with him, at various points the team definitely tried to play the "he's-too-old card" in an effort to get rid of Bill.

Regardless of how old they were, what Rausch was looking for in these skiers was potential. "Age didn't exist for me," he says. At the camp, much of which was conducted off the slopes in a gymnasium, Rausch watched for immediate improvement. He didn't want the guy who consistently finished second in the tests, but rather the natural athlete who could master things quickly and move from 25th to 8th to 1st place. That was Bill.

Looking back on Bill's skills now, Theo Nadig, the downhill coach after Rausch, says that after Bill's gift of sheer determination, his other outstanding quality was that he was an unbelievably fast learner. "If Bill decided to do it, and if he believed you, he could pick things up very, very quickly," Nadig says. "He would understand it and be able to do it."

In one of Rausch's exercises, he blindfolded each of the participants and told them to walk straight down a line 90 feet or so. Without being able to see, the skiers couldn't coordinate themselves and they all wandered off the line, many by as much as 30 feet. The second time Bill did it, he knew exactly what his feet were doing without seeing them. He was right on the line, all the way down.

Bill also excelled at the agility courses, which were sometimes timed, sometimes not, deliberately designed to put extra pressure on the participants. He was unaffected by the stress. There were 20 such exercises of motor skills and agility, and no one came close to Bill's performance on any of them.

"Bill was just *unbeatable* in these tests," Rausch says. "I knew he had it." Rausch did not feel that Bill had the racing skills yet—"He had the race technique of a 14-year-old Austrian," he says—but he wasn't concerned about that. He selected Bill as one of the top 17 racers from the camp. Without any funds for dry-land training, Rausch told the new team members that they had to train on their own at home. He made it clear that he only had enough money for 15 racers to travel to Austria to train on the glacier in September and that the two weakest skiers at a training camp at the end of August wouldn't go with the team.

Throughout the next couple months, Rausch called all the skiers to check in with them. He was not able to get in touch with Bill for over three weeks. When he finally spoke to Bill on the phone and asked him how his training was going, Bill said, "I couldn't do much on 4 x 8." Rausch says that his English wasn't very good then, but he eventually understood that Bill had been on a sailboat for the past month and didn't have room to run on the 4 x 8 deck.

Mike Brown, a downhill racer on the team, says that Rausch saw Bill as what he thought an American was—a cowboy. "He was an incredible talent," Rausch says. "But not with this attitude." At the August training camp, Bill was the weakest of the 17.

When Rausch told Bill he wasn't coming to Austria with the rest of the team, Bill was furious, but he didn't say much. Afterward, he wrote Rausch a two-page letter. In part, it reads "…and now I will train like hell because I will be the best downhiller in the world." It was signed with a smiley face and the phrase "Have a nice day." Rausch still has the letter, in his sister's attic in Austria.

After sending the letter, Rausch says that Bill was fully committed. They worked out an agreement in which Bill got in shape that fall and joined the team at the end of the year. Rausch says that Bill Marolt, then the alpine director of the U.S. Team, told Rausch straight-out that he didn't want Bill Johnson on the team at almost 21 years old, but Rausch insisted. In explaining why he believed that Bill's character could lead him to success, Rausch says, "Talent itself has never learned how to fight."

Rausch brought innovative ideas that had worked for him in Austria to the U.S. Ski Team. One night at a dry-land camp with the Austrian team in '79, Rausch touched the hood of Franz Klammer's BMW at midnight, two hours past curfew, and felt that it was "tingling, still warm." As punishment, rather than giving him additional workouts, Rausch told Klammer that he was not allowed to train. For two days Klammer had to watch his teammates, who were also his competition, train without him. Rausch says that there were no more problems after that.

The set-up of training together with teammates and then competing against them, alone, is a bit of an odd dynamic in sports, and it was probably the worst possible one for Bill. Viewing the other racers as competition rather than as teammates gave Bill free reign to alienate them, or at least alienate himself from them. When Bill first showed up, he told the rest of the team that after he was finished, no one would even remember that the rest of them had skied.

Erik Steinberg, the assistant downhill coach, says that from time to time his job duties included a request to "Take this friggin' nutcase away from the other guys."

Steinberg describes himself more as Bill's warden than his coach. Alternatively, he uses the titles parole officer, chauffeur, priest, physical trainer, and travel agent. "I saw his talent early on, but I cringed whenever he would qualify to go on to next level," Steinberg says. "Bill was a hard case. He was more work than your average six guys in terms of mental anguish."

Bill's first friend on the U.S. Ski Team was Jo Jo Weber, a kid with dark good looks from Chicago via the prestigious Stratton Mountain School in Vermont. Jo Jo, who had joined the Ski Team when he was 16, realized right away that Bill was interested in more than "getting the uniform"—he was there to win. "Billy showed up and the coaches told me to stay away from him because he was gonna be gone soon," Jo Jo says. "But I respected him because he was there with a plan."

According to Jo Jo, all the team members were warned to keep their distance from Bill, and that directive, combined with Bill's attitude, resulted in incidents such as the other racers tossing an empty chair away from the table when Bill tried to sit down with the team for meals.

Jo Jo saw that despite the taunts, Bill wanted to be somebody's friend. Soon they were rooming together, and sitting by themselves at dinner while eight other team members sat at another table.

Bill and Jo Jo shared a room at a race in 1981 in Vail, Colorado, along with Doug Lewis and a young racer named Matt Davidson. There were two queen beds and a pull-out couch in the room. Bill and Jo Jo claimed the beds, then, as Doug tells it, threatened to beat up Doug and Matt if they didn't make them Bloody Marys.

During a training camp that first season on the Ski Team, Bill also met Barry Thys, a sweet, burly kid with a mop of brown hair from Tahoe, California. These days, Barry can seem a little prickly at first, almost cynical, but once he warms up, he is open and funny with a strong empathetic streak.

Barry was 15 at the time, sick with the flu and heading to the doctor when he ran into Bill. Bill's first words to him were: "What's the matter with you, you pussy?" Barry says that he couldn't stand Bill that first year. At another camp toward the end of the season, Barry off-handedly threw out an invitation to Bill, telling him that if he was ever in Tahoe, he should stop by. That spring, with no advance notice, Bill called Barry to say he was coming over. That would become a pattern with Bill—calling someone he planned to visit only when he was in the vicinity of their place and announcing that he would be arriving soon.

He and Barry were far from friends at that point. "I knew him," Barry says, "but I never expected that he would actually show up and hang out. He showed up and never left." (Barry now refers to the phenomenon of someone coming to your house and sticking around as the "Bill Johnson syndrome.")

Bill actually stayed, on and off, for about four months. That half-heart-ed, insincere offer from a teammate who didn't even really like him at the time was the best option Bill felt he had in terms of a place to stay. He made a good decision, though—Barry's parents, Buck and Nina Thys, were warm and welcoming. The Thys's place was an open house of sorts—the living room couch was constantly occupied with a revolving cast of skiers who stayed with the family at different points. Bill started out in a bedroom known as Alcatraz (so named for a poster of the prison on the wall) and eventually moved his way into a bigger room farther up the hall. Bill and Barry ended up becoming so close that Barry was later the best man in Bill's wedding.

For stretches of time in the summers and in-between training camps for the next several years, Bill would often stay at what he referred to as "Hotel California" in Tahoe. That's what Bill called the Thys's place in a message he wrote to Nina and Buck on one of his posters, thanking them for supporting him. To this day, they still have it hanging in their hallway.

Nina and Buck are a gracious, sincere couple that even now cause people who meet them to wish they had been ski racers in the '80s so they too could have been taken care of while they crashed on that couch. The Thys don't just finish each other's sentences, but seemingly each other's thoughts as well. For example, when Buck suggests, "Bill was not the greatest skier," Nina adds, "as far as technical finesse," and Buck completes the sentiment with, "but he was dedicated to speed."

Nina says that Bill was not mean, just thoughtless and "blustery." Once, for example, Bill failed to get up off the couch he was sprawled on when he was introduced to the father of a girl he was seeing. He also used to make his dates submit to an IQ test. "You didn't expect him to help you put your coat on," Nina says, "but in his own way he was respectful."

Barry's younger sister Edith, a world-class ski racer herself, had a schedule that often intersected with Bill's, landing both of them in the Thys house in the off-season. She recalls feeling that Bill always seemed to be sparring with her when they talked, and she was never able to simply have an easy conversation with him. She liked him most when he was just hanging out with his buddies—guys who weren't impressed by Bill and who Bill wasn't trying to impress.

Nina says that Bill simply had no thought of how his comments were received by other people. For a while he latched onto the old expression "You're not a has-been, you're a never-was," and constantly chided other racers with it, even though it was clear that no one ever took it as a joke. Nina describes Bill's complicated makeup in the kindest possible way, saying simply, "There were so many things that fought with each other about Bill."

 Buck, then the president of an aerospace casting company, felt that going to college could do many things for Bill, including "smoothing off his edges." Believing that the Ski Team was as anti-education as it could possibly be, Buck tried to convince Bill to go back to school. Despite Buck's advice, Bill was adamant that he knew what was good for him. After Bill won in Sarajevo, Buck told him, "This is great, now you can go to college."

"This is great," Bill said. "Now I don't have to."

In the summer of '81, a few months after he first met the Thys family, Bill showed up at a dry-land training camp in Colorado Springs out of shape.

Bill was fairly notorious on the Ski Team for not wanting to train. Throughout his career on the U.S. team, whenever he disagreed with the team's physical conditioning program Bill would simply go free-skiing on his own. He told the press that he trained plenty, but preferred not to make a "spectacle of it" at "some rah-rah camp with a lot of other guys."

At that camp, Bill failed the physical conditioning tests, doing especially poorly in the 440 dash and the mile run. He had finished fifth in the downhill at the U.S. Nationals just a few months before, and while he admitted that he hadn't been doing much to stay in shape since, he pointed out that the ski season was six months away.

"I thought you wanted skiers," Bill said, "not track stars."

Almost a quarter-century later, memories differ on exactly what action the Ski Team took with regard to Bill's position on the team at that point. Rausch says that Bill was not thrown off the team. Marolt—claiming that Bill didn't meet criteria that "the leadership of the ski team had laid down"—says that he *was* thrown off, adding, "He didn't take it well at all."

Bill himself recalls being dumped and having to ski his way back on. Looking back now, he says: "I was kicked off a year [after I got there], when a handicapped guy, a skier, beat me in the five-mile run."

The plaque Bill received when he retired from the team simply lists his years as 1980 to 1990. The Ski Team had different levels of performance— the A team, B team, and the development team, known as the D team—and being moved down a level was often referred to as being kicked off. (For the rest of his life Bill would rank people he met in those terms, as in "He's a terminal D-teamer.")

Certainly the folklore is that Bill was tossed from the team, and that puts him in pretty good company. Both Tommy Moe and Picabo Street were considered to have been cut from the U.S. Ski Team early in their careers.

Whether Bill was technically considered a member of the team in the 1981-'82 season or not, he was kept back in the states when the team went to Europe for training camps and prohibited from qualifying for the World Cup circuit. In addition, the Ski Team did not provide him with any funds to travel or race.

Undaunted, Bill competed on his own anyway. "I am not going to let it slip out of my hands," he said at the time.

Bill also had to fend for himself in terms of his equipment. Bill's sponsors no longer considered him to be a "team affiliate," and they stopped providing him with gear. In response, Bill showed up in his beat-up Pinto in Colorado at the Raichle Molitor, USA office of Tim Patterson, whom he had known as a kid in Idaho. Tim says that although the Ski Team viewed Bill as a "malcontent," he was starting to win. He set Bill up with Raichle Flexon boots and Tyrolia bindings.

With no new skis coming in, a scenario Tim compares to taking away a gunslinger's gun, Bill hooked up with Atomic to find skis for himself. "If he wasn't tough as nails.... Most guys would have walked away," Tim says.

The Ski Team continued to enter Bill in races as long as he paid his own way. He competed mostly in NorAm races in America and Canada—the top level of races domestically. Just as when Bill was a teenager, he couldn't afford the hotels where the rest of the team was staying, and he tried to crash on the floor of another racer's room. And just like in the past, when the coaches caught him, they booted him out to sleep in his car. On the *This Is Your Life* episode about Bill after he won the gold medal, Jo Jo talked about a time a Ski Team coach woke Bill from the floor of a hotel room and demanded that he contribute something like forty bucks toward the cost of the room. In response, Bill packed up and headed out, in sub-zero weather, to sleep in his Pinto.

Some people in the ski industry say that being left behind motivated Bill, made him come back with a vengeance, gave him the incentive he needed to win. He has a different take on the situation. "They just didn't like me," he says.

Looking back, Bill Marolt says that he "didn't name" Bill in order "to get his attention." Tim Patterson says, "Marolt will say now it was to toughen Bill up, but the bottom line is Marolt didn't want him because he was a troublemaker and he didn't think he was gonna get it done."

Jo Jo says that Marolt didn't like anybody who wasn't from Colorado. Marolt had come to the U.S. Ski Team in 1978 after serving as the head ski coach for the University of Colorado, his alma mater. His first season with the U.S. team, rather than having the racers wear red, white, and blue, he dressed everyone in yellow and gold, like a Colorado Buffalo.

Later in the 1981-'82 season, Bill was allowed to attend a Ski Team camp in Vail. The team was holding try-outs to determine who would travel to Europe to compete on the Europa Cup, a circuit of races just below the World Cup level. The races were hand-timed by various visiting coaches as well as by Mike Brown, a team member. Afterward, the team told both Bill and Jo Jo that based on their results in the races, neither of them qualified for the Europa Cup squad. Jo Jo says there was no way either of them was skiing that slow. Barry recalls being surprised that Bill's times weren't fast enough.

Rick Reid, a visiting coach from Crystal Mountain resort in Washington, believes that with regard to Bill, the process was "totally loaded against him."

Reid recalls that at the camp where he was the timer, Bill raced on crappy skis with duct tape holding them together and still won just about every run. Even though Bill was so obviously talented, Reid says that the Ski Team standards with regard to Bill were literally different from those for all the other skiers. "Bill had to do so much better," Reid says. "If everyone else had to finish in the top five, they said that Bill had to consistently finish first or second. It wasn't a fair table."

Reid spoke up in a coaches meeting after the camp about his concerns regarding the unequal treatment Bill was receiving. He recalls being told that he was way out of line and that the team no longer needed him at the meeting.

Mike says that Jo Jo and Bill had a legitimate gripe in that their futures in a sport of milliseconds were ever based on hand-timing in the first place. That incredibly subjective method of timing allowed the team to make judgment calls and take, as Mike says, the "Boy Scouts" rather than the racers who were hard to deal with.

"That entire staff and how they handled things, handled athletes, how they did things, was just bordering on criminal," Mike says. "They were unbelievably cavalier in terms of people's careers and lives. They didn't know what they were doing. They screwed with us, manipulated the system, did everything they could to sort of shanghai our success. It was sheer luck some of us survived."

Sam Collins, a downhill racer on the team, has similar views of the Ski Team in that era. "I wasn't going to put my life on the line just because a coach told me to do it," he says.

"Marolt was hardcore," Andy Luhn says. "Definitely a hard-ass. There was carnage along the way, collateral damage."

Erik Steinberg was told that his first priority was the team members' safety and his second was getting them to the podium. "Even though they believed the opposite," he says. "Those guys were cannon fodder."

According to several members of the Ski Team in the '80s, the management of the team was even less concerned with the racers' self-confidence. "The coaching staff was so fucked up," Sam Collins says. "The staff was not working with you, but against you." At one point in his ski career, Sam recalls downhill coach Theo Nadig saying to his face: "We're not gonna take you because you're not good enough."

According to Mike, Marolt was in charge of setting policy, and he wanted the team run militaristically. Bill later told the *Los Angeles Times* "When you're ski-racing, you're forced into a regimented organization. It's not the Army, but it's close."

"They held a very hard line," Mike says. "They took any confidence we had and continually toyed with it, broke it down. From Marolt and trickling on down, they were constantly berating us, constantly telling us we weren't any good. Marolt didn't give a flying crap about us. Never has, never will."

Marolt certainly took an extraordinarily hard line with regard to Mike, denying him an Olympic experience in '88 based on wholly arbitrary criteria. Although the U.S. was allowed to take four downhill racers to Sarajevo, Marolt set his own standard for qualification of one World Cup finish in the top 15 or two in the top 20. That year Mike finished 18th in one World Cup and 21st in another. Marolt kept him home, taking just two downhillers.

Jo Jo left the team in 1982 following the hand-timing incident, convinced that Bill would do the same. Jo Jo had lots of other options, though, most notably his family's jewelry business in Chicago.

Jo Jo says that skiing was Bill's "ticket out." He had seen Bill's dad's place in Van Nuys, California (where Wally and Mary had moved from Oregon), and there was literally only vodka and potatoes in the refrigerator.

Bill once told the press that he saw downhill racing as a way of getting everything he ever wanted. When he told Jo Jo he was going to keep trying with the Ski Team, he explained his reasoning a little more cavalierly. "I've never worked a day in my life," Bill said, "and I'm not going to start now."

With regard to Bill's time off the team, Marolt says, "What came out of it is he discovered he wanted to be on the team and be successful." Actually, what Bill already knew was that he would be successful on his own, with or without the team.

Without the backing of the Ski Team, Bill competed in the U.S. Nationals that spring and finished fifth in the downhill for the second year in a row. At the end of that season, he placed 19th at a World Cup in Whistler, British Columbia, after finishing first in a training run. Afterward, he had to sell his skis to get home.

In November of '84, after Bill had already won the gold medal, he described his relationship with the Ski Team to *Ski* magazine like this: "They knock me down, I fight back. They knock me down again, I fight back again.

I felt like I was slipping back, like I was being punched in the ribs."

Mike feels that Bill sometimes took things too far, but that he was forced into that position by a ski establishment that refused to offer him any support. "Bill had to go outside of the system and do things his own way to come out on top," Mike says. "At every corner they were telling him, 'No, you're not good enough.' He had to put it in their face and say, 'I *am* good enough. I'll show you.'"

Mike calls Bill the most amazing individual he's ever met for being able to overcome that system. "His success in that environment is right up there with the hockey team," Mike says. "Miraculous."

By the end of the '82 season, the Ski Team had endorsed Bill again. Jo Jo says that the team didn't put Bill on again until he was doing so well that Marolt had absolutely no choice. Bill earned his way back with his skiing, not by physical conditioning, a dynamic that would be a continuing battle between Bill and the team.

In the 1982-'83 season, Dr. Gene Hagerman came to the Ski Team as the head trainer. He had a PhD in sports/exercise physiology from Ohio State University and had been working at the U.S. Olympic Training Center in Colorado Springs when the Ski Team lured him away. Everyone called him "Topper," a nickname from infancy. As the story goes, when he was born the doctor told his mother, who already had boys ages 11 and eight, having a third, much younger child "topped it off." Although he was only 35 at the time, his shaggy salt-and-pepper hair led the racers to call him "Gramps" or "Pops" as well. Topper, who refers to himself as an "industrial skier," made it clear that the members of the Ski Team needed to be athletes first, skiers second.

That summer, at the end of July, Topper had everyone on the team perform a series of activities he referred to as the "Medals Test." Bill was not doing well, and Topper let him retake the push-ups section as well as the box-jump (jumping over a $2^1/_2$-foot-high bamboo pole laid over cinder blocks). On the mile run, Erik Steinberg says that Bill just wouldn't try, and he recalls Topper saying, "This kid doesn't deserve our leniency." In response, Steinberg got out on the track with Bill and "dragged him the last half mile by the throat of his t-shirt." Although Bill was embarrassed in front of his teammates, he met the team's standard (approximately 5:45).

Topper says Bill "always had his comments" with regard to train-ing. In Austria in the fall of '82, Topper ran a training camp to work on a combination of speed and technical skills. On the first day, Topper addressed the team on the importance of dry-land training. Bill, pretending he was sneezing, started muttering "bullshit" under his breath. Later, after everyone was exhausted from uphill wind sprints, Topper pulled Bill aside and said, "You're gonna do some extras with me."

On another occasion, Bill told Topper that he had his own ideas for early morning stretches. Topper replied that he was happy to wake up Bill even earlier so they could implement his suggestions. In response, Topper says that he just got a "Bill Johnson kind of a laugh, kind of a smirk."

Meanwhile, Steinberg worked out with Bill every day, trudging up hill after hill with him whether he liked it or not. "I had to drag him around and torture the shit out of him," Steinberg says. "That was my job."

Looking back now, Bill does seem appreciative. "Eric was and is a great guy," Bill says. "My memory is terrible, though I do know he worked hard."

For the '82-'83 season, Bill was invited to race on the Europa Cup, provided that he came up with $7,400 for travel, lodging, and coaching. If Bill couldn't raise the money, he couldn't go.

The Ski Team has been heavily criticized for the method of developing ski racers by charging fees, and it is no longer practiced. In some respects, however, it seems that things haven't changed that much. At an awards ceremony a few years ago in Squaw Valley, the Ski Team honored Phil Mahre and Tamara McKinney as "Skiers of the Century." In recognition of the honor, the team presented each of them with a $10,000 check—made payable to the U.S. Ski Team on their behalf.

Bill somehow produced the money demanded by the Ski Team. Much of it was raised or borrowed by Bill's dad in five- and ten-dollar bills through donations from various clubs and whatever other funds he could scratch up. Then Bill went to Europe and won the Europa Cup title, the first American ever to do so.

Bill was, in fact, the first American to ever win even a single Europa Cup downhill race. He did so well that at the end of the season he was confirmed not just as the Europa Cup downhill champion, but the overall champion as well. His performance in the downhill races alone (winning three of them and placing second in another) qualified him as the top racer in all alpine events. Both of those accomplishments—being the downhill Europa Cup winner and the overall Europa Cup winner—were firsts for an American.

One advantage the U.S. Team had over European skiers was the opportunity to train in an industrial wind tunnel that came with, as Steinberg says, "an absolute genius helping us out." Dr. Michael Holden, a former NASA engineer and also a certified ski instructor, came to the Ski Team offering the use of the wind tunnel at the Calspan Corporation in Buffalo, New York, where he worked as an engineer.

The team stayed with families of the local race team at Kissing Bridge, a ski resort near Buffalo. They were at Calspan several days at a time, 12 to 14 hours at a stretch. The coaches ordered take-out pizza, and the skiers did their homework, played guitar, or threw a football around while waiting for their 40-minute rotation in the wind tunnel. Bill was the first one to line up.

Normally used to test the dispersion of pollutants and the airflow around buildings, the tunnel had a 92-inch fan with a 200-horsepower motor generating a 70-mph wind. Team members stepped onto a gridded platform and watched a video of a ski run, moving their bodies like they were skiing, experimenting with different positions. The changes in drag caused by their movements were measured by sensors in the platform, and a digital readout displayed their improved time. The skiers could also see themselves on a video screen, enabling them to easily correlate drag and position.

For example, in a tuck position, if a skier held his arms along the outside of his legs when approaching a jump, he generated a drag of about forty-three pounds. If he held his arms in tight against his body, assuming that he was able to maintain that position, the drag was reduced to about eighteen pounds.

The racers also used the tunnel to create custom-bent poles. Steinberg checked the monitor to see how the values changed as he made various adjustments to each skier's poles.

It was in the wind tunnel that Bill perfected his unusual body position—a low tuck with his chest below his knees and a wide stance to allow his skis to ride very flat. As Jo Jo says, "Billy walked out of there faster than he walked in."

Bill has especially thin shoulders, narrower than his hips and thighs. When he folded his body into a tuck, his back rounded, his knees in his armpits, his hands up by his chin (a position known as "chewing on your hands"), Steinberg says he "popped out" on the TV screen, percentage points faster than anyone else.

"He just killed everybody," Steinberg says. "It was a raw, God-given talent. It was built into his body. He knew he had an edge, and he was gonna make that edge work. He was not going to be denied."

In January of '83, in Valloire, France, Bill was doing a crossword puzzle the night before the season's first Europa Cup downhill race when he suddenly realized something else he'd been doing wrong in terms of his form. It occurred to him that he had been using his upper body too much, twisting his shoulders in the turns, and he decided to rely more on his legs instead. He won the Europa Cup downhill the next day as well as the next two Europa Cup races after that.

Even then the press was calling Bill, who stayed sometimes with his dad and Mary in Van Nuys when he wasn't traveling with the team, a "brash California newcomer." Reporters called Bill anti-establishment, the counter-culture candidate, a rebel. They particularly liked to pit Bill's image against that of Doug Powell, a ski team veteran from New England with short hair and nice things to say about the team, writing things like "East v. West" and "The insider against the outsider."

The truth was that Bill was on the outside of the entire team.

No one could really figure Bill out. According to his former teammates, every cliché that could be used to describe a difficult person applied to Bill. He rubbed people the wrong way, got under people's skin. He liked to play with people's minds.

When they fill in the details, Bill's old teammates say that he never gave anyone any respect or any space. He could be mean, really mean, and outright rude, often to wait staff or other service people. He was almost always gracious to his fans, but occasionally when a stranger tried to be overly friendly he would cut them off abruptly.

"He never felt bad about anything that he did," Andy Chambers, a racer on the downhill team, says. "He just didn't. It was all about him and never about anybody else. If you don't feel remorse or regret, you don't have mental clutter. Bill didn't have any of that mental clutter."

Bill especially liked to prey on weak people. Barry says that he liked to find a weak person, rip them down, humiliate them, then slowly build them back up by treating them with respect.

Bill would tell the younger races that they didn't deserve to be there. He would do petty, annoying things like take people's drinks. He would try to demoralize people, dominate them with small acts of defiance like fold-ing his arms at the end of a team meeting and blocking the door, saying, "Nobody is leaving this room until I say so."

And just like his former classmates in high school, Bill's teammates say that it was unsettling to have him around. Most of the other racers were always a little on edge when they were with him. He made them uneasy.

As coach Rick Reid says, "The chemicals in Bill's brain were always on the edge of being insane."

"Bill was a complex individual," Mike Brown says. "One minute you'd get one guy, the next another—four or five people wrapped up in one. He was all over the map, inconsistent. Sometimes he was on a rampage or a tirade, trying to put everybody down. Sometimes he was just like a normal guy. You had to see where you were at that given moment."

As a slalom skier on the team, Cory Carlson was on a different train-ing schedule than the downhill racers—who he refers to as "their own breed"—but he spent time with them off the slopes. "Bill was interested in conflict, liked friction," Cory says. "We would be out having a beer together, in a comfort zone. At times he could interject…fun. But then it would go to an uncomfortable level. He was unorthodox. Intense. Emotional in certain respects. You had to tread lightly."

Cory pauses, then continues with an emphasis that indicates something stronger than the terminology suggests: "The fact was, he was a son of a gun."

"Most of the boys on the team didn't like him," Nadig says. "I don't know what they're saying now, but back then, they didn't like him. One or two could somehow take him."

Most of Bill's teammates say that it didn't matter to Bill what anyone thought of him, and that he deliberately isolated himself from everybody else. Barry says it was all part of an act, that Bill played an invincible tough-guy character but, "There was some soul in the guy." Steinberg thought that it did hurt Bill that people didn't like him, that it seemed like he didn't care but the next minute he was actually really upset. Bill once confided in Rausch that his teammates hated him.

Andy Chambers describes the dynamic like this: "Bill had a really rough childhood and he needed a lot of attention. It didn't matter to him if it was good attention or bad attention. Bad attention didn't bother him as long as the focus was on him. He would do whatever it took. Whether that was winning races or being a jerk, it didn't really matter."

Bill's teammates say that he brought everything on himself, and while he clearly seemed to, he didn't have a lot of experience trusting anyone. In his early 20's, Bill was familiar only with being abandoned or ignored. He had never fit in anywhere, never been included. In the past Bill had been outright laughed at for being different, and he likely had no expectation of being accepted by these teammates either. It was as if Bill was so sure he would be ostracized that he reacted by deliberately pushing people away before they could do it to him.

In the off-season or between training camps the racers would often crash at each other's parents' houses, but aside from Jo Jo going to Bill's dad's place in Van Nuys, Bill never brought anyone to visit his dad or his mom. He was always on the move, always somebody's houseguest. He lived with each of his sisters when he was in Portland—Kathryn in 1981 and Vicki the following year. Kathryn was a single mother at the time, working three jobs to support herself and her young daughter, but she let Bill live with her for free. One time they had an argument at the park over some small indiscretion her daughter had committed, and Bill stormed off. Later, he telephoned Kathryn, sounding hurt. "Weren't you going to call me?" he asked.

Vicki made Bill get a job while he was living with her, and he briefly held a position at a margarine factory in Portland. He was fired early on for accidentally tipping over a whole barrel of margarine. "He didn't do it on purpose," Vicki says. "He was trying his hardest."

"You hate to blame people's parents for the problem," Steinberg says, "but Bill had baggage and he brought his baggage. I saw the scars, deep scars, in Bill's brain as an adult. He was such a bright guy, high intelligence and cunning—where did he get this anger? And it wasn't gonna change."

According to Steinberg, Bill was always putting the coaches in situations in which they "had to come down on him like a ton of bricks."

"What Bill had was an authority complex," Rausch says, "or rather a reaction to authority that caused him to say 'Forget about it, I don't care.'" Rausch felt that if someone tried to intimidate Bill into not doing something, Bill saw it as a threat. In response, he would continue to do it just to make a point, or simply say nevermind and walk away. That would certainly be the case later in Bill's life when he just quit things that weren't going his way. Rausch believes that top athletes have a trigger, and that it is a coach's job to not pull that trigger. Consequently, Rausch approached Bill differently than he did the other racers.

In '82, Marolt had given the order that chewing tobacco was 100% forbidden and that anyone caught with it would be eliminated from the team. When the team was training on the glacier in Zermatt, Switzerland, that year, Steinberg approached Rausch with a package in his hand, sent from Wally Sr. to Bill. It obviously contained round tins.

"Give me that package," Rausch said. "I'm in charge here."

Rausch met with Bill and showed him the package. Bill said it contained cookies. Rausch told him not to fool around.

"I told my father he shouldn't send them like that," Bill said.

Bill told Rausch that he was addicted to tobacco. In response, Rausch asked him why he wanted to ski race. Bill said that he wanted to be an idol for young people. Rausch then asked him if he thought he needed tobacco for that, and Bill agreed that he didn't.

"If you addressed him correctly, put something in his head, and he understood what he needed to do to be right, he would put his mind to it," Rausch says. Rausch gave the package to Bill and told him in two weeks, when they were leaving Zermatt, to let him know what he wanted to do. At the end of the camp, Bill returned the package to Rausch, unopened.

"He was never easy to deal with, but if you did it right," Rausch says, "it was good." After he left the Ski Team in '83 to return to Europe, Rausch felt Bill was no longer coached correctly and "was not understood by my successor [Theo Nadig]."

"Bill was a very difficult person to handle," Nadig says. "Easy to handle if you were only with him. He could be very, very nice, very charming. In a group sometimes, not easy to handle."

Looking back on that time, Marolt's mild observation of the situation is merely "Sometimes the really talented are tougher to manage."

During dry-land training when the team was playing basketball or touch football, Bill was just not going to be the first one to back down from a challenge. "I think he felt like people were attacking him," Doug Powell says. "But at that level you're not there to be coddled."

Whether or not Bill picked the fights, his response was to fight back physically. Steinberg came to blows himself with Bill a couple times over missed curfews and drinking and general insubordination. "He wouldn't pull a punch for any reason," Steinberg says. "He was over the top as far as wanting to fight all the time."

Yet when Bill did make a friend, he formed the kind of bond that caus-es men to say, decades later, that Bill was like a brother to them. It is clear from the various descriptions of the friendships that it was not easy to get close to Bill—everyone's praise is conditional, all beginning with "if." Jo Jo says that if Bill liked you, there was not a better friend—he would have walked through fire for you. Mark Herhusky, a skier Bill met through Barry, claims that if you were in his circle of trust, Bill was the best guy in the world. In Barry's opin-ion, if you were tight with Bill, he would have gone against anybody for you.

Andy Luhn, a racer from Idaho with a square jaw and blond hair, who would later receive the award for "least changed" at his 20-year high school reunion, became friends with Bill at that same level. After Jo Jo left the team, Andy was Bill's roommate on the road for years. Topper says that Andy was especially kind to Bill and always at his side. Barry refers to Andy as Bill's right-hand man.

Andy says that Bill was misunderstood and underrated by the clique on the team. "Bill did things his own way," Andy says. "He was not phony. Everyone can say at some point in their lives they are not acting true to themselves. Bill always acted true to his character."

Andy also recognized a core of resiliency in Bill that others didn't nec-essarily notice or tended to disregard. "Everybody has the cards they're given when they're growing up," Andy says. "There were a lot of things in Bill's life that were probably not that great. He never made excuses. To a lot of things, he said 'Fine, I'll take it.'" He took a lot, never put it on other people, never asked for help. He just said 'Fine.'"

Despite his problems fitting in with the team, Bill adapted well to life on the road. He loved traveling in Europe. He had an easier time than most skiers being so far away from home for so long. He also came home less. From the early 1980s until the end of his racing career, when Bill trained in Europe he stayed there from September through December. Almost all of the other rac-ers came home for holidays, but Bill remained in a hotel in Europe. Gina, Bill's ex-wife, says, "I don't know that Bill's family had big Christmases and Thanksgivings where everybody gathered together. Holidays were kind of painful for him for some reason. He struggled with holidays."

Bill had too much fun a few times—once in Zermatt, he stayed out at a nightclub way past the team's ten o'clock curfew. The doors of the hotel were locked when he returned and he obviously didn't want to alert the hotel staff. He climbed up to the higher floors on the outside of the building and knocked on his teammates' windows, climbing from bedroom to bedroom trying to find someone who would let him in. No one had any interest in helping him out. He finally found an open door and snuck in that way.

Another time in St. Anton, Austria, Bill went out with a girl the night after a race. The coaches had announced that the bus was leaving the following morning at 8 a.m. When Bill was not there in the morning, the team left him behind to find his own way to Zurich, Switzerland, to meet up with the team. After a series of trains and buses, he eventually showed up.

In Germany, Bill was the first skier to get a dictionary and try to learn the language. His first attempt at speaking was to piece together words in a restaurant, where he tried to ask the waitress to sleep with him. He picked up German quickly, learning it well enough that he could soon correct other people.

Bill would also have arguments over the definitions of English words with his better educated teammates, and he would virtually always be correct. Andy Chambers says that Bill was "really, really bright," and never got enough credit for his intelligence and cunning. One time some of his teammates caught Bill, who was not at all religious, reading the Bible. "If I'm going to argue with people about religion," Bill said. "I have to be informed, find things I can use to tear people apart."

Certainly Bill always felt that he was smarter than everybody else, and although that attitude did nothing to endear him to his teammates, he may well have been right. "There's a lot firing in his mind, often ahead of other people's speed," Blake Lewis says. Andy Luhn calls Bill one of the smartest people he's ever known. But beyond his IQ, in a sport with an enormous mental component, Bill held a huge advantage. The smallest amount of uncertainty, the slightest inkling of doubt, could dramatically affect a skier's placement in a race. Bill simply had no fear. As his teammate Cory Carlson says, "I don't think Billy felt pressure. He didn't weigh that."

Andy believes that Bill approached the sport differently from other racers did at the time and "won more with his head." Andy says that although Bill never trained very hard, he took it seriously and understood that he couldn't tear up his body. Instead, he focused on subtle things like body position and how to pressure his skis, small adjustments no one else was paying much attention to back then. "When we were racers, Bill figured out nuances of a sport that is not common in our country," Andy says. "He figured things out we didn't."

Bill's style was to flutter his skis on the turns rather than carve them. "He's a sloppy skier and he doesn't look as good as he should," his teammate Alan Lauba says. "But he fights for speed."

As he had as a child, Bill continued his meticulous inspection of courses. He also applied the same approach to assessing his competition. Much like he would do in Montana over 20 years later, he analyzed the level of risk he was willing to take in an upcoming race. Once in France, after a training run for a giant slalom race, Bill squatted down to examine the results. He looked at where the other skiers finished, how far back each of them was, and what his placement was in relation to them. It occurred to Andy, who was watching Bill at the time, that Bill was literally calculating how much risk he had to take in the race. Bill may have figured it correctly, but if so, it was more risk than he was physically able to withstand at the time. He crashed.

Tom Kelly, a coach affiliated with the Europa Cup in Bill's early years on the team, realized that Bill had great talent, and he says that he tried to understand him. "Off of the snow, I let him be who he was," he says. "He was a little on the wild side, a little different."

Off the snow, training was something Bill never made a priority. Motivation wasn't a problem with Bill—he wanted to win—but keeping him interested was sometimes an issue. Even so, Topper says that having him on the team brought the other skiers up to another level—they had to get better to try to beat him, and they especially wanted to be able to defeat Bill.

To vary the conditioning, Topper often introduced different sports. Although he was a natural athlete, other games often put Bill at a disadvantage. He wasn't familiar with team sports like basketball and soccer. Doug Lewis was an especially talented soccer player, and problems between Bill and Doug occurred on the soccer field early on. Bill, who thought the game was stupid—and was upset at not knowing how to play—one time just kicked the ball as far as he could, saying, "Go chase this, clown."

As Andy says, "To the skiers from the East, that was game on."

Topper also initiated a tennis doubles tournament for the team when they were training in Zermatt. Dubbed the Zermatt Open, it took place in September of 1982—a lonely time on the glacier, as Cory Carlson says. Most of the skiers on the team had grown up playing tennis. Bill, who had not, lost badly.

The following year, Topper ran the tournament again, at which point Bill, partnered with Tiger Shaw, won it. Cory and Felix McGrath played them in the finals. Cory, now a ski ambassador at the Beaver Creek Park Hyatt in Colorado, still refers to it as "that damn tennis tournament."

"Bill couldn't play tennis to save his life, but you could see his raw determination," Cory says. "He wasn't good at all, but so damn determined you couldn't believe the shots he was getting back."

A lot of people have specific opinions about the traits that made Bill such an incredible skier—his tight tuck, his loose ski, his soft touch on landings, his uncanny ability to see a line down the mountain that that other skiers either didn't see or weren't willing to risk. Yet clearly, Bill's performance on the tennis court showed that his talent went beyond a technical analysis. Asked his opinion of why Bill was able to play above his ability in the Zermatt Open, Topper says only, "Once he put his mind to something, once he set his mind…."

Coach Tom Kelly saw the same characteristic: "When Bill decided to do something, when it was time to focus, Bill's ability to zero in was unreal. Bar none. He did it. I could see the difference when he wanted to win."

Theo Nadig says that in terms of Bill's skill there were "two things—he wanted to do it and he did it."

Rausch's philosophy was that racers first needed to learn to win, and he therefore didn't want to bring them on the World Cup circuit too soon. He felt that if they skied at that level before they were ready, they would crash too often and destroy their knees and the rest of their bodies. Toward the end of the '82-'83 season, however, Rausch entered Bill in a few World Cup races—ones that he deemed easier—to give him experience. Bill placed 30th in Pontresina, Switzerland, and he finished 6th at the Arlberg-Kandahar downhill at St. Anton, Austria, skiing from the 43rd start position.

Later that month, on February 16th, exactly one year before he would win gold in Sarajevo, Bill beat a field of 94 to win the downhill at the U.S. Nationals at Copper Mountain, Colorado. On the two-mile course, Bill's speed was over 80 mph at points and averaged more than 77 mph. After winning, Bill played it fairly graciously. He ducked any reference to his competition, instead praising the forerunners for setting an accurate track and promising them all a beer.

In Aspen early that March, Bill crashed in training and suffered a concussion the day before a World Cup race. He caught his edge, splintered his pole, and landed on his head going about 50 mph. He was back racing 24 hours later, with a severely bruised chin and, he said, a headache. During the race, the skier in front of Bill fell, and the electronic timing system failed to record Bill's time. A handheld clocking mechanism, not the most reliable of back-up timing systems, had him in 36th place.

In the last World Cup race of the '82-'83 season, on March 12th in Lake Louise, Alberta, Bill was 20th. In the final World Cup downhill standings that year, Bill was ranked tied for 27th. Franz Klammer was first.

Bill was also named the Europa Cup downhill and overall champion despite skiing on the World Cup circuit and not competing in any additional Europa Cup events for close to a month and a half at the end of the season. He was called with the news while he was at the Thys's house in Tahoe, and he and Nina Thys celebrated at the coffee table in the living room with a bottle of champagne. In Nina's opinion, the team made "so little" of the achievement. Claiming that it did not have enough funds to do so, the team did not even fly Bill to Europe to accept the award in person.

That June, 1983, Bill decided that he was going to win the gold medal the following February. He announced it over dinner in a restaurant in Indiana with Jo Jo, friends of Jo Jo's family, and Bill's then-girlfriend Heather Rapp. Jo Jo responded, "That's great, Bill."

"Hey," Bill said, "I'm *telling you*, I'm gonna win the gold medal." Jo Jo tried to tell him that no one there had said he wouldn't, but Bill was unconvinced. He raised his voice and said again, "I'm tellin' you, and I'm gonna tell everyone at this table, watch me. I'm winning the gold medal and that's what's gonna happen."

Jo Jo told Bill to take it down a notch, a comment that in retrospect he admits was the wrong thing to say to Bill. Bill started screaming, "You don't believe me? You don't believe me?" In the end, everybody in the restaurant wound up assuring Bill that they believed.

After his victory, Bill called Jo Jo from Sarajevo, tracked him down at a girlfriend's house. "I did it," Bill said. "I won."

Twenty-one years later, Jo Jo still tears up relating the story.

After dinner one night in the fall of '83, Blake went to the ski room to work on some skis and Bill asked Blake's then-girlfriend (now wife) Dañela to go for a walk. In the course of that walk, Bill told her that he was there to win a gold medal and he didn't want her to interfere with his relationship with Blake. "I'm going to win this," Bill said. "Don't get in the way."

That '83-'84 ski season was the first year Bill skied on the complete World Cup circuit with the Ski Team. Before the season started, in November of '83, he went on a trip with his sister Vicki to Mexico. As Vicki says, Bill was coming back from somewhere and leaving again soon, but there was a break in between and they decided to head out of the country. A sponsor had just given Bill a Windsurfer (every member of the U.S. Ski Team received one) and they put that on the top of the car along with some couch cushions. They traveled light—the stuff they packed included $200 in cash, a deck of cards, a loaf of bread, jelly, a jar of peanut butter, and some Dr. Pepper.

They had no destination. Past Ensenada, they stopped long enough to stay in a room with cockroaches, then headed south and took a dirt road to the beach with a bottle of Jose Cuervo. The beach was long and white with no seaweed and with clams all over the place. They drove right up onto the beach, sat in low chairs, and cut cards for shots of tequila until Vicki couldn't do it anymore. They slept in sleeping bags in the car, rotating turns for the front where the steering wheel pressed in. The next day, hung over in 105-degree heat, they tried to dig the car out of the sand where it had gotten stuck when the tide came in. In the end, they had it towed.

From there, Bill and Vicki drove south toward the gulf side of Baja, where they found what Vicki calls an oasis. It was a little protected cove—the perfect spot to windsurf. When the peanut butter and jelly ran out, they bought a can of beans and heated them on a fire. With no silverware, they used clams to scoop them out. "It was pretty awesome," Vicki says. "There was no sense going anywhere else. We found paradise." They ended up running into two doctors who knew how to "find food under water," and snorkeled and water-skied with them for the next week. When they got back to California, Vicki took Bill straight to the airport, and he flew off to Europe to race.

In January that season, a month before the Sarajevo Olympics, Bill competed in a World Cup race in Wengen, Switzerland. He was starting in the second seed. The seeds are based on rank—the first seed consists of the top 15 racers, the second seed is the next 15, and so on. It is almost always preferable for a racer to be in the top seed so he can race early, before the course gets too rutted from the paths of other skiers.

Austrian downhillers Anton Steiner and Erwin Resch were actually posing for victory photos at the time Bill was racing. In their pre-race comments, John Tesh and Billy Kidd, calling the competition for CBS, discussed how Bill tended to ski out of control. "They want to keep him on the team now because he is really a fast skier—he has the fastest run at training very often," Tesh said. "But very often he's too fast, he can't keep it together all the way."

That was almost exactly the scenario during Bill's run, except that after he lost control and skied off the course, he somehow gyrated violently enough to keep his skis under him and finish the race. A decade later, Bill claimed that in the "hundredth of a second" he had to consider his situation after he lost control, he thought, "If I can just get my feet together when they come back, maybe something good will happen."

What happened was that Bill won the race, becoming the first American man ever to win a World Cup downhill. The crowd was actually hushed as his time flashed on the scoreboard. The photographers put down their cameras, and the reporters stopped interviewing Steiner and Resch. Bill skied over and stood between them.

After Bill's victory, there were suggestions in the press that due to improving weather conditions, skiing later in the race had actually benefited Bill. Looking back now, Franz Klammer agrees. "In Wengen, he had an advantage with the weather—[the course] was faster later on," he says. "Other guys had the same advantage, but he took it. Then he wins and he thinks he's invincible."

Bill wasn't unbeatable at that point, though—not yet. The week after Wengen, he placed 45th in the Hahnenkamm World Cup in Kitzbuhel, Austria. Klammer won the race. The following week, Bill was 31st at a World Cup at Garmisch-Partenkirchen, West Germany. In the last World Cup race before the Olympics, in Cortina, Italy, on February 2nd, Bill finished fourth.

The Cortina race was the last chance to make it to the Olympics—everybody was still trying to qualify, and tensions were high. Andy Chambers had finished behind Bill in races something like eight times in a row, and Bill was in Andy's face teasing him about it. "We were not close," Andy says, "and we spent a lot of time together."

In the ski room before the race, Bill and Andy had what Andy now refers to as our "little silly-ass fight." When Bill came into the room he apparently wanted something to go his way. "Who knows what he wanted?" Andy says. "He was just trying to establish his dominance, just struttin' around bein' Bill." Andy told Bill that Bill couldn't do what he wanted because Andy was already there, and when Andy wouldn't move, Bill picked up Andy's ski and threw it off the bench. Violence ensued. In the course of the fight, Bill punched Andy in the jaw and pulled his t-shirt over his head.

Bill also pushed Andy into about 25 or 30 pairs of finished race skis. Once the skis were prepared the racers weren't even supposed to touch them because the oil on their fingers could affect the wax, and there they were sprawled out on the concrete floor. Blake scrambled around trying to protect the skis while team members pulled Bill and Andy apart.

"I would have hurt him because he would have hurt me," Andy says. The ski room was on an upper floor, and in retrospect, Andy feels that he should have been worried about one of them flying out the window. After their fight, Bill liked Andy more than he had beforehand. "The only thing Bill respected was if you stood up to him," Andy says.

Alan Lauba says the same thing about Bill. "He respected someone who could challenge him, who said screw you. Then he would shake your hand."

After Cortina, the U.S. Olympic downhill team, consisting only of Bill and Doug Lewis, headed for Yugoslavia. Prior to his victory, Bill took the time to send a postcard from Sarajevo to Mark Herhusky in Tahoe in which he described the frenzy he was causing in the world media with his brashness as simply, "More trouble in 'Paradise.'"

Back in Van Nuys, Bill's dad and Mary were home listening to the radio. With the time difference in Europe, they were up very late at night, listening and waiting to hear if Bill won. For Mary, who had known Bill since he was an adolescent, it was obviously a powerful night. Over twenty years later, she still remembers it well, and she clearly recalls something Wally told her in the midst of their anticipation during the long wait that night.

"You know, I sort of don't want him to win," he said. "It could be the best thing that could ever happen to him but it could be a really horrible thing for him. I think it could be more than he can handle."

CHAPTER FIVE

"He woke up as if a newborn and needed to relearn everything from holding a spoon to talking."

– KATHRYN PUNDT, Bill's sister

Skiing wasn't the first thing on Bill's mind when he awakened from his coma three weeks after the crash that almost killed him. He was more concerned with seeing his wife, who was no longer his wife, and his sons, one of whom had died ten years earlier.

When he woke up in the hospital, Bill knew who he was. That is, he seemed to know that his name was Bill Johnson, but he didn't necessarily know who Bill Johnson was. Initially he recognized only his ex-wife—"Hi, Gina"—and his mom, whom he spoke to for the first time in a year and a half. He had no memory of having cut off contact with his mother. He also did not remember his divorce or his father's death (in 1995), and he was extremely upset when informed.

Bill had been flown from Montana to the rehab unit on the fourth floor of Providence Portland Medical Center in Portland, Oregon, on April 11th, 2001. Although he still appeared virtually comatose at that point, he was able to respond to some outside stimulus when he was brought to Oregon, and he had drawn up his knee in bed on his last morning in the Montana hospital, an encouraging sign. Doctors determined that he was in a transition phase. It was in the hospital in Portland, on April 14th, that Dr. Molly Hoeflich, Medical Director of the Acute Rehabilitation Center, officially declared that Bill was waking up.

Contrary to how it is often portrayed in the movies, coming out of a coma is not necessarily a dramatic event; it is measured instead in terms of things like finger twitches. At the time when Bill was no longer technically comatose, he was making slight movements on his own and responding to simple verbal commands such as, "Squeeze my hand" (which he could initially only do with his left hand). He would open his eyes spontaneously and sometimes in response to a request. In the course of his awakening, he actually spent another several weeks semi-conscious. He then gradually, steadily, began to learn the most basic skills of life all over again—how to talk, walk, use the bathroom.

"There was nothing pretty about any of it," Kathryn says.

Bill was not able to communicate easily for a long time after waking up. As early as April 17th he was trying to mouth words, but he had a tracheotomy tube in his neck for almost a month to help him breathe, and he couldn't speak with it in. He had to re-learn how to maneuver his tongue and lips to talk.

He could not always get the right word for the right object. He used a very unusual way to communicate his message, using analogies and wordplays. Once he referred to a glove as a "breeder," envisioning a cow's udder. The words he used were at first difficult for friends and family to interpret, but when they searched for the meaning they realized that they made sense in a philosophical sort of way. Kathryn recalls feeling that she was back in the 17th century, when wordplay was clever and sly with very subtle meanings.

As soon as Bill learned how to plug the tracheotomy tube with his finger to talk, he would not shut up, to certain family members at least. He talked more than Kathryn (whom he called Yvette for no apparent reason) had ever heard him talk—about everything. He was also very flirty with any attractive girl who entered his room. He would exaggeratedly kiss his nurses' hands. He would beam at them and call them by names he made up for them—colorful, stripper-sounding names—Colette, Amber, Angelique, Dominique, Chantal, Desiree.

Other times, Bill had to be prompted to talk. Often his conversations with friends and family were brief and one-sided, with Bill not so much talking as just responding to questions. Less than a minute later, he would have already forgotten the topic. Bill himself never asked any questions.

He did not talk about the accident. When he was asked about it, he said that he did not remember it. Questions beginning "Do you remember" tended to confuse and agitate him. To this day, he has no memory of the crash. He watches television footage of himself hitting the mountain head-first and flopping in the air like a rag doll, and he laughs, as if he is watching some type of blooper film.

John Creel, Bill's coach during his comeback, thought that even if Bill didn't remember it, he understood what had happened. Bill still talked to him in all-out, go-for-it ski racer terminology, but now his outlook was resigned. One day in the hospital, while Creel was holding Bill's hand, Bill looked up at him and said, "No more spinning the wheel."

Meanwhile, Creel told *People* magazine that it wouldn't surprise him if Bill were making turns on the slopes by the next winter—a seemingly ludicrous statement. At the time, it wasn't even clear if Bill would ever walk again.

Initially Bill had the emotional outlook of a child. Words and ideas seemed to float freely in his mind. Early on, DB described him as "about a two-year-old." The headlines in the press were full of catchy titles: about the downhill racer's uphill climb and Bill's "real" comeback. At the same time, DB was quoted in the press as saying, "You wonder why his life wasn't just taken, why he has to go through this."

Bill's attitude changed from minute to minute, mood swings typical of a recovering head-injury patient combined with Bill's already mercurial personality. One night, for example, Bill asked Kathryn to stop giving him a foot massage, then seconds later glared at her and demanded to know why she wasn't rubbing his feet. He was especially confused, and often combative, when he was tired. Looking past the hostility, a friend or family member stayed with Bill every night while he was in the hospital in Portland.

It was usually only after repeated visits that Bill was able to recognize the faces of anyone besides Gina and DB. And even then it wasn't apparent if he remembered them from his past or from the repetitiveness of the visits themselves.

While Bill responded to his name, it was unclear whether or not he initially identified and remembered himself as a famous skier. At one point, for example, he asked where the TV cameras were. As there actually had been television cameras snooping around the hospital, Bill's friends were unsure whether his comment was prompted by having seen a camera or from independently remembering that he was a celebrity and wondering why cameras weren't there to document his hospital stay.

Similarly, friends who visited Bill brought him lots of skiing pictures to put up in his hospital room to try to revive his memory, and it was hard to tell what Bill really remembered and what he learned by seeing the pictures. And it was impossible to separate what Bill knew on his own from what his family was telling him. "The family strongly identified with Bill Johnson the skier," Hoeflich says. "That was part of the milieu."

In the Portland hospital, Bill talked about having died and said that because he was brought back to life, he was God. Sometimes he would say that he was brought back to become president to right the world. Sometimes even now, when he is tired or after a long day, Bill will tell you that he is going to be president.

Asked to look back at that time now, Bill recalls that his first thoughts upon waking from his coma were these: "I am told I am on the right planet but I don't think so, something is gone, 'cause I was told this is planet Earth and I am alive."

CHAPTER SIX

**"There is basically nothing I can't do right now or at
any other time."**
– BILL JOHNSON, 1984

H e was on the cover of *Sports Illustrated* on February 27th, 1984, with the
caption "Flat Out for Glory." He met President Reagan (who gushed
that Americans were "all on the same team in cheering [him] on.") He went
to the Playboy mansion. He did the talk show circuit: *Good Morning America*
and *The Tonight Show* with Johnny Carson (Carson, when discussing Bill's
delinquent youth, advised him to "only take things on a mountainside,
because then you can get away very quickly").

Bill competed in a celebrity grand prix race, after which he pro-
claimed that it was fun to drive that way legally. He went on *This Is Your Life*,
where the guests from his then barely 24 years of life were his father, mother, brother, sister Kathryn, grandmother, school guidance counselor Bob
Hansen, then girlfriend Heather Rapp, Judge Coumont, and Jo Jo Weber.

He was a guest on local TV and radio talk shows and attended a variety of Olympic fund-raising events and celebrity parties. He appeared at
autograph signings, where he would often sign his posters "Ski to Die."
(Around this time he told a local Oregon paper that Ski to Die was "an exclu-
sive club. I'm the only one."). Sometimes he wrote, "Faster, faster, faster, until
the thrill of speed overcomes the fear of death, Love, Bill."

He bought a Ford pickup truck. He bought a Porsche 911. He bought
an Audi Quattro, and kept it in Austria to drive when he was there.

And in the midst of all of this, Bill was untouchable on skis. After the
Olympics he won the U.S. Nationals at Copper Mountain, Colorado (two days
after appearing on *The Tonight Show*), and he won the last two World Cup

downhills of the season—in Aspen, Colorado, and Whistler, British Columbia. He won, quite literally, everything else there was to win that season.

His Olympic victory has been called a fluke, his step onto the podium a flash in the pan. But he was not just on top for 1:45.59. On February 16th and for the remainder of the 1984 season, he was the best downhill skier in the world.

He competed in the World Cup in Aspen just over two weeks after his Olympic victory. The race was postponed (for a day) due to fog and snow, just like the races in both Wengen and Sarajevo had been delayed.

The downhill course at Aspen was in no way designed to favor Bill. It had a curvy bottom section that required tight, exact turns. "Aspen is not a gliding course," Topper Hagerman says. "You have to turn those babies at some high speeds."

During the training runs, a Canadian coach announced that the course wasn't for Bill because racers had to finish their turns on this one. In the training runs, Bill finished 30th in one (caused by a single mistake) and in the top six in the rest.

Another factor working against Bill was that he was racing in the second seed. The points that determined the racing order for the rest of the season had been calculated prior to the Olympics. Despite Bill's victory at Wengen, he had not had strong enough finishes before the Olympics to make it into the first seed for post-Olympic World Cup races.

As a result, Bill was the 19th racer down the hill. By the time he started, the soft snow had been chewed up and gouged, pushed into washboards on most of the turns. Nonetheless, Bill won the race, and he won it not in the flats near the start but in the technical turns at the end.

Ahead of Bill, Anton Steiner and Helmut Hoeflehner, both from Austria, were tied for first at 1:49.85. On the relatively flat first section of the course, Bill was only in fifth place. By the second split time he had moved into third. It was on the twisty bottom third of the course where Bill actually gained time, holding his tuck while carving defined turns and clattering over the top of the jarring ruts. He finished in 1:49.60.

Somehow, Bill had learned to turn. Bill Marolt, who says, "of course he could turn," also believes that Bill's confidence had caused him to make incredible leaps in his technical skills—"I've never seen anything like it," he says.

"To win World Cup downhills," Bill said at the time, "you have to be very close to the edge."

The following week, Bill competed in the final World Cup of the season, in Whistler, British Columbia. Despite again racing from the second seed, this time in the 18th start position, on a course that was both icy and precise, Bill won that race as well.

It was with this victory, even more so than his Olympic win, that Bill earned the respect of the ski community for his downhill skills. He skied a technically perfect race on a course not built for gliders. Even his worst critics, who claimed that Bill capitalized on delays by gliding over fresh snow, had nothing to say in response to this result.

Bill's rivals were impressed as well. "Bill climbed up two levels of ski racing," Klammer says. "He was thinking he owns the world and no one can stop him. He was a different downhiller, a more complete downhiller, after the [Whistler] victory. Making turns. Before, he was just gliding and being cocky."

Bill was, simply, unbeatable. He was on such a roll that he couldn't do anything wrong. In a sport where the slightest hesitation will keep a racer off the podium, no one could compete with his state of mind. As his Olympic coach Theo Nadig says, he was "on Cloud 7." In sports there are always stories of momentum, confidence translating into success, winning streaks. But to the people around Bill at the time, this seemed like more than that.

"Some people are religious, some are not religious," Barry Thys says. "There was some magic surrounding that guy at times."

Barry pauses, then adds, "And there was a black magic streak following him as well."

To put Bill's three World Cup downhill wins in one season in perspective, another American man didn't win even one again until some 70 races later, when AJ Kitt did it in 1991 on the Oreiller-Killy course at Val d'Isere, France. Later in his career, Bill shrugged off criticism that he was just a glider with the response: "I won three World Cups and the Olympics—I must've made a few good turns."

Bill remained on the U.S. Ski Team for another six seasons, but that World Cup race in Whistler was the last race he would ever win. Other athletes lose their focus due to injuries—Bill was distracted by victory, and by being, as teammate Alan Lauba states, "high on the hog." In the summer of 1984, Bill was on what he later referred to as the "champagne circuit."

It was clear to Bill from literally the moment he arrived back in the U.S. that his life had changed. His flight landed in St. Louis, and pro wrestler Hulk Hogan, who was not scheduled on that flight, boarded the plane just to meet Bill.

The press interest in Bill was relentless, and his family was involved in it as well. Immediately afterward, over 70 TV stations with 100 reporters tried to squeeze inside his father's little place, cameramen fighting to get in the door. The phone rang constantly. Bruce Jenner, gold medalist in the decathlon in the '76 Olympics, called Wally Sr. and Mary to say he wanted to be the first to congratulate them (he was). Mary has no idea how he got the number.

"I think [Wally] got caught up into it," Mary says. "How could you not? It was in our life whether we wanted it or not." During Kathryn's wedding reception, a photographer from *People* magazine showed up at the house to takes shots of the family holding up signs congratulating Bill. DB answered her phone, "Home of the gold."

His childhood coach, Matt Greenslade, says that when he won the gold medal, "He was suddenly riding at the front of the bus family-wise."

"Bill put my mom in the limelight," Vicki says. "She ate it up, felt it was her right. My dad was the same. It was just the way it was."

But the person most enveloped in it was Bill himself. It didn't help that everyone around him was telling him he had it made. Shortly after his Olympic victory Bill attended a testimonial dinner in Los Angeles where Mayor Tom Bradley said, "Welcome to the new world…flooded by adoration you will now enjoy some of the luxuries of life that will come because of the new income flood…."

Bill was swarmed with people wanting something from him, but he wasn't as upset with people angling for a slice of his money or his fame as he was with anyone who tried to take credit for his success. Bill saw his victory as a personal endeavor, an individual achievement. He believed that no one else had done it for him. And it was true, to a large extent. Although many of Bill's problems along the way were clearly self-inflicted, he alone had the motivation to refuse to hear that he wasn't young enough, that he wasn't good enough, and to come back fighting every time. He stayed on skis not despite everybody telling him he couldn't win, but because of it. To show everyone. Now that he had shown them, he didn't want to share the glory.

But the result of Bill displaying his I-did-it-my-way attitude like a banner was that he became beyond insufferable. He lorded over his teammates that he was the star. Barry Thys's sister Edith, who prior to Bill's Olympic win had sat with him at the same breakfast table for months when he lived with her parents, tended to stay away from home when Bill was visiting. "He went right into his rock star existence," Edith says, "and you'd have to hear about *everything*."

Tim Patterson, who handled Bill's boot and binding sponsorships, says that the difference in Bill was dramatic. Back in the United States for the Nationals, Bill's equipment sponsors were eager for photos of Bill, the champion, wearing their equipment. It was, in fact, why these companies were paying him. But Bill's response to being yanked in a bunch of different directions was to stop cooperating.

"As soon as Billy rings the bell, things changed," Tim says. "He was being a complete asshole. Every time he turned around he wanted money in his hand." (As would be the case with several other people throughout Bill's life, despite his behavior, the bond was strong enough that not only did Tim maintain the friendship, he was one of the first people at Bill's hospital bed after his accident.)

Throughout it all, Bill was still there for his closest friends. He arrived at the U.S. Nationals at Copper Mountain, Colorado, in a helicopter that touched down on the top of the course. When he stepped out, he was immediately surrounded by reporters, as Barry says, "kissing his ass." In the midst of the crowd he spotted Barry and Mark Herhusky, tired and dirty from weeks on the road ski racing.

"Come on, boys," Bill said. "You're with me."

He blew off all the questions and the fawning over him and took his two old buddies back to his hotel, where he moved them into his room. The first thing they did was shower, then shared some of the chocolate-covered strawberries (which Mark couldn't believe someone had sent "in the middle of *March*") and champagne that filled Bill's room.

With just about everyone else in his life, however, the dynamic shifted after Bill won the gold medal. Bill's brother says that his win "amplified his edge a bit." Kathryn says that Bill began to treat her more like a fan. Mary says that Bill started thinking everything he did was right. "How could it be wrong?" she says. "He won."

Bill's attitude had ramifications in terms of financial opportunities as well. "[Sponsors] ditched him," Tim says. "They were just plain sick of him. He had it by the balls but it got away from him."

In Sarajevo, after Bill phrased his response to what the medal meant to him in material terms, *Sports Illustrated* somewhat famously, and anonymously, quoted an American reporter there as predicting a bad end for Bill, saying, "There's a gold medal that's going to end up in a pawn shop." As is often the case, people will remember the spirit of a remark that like in a magazine but will have the details slightly off. Looking back, Tim recalls the *SI* quote as predicting a scene of Bill, twenty years down the line, sitting in a bar with his gold medal as the only thing he's got left.

"Everybody could see it coming, and prayed it wouldn't happen," Tim says. "Now, it's almost worse."

When Bill returned home at the end of the racing season, he bought a house in Malibu at his dad's urging. Family – or a least the concept of family—was everything to Bill, and financially, it cost him. He allowed his father to be his agent, even though Wally had no experience in that field.

"Bill had the biggest abandonment issues," Vicki says. "He just dealt with it as his lot in life. That's what caused his anger, that's probably why he won the Olympics. All my parents understood about Bill was the money, and how much they could friggin' make off their kids. He wanted them to love him. He wanted some attention. He didn't get any until he started winning."

Most of the people connected to the Ski Team confirm that Bill's parents hadn't really been in the picture prior to his victory. "I didn't know he had parents," Doug Lewis says, "and then there they were."

Mike Brown witnessed the same dynamic. "His parents were all of a sudden back in his life, and all they wanted to do was take as much as they could get from it," he says. "His father ignored him until he won the gold medal, then he was his best friend. Not a conventional father-son relationship, kind of like two college buddies. It would be like 'Let's go out and pick up girls.'"

Blake feels that Bill's father never gave Blake, or anyone, credit for playing a role in Bill's success. "I don't remember his father prior to the season. After the success, he was around," he says. "His father saw Bill as his meal ticket."

Wally had always said that he would retire when Bill won, and he was true to that word. Allegedly, in Bill's first call to Wally after his Olympic victory, he asked his dad if he had quit yet.

"Wally was trying to get into Bill's pockets," Erik Steinberg says. "It was unsettling the way Wally was living vicariously through Bill. I always suspected Wally, and I was always nervous when he was around. He was always present but silent. I'm not sure how he was influencing Bill through silence, but it always gave me the creeps."

Tim Patterson describes Wally's sudden presence on the scene as a "circus of sorts." Bill Egan, who coached Bill later in his career, recalls Wally's involvement as something short of positive. "His old man was such a shyster," Egan says. "[Wally] had real problems, guys after him."

Blake believes that Wally convinced Bill to let him manage him, telling him they could do it on their own. Bill seemed to refuse to believe that there were experts out there who could manage his fame better than his dad.

Sports agents have connections. They understand how to lay groundwork, and they know how much to ask for and what offers to accept. "It was not Bill's dad's business—in so many ways," Debbie Armstrong says. "It takes a lot of work to get yourself on a Wheaties box."

In addition, finding the right sponsors for Bill was a particularly tricky proposition. Most companies want athletes, especially Olympic ones, to be wholesome, not outlandish. Sponsors want their products associated with good sportsmanship. The behavior that got Bill the most attention from the media was not necessarily the kind of impression companies wanted tied to their product.

After the '84 season Bill told the *Los Angeles Times*, "I try to come off with the cheesecake image, or whatever" (to which the reporter, Scott Ostler, wrote "I think he meant apple pie"). But meanwhile, the press was running with the car theft in Bill's background, and it wasn't because reporters had dug up this fact. Bill was the one who informed the media about his past, apparently because he thought it made a good story.

Phil Mahre's impression of the situation was that Bill wasn't promoting skiing as much as he was promoting himself. Around this time, Bill told a reporter that even bad publicity is publicity and claimed—correctly, at least at that time—that whatever he did brought attention. He went on to say that the Ski Team didn't understand marketing.

The way he was handling things, Bill clearly didn't understand public relations himself. Not happy with the criminal aspect of Bill's image, his sponsors were even less pleased that it was Bill who brought it to the world's attention.

His criminal background did make a positive—and lasting—impression on at least one person who saw it. Bode Miller remembers the personal segment about Bill from the '84 Games. "Him getting in trouble, juvy—it just was cool," Bode says. "Seeing his life before the Olympics was definitely inspiring. You could tell he used ski racing to achieve what he couldn't have otherwise. All really inspirational stuff. He's got that classic American overcome-the-obstacles story."

In interviews around this time, Bill complained to reporters that he had no time to relax. He often seemed bored when answering questions. Other times he came off as calculating, eliciting descriptions such as, "The blue eyes do not read—they look almost cold." He often spit tobacco juice between questions, and he tended to wander off when he was finished talking.

Bill's brother feels that Bill had a hard time with his celebrity status. "He didn't have social graces," Wally says. "He pissed people off. People wanted to get close to him and he would say 'Do I know you?' He didn't like people's bullshit."

Still, Bill did tell *Outside* magazine in the summer of '84, "I'd just as soon be their American hero as some other jerk."

Agents that handle sports figures always say it is better for an athlete to make $50,000 a year for 50 years than quick cash, but Bill's dad didn't agree with that philosophy. There is a short window for athletes, particularly Olympics ones, in terms of endorsements, but a longer one for motivational speaking. Mike Eruzione, the 1980 U.S. hockey player who scored the winning goal against the Russians in Lake Placid, claims that he is as sought-after today as he was a quarter-century ago, reportedly commanding as much as $25,000 per engagement.

The system has since changed, but when Avery Brundage ran the International Olympic Committee, there was a policy of complete amateurism. To retain their amateur status, athletes had to launder their income from endorsements or sponsors through the team. The Ski Team took a cut of the money as it passed through.

The team no longer takes a percentage of skiers' earnings, but the past is another story. In the '80s, Phil and Steve Mahre were supposedly effective at negotiating better deals for themselves. The day Bill won the gold medal,

Blake recalls walking with Marolt and Marolt's wife Connie in the athlete's village in Sarajevo and discussing Bill's victory. According to Blake—who says that this particular memory, even down to the fur coat Connie was wearing, has stuck in his mind ever since—Marolt said, "I don't want another Phil or Steve. We've got to control this."

Immune from being controlled, Bill referred to himself as the "clout" and the "cash cow" for the Ski Team, and addressed the issue of the team's involvement in endorsement money in at least one bitter meeting with team officials. Bill's dad also went public, telling the press that the percentage the Ski Team took was such that "the kids barely get bubble gum money for most of their commercials and appearances." Many of Bill's teammates and coaches credit Bill's success in structuring his share of his earnings as breaking ground in this area.

Money has only come into the sport of skiing recently. "Before, you had to do it just because you wanted to do it," Ski Team spokesperson Tom Kelly says. "There was less motivation to stay in the sport." The IOC gradually loosened the rules regarding endorsements, and skiing was on the forefront—by the 1985-'86 season, racers could wear sponsor's names on their headgear. Skiing also pioneered cash prizes in sports. Kelly says that by 1990, top ski racers could easily make a half-million dollars a year on prize money alone.

Doug Lewis makes the comment that if he had won the gold in '84 he would own five ski resorts now, and that sounds about right. It was not to be for Bill. Potential sponsors came to him, but his father pushed too hard, demanded outrageous payouts, and was left with nothing. Aside from incentives from his equipment sponsors for wearing their gear—Raichle boots, Tyrolia bindings, Scott poles and goggles, (later) Bolle and Cebe goggles, and, of course, Atomic skis—Bill did no commercial endorsements whatsoever. No cars, no soft drinks. No Wheaties box.

At the end of his career, Bill was asked whether he had, in fact, made millions. He answered that he had "probably gone through a couple," but that wasn't true. Even so, with his sponsors paying him base payments for every piece of equipment he used (for example, $100,000 a year just for his boots and bindings) and hefty bonuses on top of that for every win, Bill did make several hundred thousand dollars in 1984 alone, and probably close to a million over the course of his career.

"He thought the money he made was going to last him forever," coach

Jim Tracy says. "And if it was managed better, it probably would have. But Billy was Billy. His style wasn't conducive to planning for the future. He lived for the moment."

Bill went through his income quickly. "Money is a concept to Bill," his brother Wally says. "When he went out, whatever was in his pocket was out on the table. He doesn't get the management of it at all, he never did."

Bill cashed in on his medal for fast money in the form of a 1985 made-for-TV movie called *Going for the Gold: The Bill Johnson Story*. It stars Anthony Edwards as Bill and Sarah Jessica Parker as his (fictional) girlfriend at ski school. It is made-for-TV movie-making at its very worst, and it plays a bit loose with the details. As Doug Lewis points out, in Bill's real life at that time, "There was no dog. There was never a dog." (Bill's sister Kathryn says that earlier on there actually was a black Lab that Bill traveled with—until a neighbor shot it.)

The Ski Team, without Bill, got together to watch Bill's movie at a ski camp in Mt. Bachelor. "That was a pretty good hoot," Andy Chambers says.

Bill was paid $200,000 for the movie, from which Wally bought a $23^{1}/_{2}$-foot SeaRay cabin cruiser for himself as his commission. Bill believed that he was supposed to receive royalties from the movie, but he never did.

The boat ended up being a very controversial item in the Johnson family, with Bill, as an adult, still being torn between his parents' squabbling. "Mom was very jealous of it and when Bill sold the [Malibu] house, she drove Bill's truck down to Malibu and picked up the boat," Kathryn says. "Dad immediately called Bill and Bill told Mom to take it back. I think Dad had to retrieve it. Bill was caught in the middle."

Years later, needing money, Wally sold the boat to Kathryn, who later sold it to someone outside the family.

Bill's future wife Gina would later sum it up like this: "They are not a close family. They don't work as one, they work for themselves."

Bill also paid his father $3,000 a month (for the next year or two) to manage him and cover the house payment, and he let Wally live—and have parties—in the Malibu house, where with his international travel schedule, Bill himself rarely stayed.

The fact that Bill's father took advantage of him seemed clear to most everyone around him, but at least one of Bill's teammates saw it a slightly different way. "To me, it's like how dysfunctional can you say it was, how bad?"

Sam Collins says. "Not really having the support of your family—there were just a lot of issues. But Bill wanted his dad to be part of his life, no matter what. Bill wanted his dad there and he didn't care what that meant."

Family members are surprisingly easy on Wally—he had sacrificed for Bill in the past, he needed the money, Bill wanted his help. And in his own way, Wally always seemed to believe in Bill. It may have been akin to betting on a horse, but he did front the bills for Bill for a long time to keep his son on skis. Even when his businesses were failing, he put all his money into Bill. He gave Bill a credit card and paid it off for him. He picked up the tab when Bill would buy rounds for everyone in a bar. He called friends and begged for $500 at a time to pay Bill's expenses.

Wally took a gamble on Bill, at least financially, and it paid off. Kathryn believes that in return, he was entitled to reap some of the benefits. "If Dad took a 'manager's fee' off the top, I say he deserved it," she says. And in the epitome of a backhanded compliment, she says, "Dad took no more advantage than [Mom] did."

The rest of Bill's family enjoyed his generous nature as well—at one point he bought an apartment building in Portland as an investment, and just about everyone in his family lived there rent-free at one time or another. (Bill's sisters did manage the units in exchange—they disagree on the amount of work that entailed.)

Bill also bailed his sister Vicki out of Mexico twice. The first time she was car-jacked and never got her car back, so Bill sent her an airline ticket, then paid off all her credit cards when she got back, about $2,500 worth, so she could have a fresh start. The next time she was in Mexico for a year having, as she says, "way too much fun." Bill wrote her a letter that whenever she was ready to come back to let him know. When she called him, he had a plane ticket waiting for her at the airport. "He never asked for anything in return—anything, ever," she says. "To Bill, family is family."

Bill's sense of loyalty—and resultant loss of money—wasn't limited to family members. He also maintained his relationships with equipment sponsors that had always stood by him, turning down significantly more money from new companies that approached him to wear their gear. While he wasn't always accommodating to the sponsors he had, he did remain faithful to them.

In between celebrity parties Bill managed to give back to his hometown, returning several times to Oregon. In June he came back to attend a "Roast and Toast" to fund the Mount Hood Ski Education Foundation, formed to provide qualified young skiers from lower income families the opportunity to pursue ski racing. He was also in town to attend a junior award ceremony at Mt. Hood where each kid got their picture taken with Bill's gold medal around their neck.

On July 5th, he returned to be the grand marshall of the Sandy Mountain Festival parade and accept a key to Sandy from Mayor Ruth Loundree. (The Mountain Festival committee had picked the theme "Salute to the Olympics" in hopes that Bill would accept their invitation.) In the parade he rode in the back of a red Mustang convertible, driven by the daughter of the same police chief who had been involved in Bill's arrests as a teen. DB rode in the car with Bill wearing a t-shirt emblazoned "I'm Bill Johnson's Mom."

Since Bill had moved around so much within his family, never really having a solid home base, once he became famous there was quite a bit of confusion about where he was from. Many of the spectators in the parade in Oregon, for example, held signs saying "Welcome Home, Bill!" Bill usually listed his address as either his Pinto or his father's place in Van Nuys, California. The press ran with the California-boy angle. On his show, Johnny Carson introduced Bill with the line, "He comes from the ski capital of the world—Van Nuys."

Between celebrating and taking time for various appearances and commitments, the summer of '84 took its toll on Bill. During that time Bill told friends that he was staying in shape by water-skiing and windsurfing— not exactly the strictest of training regimens. When he returned to the Ski Team, Alan Lauba recalls, "Bill took the full summer off. He enjoyed the summer. He drank a lot of beer, partied a bit, was his cocky self. When he came back, he forgot where he was. The will, desire, passion to win—he didn't have that feel. He lost the edge to ski perfect."

Even at the height of his stardom, Bill's unwavering sense of entitlement continued to be a destructive influence in his life, causing him to alienate people and hurt himself. "He had money and fame and yet no one would give him respect," Steinberg says. "He had no respect, no endorsements. It just killed him. Rotted him from the inside out."

Bill's teammate Cory Carlson has a similar impression: "The tragedy is that he wasn't able to enjoy his success. I don't know that he was very happy. He should have been living a dream, set for life."

Bill would constantly ask people, condescendingly, "Do you know who I am?" Bill said it to a Canadian Mountie once, when Steinberg was behind the wheel. Twenty years later, during a traffic stop with a more dramatic outcome, Bill would say the same thing to a policeman. Bill announced it so frequently, and so haughtily, that the other skiers on the team took to mocking Bill about it—for example, pointing at Bill and asking the counter person in McDonald's, "Do you know who this guy is?"

A year after Bill's victory, Steinberg took him to a nightclub in Los Angeles to celebrate his 25th birthday. They went in Bill's Porsche, which Bill kept in the billiard room of his house in Malibu. He didn't have a valid driver's license and the car had Oregon plates. At one point Wally had backed Bill's pick-up truck right into it. The car looked like a rental—fast food wrappers and spilled beer everywhere. Bill didn't care.

When they went out that night, Steinberg was dressed in wool pants and sandals. Bill had on a silk shirt, jeans, and thousand-dollar cowboy boots. The guy at the door wouldn't let them in. In response, as Steinberg expected he would, Bill asked the bouncer if he knew who he was. "I don't care if you're the Shah of Iran," the bouncer said, "you're not coming in here in sandals and cowboy boots." When they got back in Bill's car, he revved the engine, popped the clutch, and drove screaming across the parking lot. There was a wood barrier across the lot. Bill executed a 90-degree skidding police turn, smashed right through it, and kept on going. "Happy Birthday, Bill," Steinberg said.

Bill was partying a lot in this era (Jo Jo smiles at the memory and says "Aspen in the '80s"). Former snowboarders recall a time in South America when Bill was ranting against snowboarding as a sport, as well as the athletic abilities of the people who participated, all while rolling a joint. When Bill would visit "Hotel California" in Tahoe, there was usually some pot smoking in the snow cave. It's unclear whether this ever directly affected Bill's skiing—after crashing once, he told Doug, "That's the last time I get high before a race," but Doug couldn't tell whether or not he was kidding. In the fall of '84, at a press conference in a beer garden in Switzerland, Bill was asked by a reporter if it was true that he had a drug problem. In response, Bill winked and said, "No, it's not a problem. I can afford them."

In Malibu, Bill's dad was partying excessively as well, with life-altering results. At one point Bill left his dad in the Malibu house without any cigarettes or any money for alcohol in an attempt to get him to clean himself up.

"Bill was angry and bitter that Wally wasn't the father he wanted him to be," Mary says. "Even at the end, he refused to give up the image that he wanted for his father." When Wally wouldn't agree to go to rehab, Bill ended up selling the house.

Now and then, Bill's belief that he could do whatever he wanted to do because he was Bill Johnson backfired badly, including almost getting him thrown off the Ski Team again on at least two occasions. One time, in the summer of 1984, Bill showed up an hour late for a team meeting at the Mammoth Mountain Inn. He arrived in cut-off jeans, no shirt, no shoes. He jumped right up onto the front desk in his bare feet, announced his name, and asked where his room was. Erik Steinberg escorted Bill back to the team van and told him he had lost his privilege to be at that training camp. Bill showed up two weeks later at a camp in Bend, Oregon, forgiven.

Another incident took place at a McDonald's in Cranbrook, British Columbia. At that point Steinberg was in charge of enforcing Marolt's no-tobacco-chewing rule. To test him, Bill began to spit tobacco into a cup right in front of Steinberg's face. The situation ended with Steinberg and Bill throwing punches and Bill being kicked off the team for about 20 minutes. Bill's ski bag and duffle actually came off the van, but then, to Steinberg's shock, Bill began to shed some tears. Steinberg let him back in the van.

Ironically, the American Tobacco Company was, in those days, a sponsor of the U.S. Ski Team, funding the wind-tunnel project, a training device called a Berg Und Fal (similar to the barrels elephants stand on at the circus), and all the Copenhagen, Skoal, and Happy Days the team could (not) chew.

Bill was never a team player, but there were times when he tried to support his teammates. To Sam Collins, Bill acted as a coach and a mentor, helping him out quite a bit.

In 1985, Doug Lewis won the bronze medal in the World Championships in Bormio, Italy. Bill finished 13th, due to what Steinberg calls Bill's time on the "rubber chicken" circuit. After the race, while Doug was still at the mountain doing interviews, Bill went back to the hotel and borrowed a bunch of magic markers. He found a big poster and on the blank side he drew a beautiful to-scale flag with all the stars and stripes and wrote, "Congratulations, Lewie, you're the best, you rock." He posted it in the front window of the hotel for Doug to see when he returned. The only handwriting on the sign was Bill's, and he didn't sign his name to it. "It was the only time I saw Bill do an unselfish act," Steinberg says. "It was touching to all of us."

Topper, like many people who discuss Bill's historical contribution to skiing, ends his comments with a qualifier—in his case, "whether you liked the guy or didn't like the guy."

Jim Tracy and Bill Egan both coached Bill toward the end of his career on the Ski Team, and they express their praise of him similarly. "Bottom line, he's a champion. He did a lot for our sport," Tracy says. "Regardless of what people thought about him."

"Bill was one of the greatest skiers that ever lived," Egan says. "But he just was able to screw that whole thing up."

Topper's answer to the simple question of whether he liked Bill seems to sum up the attitude of many people associated with him. Topper pauses, and seems a little taken aback. "Did I like him? There were times I didn't like him. I wish he would have appreciated people more, been more congenial, more respectful. I thought I got along with him, helped him do some things," he says, then pauses again. "But yeah, I liked Billy. I did."

Just like Topper, Steinberg's first response to being asked if he likes Bill is to repeat the question. After a moment he comes up with: "Oh, God. It's like if you have a brother who's always stealing money from you. I'm always there for him. Do I like him? No. Do you get to choose your relatives? No."

Andy Luhn, always Bill's biggest supporter, defends him once again. "He was not Mr. Nice Guy, but people see what they want to see," he says. "They want to take someone that's been up high and put him down low. I'm not saying he was a prince, but mostly what I see is that he didn't hold anybody back. He didn't make anybody go slower."

Once Bill won the Olympics, Nadig claims that he got even more "out of the hand" in terms of coaching. He essentially refused to train with the team or take any advice from its coaches. "After, Bill thought he was the boss," Nadig says. "It was very difficult to keep control of Bill afterward, to help him."

Tim Patterson recalls Bill getting "mean and nasty" with Nadig. "Bill was the king," Tim says. "He wasn't going to be coached by anybody, wasn't going to listen to anybody. [His win] was because of him, it was because of no one else." In fact, Tim feels—and he is not alone in this belief—that Bill's attitude cost him a chance to compete in the next Olympics. "Theo hated him so bad he wouldn't even let him defend his title," he says. "He was so damn mad at Bill by then, and he got back at him."

All the distractions—all the people pulling at Bill, trying to get a piece of him, the hype, the media, the autographs, the obligations—drew Bill's energy away from ski racing, making it difficult for him to concentrate.

Franz Klammer says Bill "obviously didn't dedicate himself that much anymore." Phil Mahre and Doug Lewis believe Bill felt that all the adulation he was getting from his fans would somehow translate into success on the slopes. "He thought he had arrived and didn't have to work anymore," Phil says.

"He thought it was gonna be easy—he had money, everybody thought he was God," Doug says. "He didn't work, and everybody else caught up."

Not surprisingly, as a trainer Topper stresses that Bill's lack of conditioning played a key role in his future performance. "Skiing is a serious business—you have to train for it," he says. "Bill did not appreciate conditioning as much as others. When you take the summer off, you're asking for a tough road, very tough. Muscle, strength, power, endurance, it's gonna catch up to you. You might get through it, but you're not gonna place well."

Bill may not have been putting in the training time, but judging from his response to his finish in a World Cup Super-G in France the following season, his competitive edge remained. (Bill trained on Super-G courses now and then and he also competed in them occasionally.) Barry Thys was in the same race, toward the back. The scores were flashed at the end, but due to the crowd of reporters surrounding Bill, Barry couldn't fully read his time. He asked Bill if he could read the tenths of a second posted next to his name. In front of all the press, Bill yelled over to Barry: "Let me tell you something. We lost. You sucked and I sucked. There's first place and there's everything else."

Andy says that Bill took a scientific approach to his race finishes. Rather than just proclaim that he had to be faster to win, Bill would review his performances painstakingly, making notes on each of the section times of his run, trying to figure out why, in each individual section, he hadn't been the fastest.

The combination of an infatuation with the limelight and a lack of conditioning would likely have been enough to keep any ski racer from the podium. But in Bill's case, it was more than that. He also had to return to an environment where, justified or not, virtually nobody liked him. Despite his victories, Bill was still alienated, probably more so. When he was no longer winning, the administration of the Ski Team looked at it as validation that their way was better. It would have taken a massive amount of energy for Bill to overcome a heated organization that hated his guts, and some say, awaited his fall.

"Marolt just couldn't wait for him to fail," Mike Brown says. "They wanted us to know that. They made that abundantly clear. They couldn't wait for him to fall off his pedestal."

But perhaps the best explanation for why Bill never won again is that he already had. His goal was to be the best skier in the world, not *stay* the best skier in the world. He had no encore planned.

"It engulfed him so much," Debbie Armstrong says. "There was especially a lot swirling around him. He didn't necessarily have the skills to deal with it all. He had done all he needed to do…he just let it go."

Barry says that Bill wasn't as hungry anymore. Bill hadn't just done everything he wanted to do in the sport—at age 23 he had pulled off his wildest dream for his whole life as well.

"The medal meant the world to him," Blake says. "It was his life's goal. It was his only goal. It came back to bite him. What do you do after that with the same intensity? How do you refocus?"

Phil Mahre believes that if an athlete makes the quest for a gold medal their goal in life, they are setting themselves up for a future of disappointment. "If you don't accomplish that goal, your life is over," he says, "and if you do, your life is over as well."

Bill never seemed to have a vision for himself beyond winning the Olympics. He didn't consider retiring, but he also didn't necessarily see himself as having a long and fulfilling career in the sport. It's not clear if he assumed that he would continue to win, or if he just figured that it wouldn't matter that much if he didn't. Most likely, he simply didn't think that far ahead.

The problem was that Bill's personality was not as laid-back as his career plan. As Doug Lewis says, "When you're losing and still a cocky bastard, it doesn't work."

And then there was Bill's family. "There were negative influences on him—people came back into his life," Nadig says. "As soon as he was Olympic champion, people came back and they try to take a little away, get a little of the money, the fame. I thought they were bad people. They didn't know the sport, what it was going to take. His father was an alcoholic, and his mom was weird, really weird."

For the entire '85-'86 ski season, DB and Jimmy traveled with the Ski Team in Europe. Doug Lewis uses the same term as Nadig to describe the experience: "It was a weird dynamic, with Bill's parents at the dinner table with the team on the road—just weird."

To be closer to the team—and to ski for free and gain access to press parties—Jimmy worked as a cameraman, taking film of the team while they were training, and DB did some reporting. She wrote from a mother's viewpoint and also submitted articles to local ski publications without a byline, interviewing her son and beginning her articles with lines such as "We caught up with Billy…."

"Bill's mom…. Bill tolerated her," Blake says.

"Her private life was so messy," Nadig says. "It was not a healthy thing. She didn't direct Bill. At that point that she should give him support and guidance in his life, she was just hanging out with him. It was kind of sad, you know?"

DB says that Bill was awful to her, at least when she first began traveling with the team. Jimmy feels that Bill didn't like his mother being there and giving the team members hugs and wishing them luck. "He just didn't want to have his mom hanging out with the guys, telling him what to do," Jimmy says.

"He didn't want me to open my mouth," DB says. "He wanted me to be quiet and not say anything. He didn't want me to be a mom."

Several members of the Ski Team recall that DB did not seem as concerned with Bill's career as she was with the perks of traveling with him. "Bill's mom did a bit of coat-tailing," Mike Brown says. "She was an odd person. And it seemed kind of odd that she would just become part of his entourage. I didn't see it as a big support thing—more like what she could get from Bill at any given point, what she could experience from hanging around Bill."

There were several whirlwind shopping trips on the circuit that season—DB and Jimmy went with Bill to Descente, the U.S. Ski Team's sponsor, in Austria, where everyone picked out various outfits for free—warm-up jackets, ski pants, downhill suits, sweaters. While in Europe, Bill's family also brought home several sweaters from Steffner. In addition, DB recalls a couple trips into the Obermeyer facility in Colorado for clothing. During this time Bill, as well as his entire family, was also receiving free skis and equipment from Atomic.

DB parlayed her contacts from that season into two businesses. Since 1986, she has owned and run ProSports NW, which manufactures race bibs, gate panels, and signs, as well as Gresham Flag & Banner. Jimmy is now a precision machinist at Cascade Microtech.

Bill has always maintained that there are only two acceptable outcomes to a race —win or fall—but after the '84 season, he wasn't doing either one. Conditioning and motivation aside, Bill wasn't winning because he only won when he skied to die, when he risked his life to win, and he no longer wanted to take that gamble. He didn't have to. He had nothing left to prove. Just like his early days on the Ski Team when he assessed the risk necessary to win, he likely knew what it would take to win, but wasn't willing to do it.

During the '86-'87 season, that drive may have been back. It seems that Bill, looking ahead to the end of his career or more immediately, to another Olympics in '88, weighed the risk and made a conscious decision to ski that way again. Of course accidents can always happen, but if a world-class ski racer is not going all out, it is not so difficult to get from the top of the mountain to the bottom without falling. Bill didn't win that season, but he did try hard enough to fall.

That season, Bill was winning a race in Aspen when he wrecked. Then, in Val Gardena, Italy, he had another accident—a horrifying crash that ended his season, and, some say, although he would return to the team for another three seasons, his skiing career as well.

On the downhill course in Val Gardena, there is a high-speed section near the bottom known as the "camel bumps"—a big bump, a little one, and a drop. There are at least three potential lines for a racer to take through them. Bill was going about 60 mph when he fell. He slid on his side until one of his edges caught, twisting his leg and throwing him into the air. He came to a stop with a fractured right shoulder and a mangled left knee.

In later interviews about the crash, although he didn't break it down into a list, he essentially identified three separate factors that caused the accident. The first was that he was confused by spectators waving their arms. The second was that for a split second his mind went blank and he hesitated, trying to remember which line he'd decided to take. He did not learn from the third reason, which, fifteen years later, would contribute to his downfall: "I was on a really fast pair of skis," he said, "moving faster than I was prepared for."

Other racers feel that Bill's lack of physical conditioning at the time may have made him more vulnerable to injury. He ruptured both his medial collateral ligament (in three parts) and his anterior cruciate, and he scraped the bones together on the lateral side of the joint, roughening the bone ends.

Dr. J. Richard Steadman operated on Bill's knee in South Lake Tahoe, California, on December 15th. He patched the ligaments together, repositioned the good parts, and created a new ligament out of knee tissue. He then inserted two screws and a pin to hold it all together.

After the knee surgery, Bill's back began hurting so badly that he couldn't do his rehabilitation exercises. He had had back pain since going over a man-made training bump wrong at a Ski Team camp in May of 1985. At the time he didn't even fall, but he knew right away that he had hurt himself. The injury put pressure on his spinal cord, eventually causing chronic pain. For a while Bill had traveled with a masseuse who doubled as his girlfriend, but once they broke up he had no relief from the pain.

On January 13th, less than a month after his knee surgery, Bill had a second operation, this time on his back. Dr. Courtney Brown, who performed Bill's spinal surgery in Denver, said at the time that he was surprised that Bill could even stand up straight. In a two-hour operation, Brown removed two ruptured lumbar disks from Bill's back. Afterward, Bill went back to Tahoe to a clinic for rehabilitation and, as it turns out, to meet the love of his life.

In the final scene of *Downhill Racer*, as the Robert Redford character is hoisted up on the shoulders of his adoring fans and the credits roll, he is asked by a reporter what his plans are now. His response is: "Just to slow down, I guess. I don't know. I don't know. I don't know." Having virtually lived the entire plot of the movie to that point, Bill appeared to take this part to heart as well. After the '84 season Bill did slow down, at least on skis, and he has essentially spent the rest of his life not knowing what to do next.

In real life, a lot more stuff happens after the climatic event. Referring to Bill's life, his step-mom Mary says, "Reality isn't always beautiful. Every story doesn't have a happy ending." In truth, happy endings are generally for stories that haven't finished yet.

CHAPTER SEVEN

"Bill always said he wasn't afraid of anything—except women."
– GINA JOHNSON

Bill was only out of the hospital three days after his back surgery when he met Gina Ricci, a vivacious 21-year-old brunette who already had a boyfriend. He was unshaven and hunched over and not, according to Gina, looking particularly attractive. But he refused to let her dance with anyone else, so he threw down his crutches, took off his back brace, and danced with her all night.

Bill has always said—and still maintains—that the evening they met was supposed to be a fix-up between his friend Barry Thys and Gina, and that he stole her away. Barry backs up Bill's story, saying it was a terrible idea to take Bill along on his blind date. "I never had a chance," he says. "Bill saw her as we were walking in. By the time I got to the table he was already saying I was not part of that deal." Gina denies the set-up version—she was home in Tahoe visiting her best friend Erika at the time, and her story is that she was excited for a girls' night out with a stop for a quick drink with Erika's long-time friend Barry and his friend Bill. Besides, she had been dating her high school boyfriend for the past five years.

At the time, Gina was living in Fresno, California, working as a district manager for a chain of eleven retail stores in the Bay Area called Above the Belt. She had received her associate degree at night and then started learning on the job, moving up to management quickly and relocating to Fresno to open another Above the Belt store there. She split her time between running the Fresno store and the Sacramento branch, with time off for an occasional get-away weekend in Tahoe, her hometown, in between.

Gina's first context for Bill was that he was selected to the Olympic team in 1984 and Erika's brother Hans was not. Gina, attending the Fashion

Institute of San Francisco at the time, remembers watching the race with Erika amidst a fair amount of antagonism surrounding Bill's placement on the team. Her only memory of Bill's victory is that she was happy an American had won.

The night Bill met Gina the quick drink turned into dinner, with Gina and Erika saying they were going to Jake's restaurant and Bill and Barry inviting themselves along, even though they had already eaten. Then they ended up at a dance place, and when Erika got swept up with old friends and Barry was confronted with an ex-girlfriend, Gina and Bill were stuck with each other.

"Bill could really look stunning when he would shave and dress up. But that night he wasn't anything about that," Gina says. She recalls him as being very confrontational, even while, presumably, he was trying to make a good impression on her. She stood up to him, gave it right back, but she didn't fall all over him. She thinks that approach added to her appeal, because she suspected he was probably used to a lot of female attention. "I didn't say 'Oh, Bill, Bill.' I wasn't star-struck at all," she says. "I wasn't thinking about dating him, and I think he was kind of taken aback by that a little bit, thinking 'Wait a minute, doesn't she like me? Everybody else likes me.' I think I was kind of a challenge to him at that point."

Gina, a petite girl with an essentially perfect figure, long, curly brown hair, and flinty green eyes, likely didn't need to throw herself at anybody. Her face was open, in an All-American sort of way, but with a hint of her Mediterranean background in her coloring. Gina was the rare and ideal combination of wholesome and sexy. She talked fast and made lots of straight-on eye contact and managed to seem tough and innocent all at the same time.

The day after Gina met Bill, Erika's brother was racing in a pro race, and Gina and Erika went to watch him. Barry and Bill showed up at the race. "It was very strange," she says. "The whole thing is televised, and all of a sudden all these cameras are walking over to this guy I've been dancing with all night."

Gina claims that she was not awed by Bill's fame when she first met him, but given the situation, it would have been hard for her not to be. She was, after all, only 21 years old at the time. "I thought 'Who the heck is he, you know? What is this all about?' I was surprised by how everybody was so taken that Bill Johnson was there," she says. "He won a race, but what's the big deal? I didn't really understand what it meant to be a gold medalist. I had no idea." Bill came over and sat by Gina and they talked for a little while. He and Barry were going gambling and they asked if she wanted to come with them. Erika went home with her brother, and Gina went with Bill and Barry. That second night, Gina says, Bill cleaned himself up. She won a bunch of money at the casino and then they went to dinner. She recalls thinking "Oh, you are kinda cute"—just before she kissed him.

At the end of the weekend, Gina had to leave Tahoe to go back to work in Fresno, about three hundred miles away. Bill asked for her number and called her twice. They had long conversations. He told her about his house in Malibu and talked about stopping in to see her on his way down the California coast. Then he didn't call for a week or two. Gina didn't know how to get in touch with Bill directly, so she sent a message to him through Barry. When Bill got back to her, she asked him if was coming through Fresno anytime soon. He told Gina that she was "geographically undesirable." He said he would have called her when he went to Malibu, but he wasn't sure when he was going there next. "He would have kept my number until he got in the area," Gina says. "Which was kind of his way of doing things."

But during that call, Bill decided that he did want to see Gina. He told her that he was staying in Oregon with his mother for a while, recovering from his surgeries, and he asked her what she was doing that weekend. When she said that she was off for the next three days, Bill told her to buy a ticket and fly up, that he would pay her back for it when she got up there (actually, he only paid her half).

"Tonight?" she asked.

Bill picked Gina up at the airport in his truck and took her to see the Columbia River gorge. She spent the weekend at DB's house, but the second day she was there Bill flew out to Denver for an appearance and left Gina to stay overnight with his mom. "I'm like, 'You're leaving me here?'" Gina says. "It was very strange. And it was kind of how our whole relationship was. He didn't really tell me the details in advance, here's the plan. It was always like I had to wait to see what was gonna happen, what's next."

Gina's sister Rochelle says that Bill's "grand personality" is what drew Gina to him. "He attracts people, he keeps you on edge wondering what is going to happen next," Rochelle says. "It's not the same thing day in and day out."

Gina recognized that the dynamic was odd, but in the context of Bill's celebrity, it had become exciting for her in a way as well. "Most of our planning I had to hear from him giving interviews on the phone," she says. "I was just so young and naïve and so taken by it all."

During his second dinner with Gina in Oregon before he left town, Bill turned to her and said "So, what do you want to do for the rest of our lives?" Gina realized that he meant it. "I looked at him and I thought, 'This guy's nuts,'" she said. "I couldn't figure him out. And he was serious, he was serious. He had decided, that was it. He wanted to marry me."

Still recuperating and unable to ski, Bill continued to travel constantly. "He liked that, living out of a suitcase," Gina says. "He wasn't real good about having a home base. He didn't have to. Home was wherever his suitcase was." Bill was doing TV commentary during some downhill races in Aspen in March, and he invited Gina to come with him for her birthday.

By all reports, Bill had never been the suavest guy on the Ski Team. "Billy was never a very polished individual," Jo Jo says. But he put on a good act now and then. After he won the gold medal he was quoted as saying things like, "There were only ugly guys on the tour before me, so now maybe we'll have some good-looking chicks following us." When he met Gina, however, he fell hard. He spent the week with her in Aspen introducing her to people as his wife (Gina told everyone it was actually their third date). "He was in love, crazy in love," Barry says.

"He was not the kind of guy to judge people on their looks," Mark Herhusky says. "But he saw Gina—she was gorgeous and she was his prize. He thought they were going all the way to the top."

When Gina returned home from the trip to Colorado, she talked to Bill frequently on the phone. Then he called her one night and said, "Guess where I am? Fresno Street." Gina had no idea he was coming, and he was about 15 minutes away. She spent most of that time putting all her boyfriend's pictures away (he was living in Sacramento at the time, and she hadn't totally broken it off with him yet).

Sounding exactly like Barry describing how Bill showed up at his parent's house years earlier, Gina says, "He came, and he never left." There was never any talk of living together. Bill brought just one bag of clothes—socks, underwear, white t-shirts. He always traveled very plainly, his clothes always folded, neatly organized. He could live out of that one bag for months—he had had lots of practice while he was with the Ski Team in Europe.

The first week Bill was there, he contacted a rehab facility to help him with his back and his knee. The second week, Gina unloaded his bag. That was it. He had moved in. "It happened so fast and so easy," Gina says. "It was pretty exciting." Gina believes that Bill's accident at Val Gardena had shaken him enough to change his thinking—made him reexamine where he was in his life and caused him feel that he needed to go to the next stage. "All of a sudden at that time he was ready," Gina says. "I was the one. He knew I'd be a great mother. Children were huge to him—he wanted four."

During their first three months together, Gina and Bill were extremely close. He didn't so much ask Gina if they were getting married as announce to her that they were. "He would cry, he was just so sentimental," she says. "We would talk and talk and talk, he would tell me things and ask me things. He really opened up to me."

Bill didn't go into too many details about his past, but he did stress to Gina how important the concept of family was to him. "His family was so estranged as a child, he really yearned for having that European style where gramma washes the clothes, mom and dad run the restaurant, and everybody lives in one big home and all work together and help each other out," she says. "He really wanted that."

The relationship kept up its initial speed. Bill and Gina got officially engaged that summer and were married less than ten months after they met. Bill had asked Gina her ring size before flying out to see Jo Jo, who was working in his family's jewelry business in Chicago, and he gave her an engagement ring—with a 1.2 carat, Marquis-cut diamond—at Jo Jo's wedding rehearsal dinner.

"And then things kind of switched," Gina says. "It was 'I've got her.' All of a sudden I felt like the whole dynamic changed." Gina would frequently catch Bill watching girls, and he would respond by telling her that it was all right for him to look at the menu. "Maybe it was my insecurity, but he was definitely a flirt," she says. "I was really nervous about him traveling without me. I wasn't real comfortable. Because people would *flock* over him."

That summer Bill and Gina visited Bill's dad and went boating with him on Lake Powell. By that time, alcoholism had gotten the best of Wally and he was drinking, literally, two-fisted. "He smoked from the first thing in the morning until he passed out at night," Gina says. "He did absolutely nothing but sit in front of this little teeny table in this one-bedroom apartment. It was the just the most bizarre thing I've ever seen in my life."

When Bill met Gina's family, he caused an unusual first impression, calling Gina's mom a bitch the first time he met her. The family, including Gina's mom, Linda, and her sister, Rochelle, was camping in Yosemite. The incident occurred at the dinner table at the Awani Hotel. Linda's in-laws were there, and some of their friends. Rochelle, 15 at the time and by her own admission more concerned with curling her hair before she went hiking than anything else, remembers that Gina showed up smiling and happy with her new boyfriend. At dinner, an older gentleman offered to make up a bed for Bill and Gina to stay overnight in his mobile home. Bill's response was to say, "I'm not staying in some mobile home." When Linda suggested that the remark was inappropriate and that she felt Bill had had too much to drink to safely drive her daughter back to Fresno, he responded with the name-calling. It more or less set the tone for the family's relationship with Bill.

In a karmic twist given what was to come, before Bill and Gina left Yosemite that night Bill also said to Linda, within earshot of the rest of the family and friends, "These people are trailer trash. Do you know who I am? I don't do that. I don't stay in trailers."

Bill married Gina on October 30th, 1987, in the town hall of Wagrain, Austria, right next to the Atomic factory. Gina had gone with him on the World Cup circuit, living out of two bags between them for four months. She was the only woman traveling with the team, and it was awkward being in Europe as Bill's girlfriend. In the past the Mahres had brought their wives, but they were retired now. Gina decided that if they were going to get married anyway, she would rather travel as Bill's wife. The director of Atomic and his secretary (who didn't speak English) were the witnesses. Gina wore white sweats for the ceremony, Bill wore blue ones.

When Gina first arrived in Europe with Bill she didn't realize that, as she says, "The team didn't like him." The team was particularly unhappy with Bill at that point due to some negative comments he had made—about the Ski Team in general and the qualifications of the younger skiers on the team specifically—while doing the TV commentary in Aspen.

Rather than smooth things over, Bill separated himself even further from the team. "At that time he was calling his own shots," Gina says. "We'd arrive in Europe and if the Ski Team was doing something he didn't want to do, he'd say 'I'm not doin' that. I'm going here.' The coaches were not in charge of Bill. Bill was on his own program. And that created here's Bill and here's the team."

In keeping with the way Bill had behaved at the beginning of their relationship, he rarely told Gina where they were going from week to week or what was going to happen next. Still, at the time, it was thrilling for Gina. They were meeting famous and important people and staying at lavish hotels. "We'd show up in Zermatt—I didn't know what Zermatt was," Gina says. "We put everything on the train, we park the car, we get up to the top, we go to bed, we wake up in the morning, I open the curtains and there's the Matterhorn. I had no idea that was going to be there."

The first ski season that Bill and Gina were together ended in an Olympic year. The 1988 Games were in Calgary, and Bill expected to be there to defend his title. He was coming off some dehabilitating injuries, however, and he had been spending more time in rehab than in training.

The selection criteria had changed since 1984, and the coaches planned to take four racers this time. Bill didn't appear outwardly concerned about his chances, telling reporters that all he needed were some top twenty finishes in December and some top ten and top three performances in January. The first race of the '87-'88 season was in Val d'Isere, France. Bill finished 73rd. The second race was in Val Gardena, Italy—Bill finished 81st.

In Val d'Isere, Bill was interviewed for *Sports Illustrated* by William Oscar Johnson. In the course of that interview, an uncharacteristically humble and insightful Bill said the following: "If I had to do it over, I wouldn't have spent the summer of 1984 on the champagne circuit. It was chaos. I never knew where I was. Someone would call my mom, someone would call my dad, someone would call my semi-agent. They'd all book me in somewhere, and I'd go and play celebrity. I thought it was going to be a once-in-a-lifetime chance—all the fame and fortune. Actually it wasn't that great. In retrospect I think that if I'd quit racing completely in '84, I could've made maybe $2 million. As it was, I didn't really commit myself to racing, either. My plan was to wait for this season—you know, sort of hang out until the next Olympics and try not to get hurt, and then go in and do it all over again. Maybe it would have worked, but then I went and blew the not-getting-hurt part. Now I've got to come back a long way."

In terms of forecasting another Olympic victory, Bill went on to say that there would be no predictions unless he was in top form, and discussed the possibility of "slim pickings" for himself in Calgary. He never, however, seemed to believe that he wouldn't go at all. As he told another reporter: "There's no way I'm not one of the four best downhillers in America."

Bill wasn't the only one convinced that he would go to the Olympics again. Doug Lewis, who did make the '88 team, says that both Gina and DB truly believed that Bill was going to go back and win another gold medal. He remembers trying to prepare them for the likelihood that Bill wasn't even going to be able to compete. "In '88, Bill had no results," Doug says. "Sometimes he was five seconds out. He was nothing."

The injuries clearly were an issue, sapping Bill's strength and, some say, his talent. Afterward, Bill didn't have the power to maintain his speed. Healing one part of his body would have been hard enough, but Bill was recovering from surgeries to his back as well as his knee.

In any event, the results didn't come. Bill's friends Barry and Mark have their own theory as to why. "When he got hurt, he got fear," Barry says. "Before that he never really had it."

Even so, referring to Bill's chances of winning another Olympic medal, Bill's former teammate Andy Luhn says, "I wouldn't have put it past him that he could have gathered it up." Part of the way through the season, alpine program director Harald Schoenhaar stated that Bill was fifth in line, and that he needed some pretty good finishes to make the Olympic team. In announcing that Bill would not be competing for the United States in the 1988 Olympics, Schoenhaar said that Bill had the same opportunities as anyone else on the team but wasn't able to take advantage of them.

The coaches' selection criteria in naming the Olympic team was supposed to be straight-forward—not leaving room for subjectivity or an exception allowing reigning champions to compete. (There was precedent for that elsewhere—despite winning gold in the downhill at the '76 Games in Innsbruck, Franz Klammer did not qualify for the '80 Austrian Olympic team.)

But in fact, Bill Egan, a conditioning coach on the team at the time, recalls that there was a lot of controversy surrounding who made the '88 Olympic team. Many of Bill's teammates say it was more like animosity. "The team was weak, no one made the qualifying criteria," Egan says. "We went with young guys, built for the future." Referring to the inexperience of the racers selected, Bill's former teammate Sam Collins says, "Bill wouldn't have done any worse than the other racers that were there."

Mike Brown claims that Nadig didn't like Americans in general and Bill in particular, and kept Brown off the team in '88 because Brown wasn't one of Nadig's favorites. According to Mike, Nadig took Mike's spot away from him the day before the team was officially announced, then came up to him and said, "I got you."

"And I was trying to play by the rules," Mike says. "If it happened to me, I can guarantee it happened to Bill."

Bill was understandably upset, but he did not improve relations with the Ski Team by telling reporters that his teammates who were selected to go to the Olympics had no chance for a medal. (In fact, no American did win a medal in any alpine skiing event in the '88 Olympics. The highest American finish was by Edith Thys, Barry's sister, who finished 9th in the Super-G.)

Gina says that at the time, she didn't realize how upset Bill was about not competing. "He was real quiet about it," she says. "He wasn't really good at communicating those kinds of things. He would just become either quiet or irritated, that was the only way I knew something was wrong. But he wouldn't really say he was heartbroken about not going to the Olympics. He would *never* say that."

Bill watched the Olympics that year from his mom's house in Oregon. He stayed there to take care of her dog while she and Jimmy, and also Gina, who wanted to see what the Olympics were all about, went to Calgary without him.

On July 9th of that year, Bill and Gina had a second wedding ceremony for family and friends, at the Olympic Village Inn in Squaw Valley, California. All of the members of Bill's wedding party had been teammates with him on the U.S. Ski Team. Barry, who was with Bill when he met Gina, was the best man. The other groomsmen were Jo Jo Weber, Andy Luhn, and Alan Lauba. Barry ended up too drunk to make the toast, so Jo Jo did it.

Bill was satisfied with having eloped with Gina, and he had been against spending the money to have a formal wedding ceremony. As the ceremony concluded, just when Bill and Gina began to walk back down the aisle together, he turned to her and said, "I hope you're happy now. You got what you wanted." Gina's mom knew she was devastated, but Gina went on to the reception and smiled for the guests. The photographer recorded beautiful pictures.

Both of Barry's parents felt that Gina was, in fact, star-struck with Bill, and they wondered if she really knew who he was when she married him. Vicki had doubts about the marriage initially—thinking that Bill was marrying Gina for her beauty and she was marrying him for his lifestyle—but she believes that they learned to truly love each other in the end. At least initially, Bill and Gina seemed happy. "They were good with each other," DB says. "And really pretty good for each other. They were fun to watch."

Edith saw the relationship differently. "There was nothing about those two that ever felt at ease," she says. "But then how could you ever seem at ease with Bill?"

Gina's mom, Linda, thinks her daughter was better for Bill than he was for her. She saw Gina as stressed much of the time, even during times that should have been joyful. Still, she says that Gina had high expectations and could be "very sassy," so initially Linda stuck up for Bill. On one occasion when Bill had Gina's sister in a chokehold on the neighbor's lawn, it was Gina who called the police and Gina's mother who bailed him out of jail at four in the morning.

Around the time Bill first got together with Gina he asked his mother—who, like his dad, had no experience in the field—to be his agent. DB also ended up managing Bill's money. Between having his dad and then his mom as his manager, Bill was represented by Jon Franklin at IMG.

By the time Bill signed with IMG, about a year after the Sarajevo Olympics, he was no longer winning. To the extent that anything along the lines of a Wheaties box would ever have been an option, it was basically too late. Franklin got Bill a few deals—including one with a computer company who used Bill to bolster their claim that they were a "high-speed performer"—but in general there wasn't a lot happening.

Marketing Bill's brash image was clearly a challenge for Franklin, and he was never completely sure how Bill was going to react in certain situations, but sometimes Bill surprised him. One time Franklin was walking through an airport with Bill when a woman stopped Bill to tell him that her husband loved him and thought it was so great what Bill had done for America. Franklin recalls cringing, feeling it was possible that Bill might say something along the lines of, "Screw your husband, I did it for me." Instead,

Bill told the woman what he sincerely believed at that moment. "Well, that's why I did it," Bill said. "For guys like your husband."

Stories about the dissolution of Bill's relationship with IMG vary. One version, told by some of Bill's friends, is that IMG dropped Bill after he repeatedly arrived to appearances late and confrontational, if he showed up at all. Bill says he left IMG because he didn't like giving them a percentage. According to Franklin, they mutually agreed to end the relationship—IMG wasn't making much money from Bill and what they were getting Bill wanted to keep for himself.

Gina says that Bill chose his mom to manage him because he wanted her to take care of things, pay all his bills. But maybe what he really wanted, what he had always wanted, was for his mom to finally take care of *him*.

With DB in control of the money, Gina never knew what they had or what she could spend. She never saw any bills. "Bill said 'It's my money, it's not your business. My mom and I will handle it,'" Gina says. "I wasn't to have anything to do with any decision-making at all." When Gina was employed she had been running two stores. Now all of a sudden she was no longer working and dependent on Bill—and his mother. It was hard on her, and it made her nervous. Bill simply told her that he was taking care of her and she would never have to work another day in her life again.

Gina, along with every one of Bill's friends and all three of his siblings, felt that Bill needed a manager who was in the business. He might have had different opportunities with a management company, and, at the very least, he would have avoided what everyone saw as inevitable.

 Never has a case for the division of family and business been so starkly made as by one particular investment that DB made for Bill during this time. It happened at the beginning of Bill and Gina's marriage, around the time they were looking for their first house. DB recommended that Bill give $70,000 to her brother, Bill Morris, to invest in a scheme in Canada, no details of which were ever made even slightly clear except the payoff, which was supposed to involve a tripling of the investment in a matter of months. DB told Bill that she herself was investing $10,000. According to Vicki, her uncle promised to sell his house to pay Bill back if anything went wrong. Bill sold his Audi and financed his Porsche to come up with the money.

Afterward, it turns out that DB had failed to get anything in writing. There was no paperwork at all. The get-rich-scheme failed utterly; the money was never seen again—at least Bill's share.

DB later recovered all or at least a portion of her investment (according to Vicki, her uncle returned all of her mom's investment to her; DB claims that she only got $2,000 back when she told her brother she needed it for taxes). Morris flat-out refuses to shed any light on the situation whatsoever, abruptly cutting off discussion with the following comments: "You're not going to get anything from me. That's a thorn in my side. It's caused me enough grief."

Barry and Mark say the deal "crushed" Bill, because he lost the last bit of his money and also because he had trusted his family. At the time, Bill threatened to talk to his uncle in person about the venture, but DB talked him out of it. Apparently in response to the situation, DB and Morris's mother cut Morris out of her will. It is unclear if Bill's grandmother said, or even intended, that this shuffling of her inheritance would result in Bill receiving his investment back when she died. In any event, it was certainly Bill's belief that it would all be made right in the end. He told Vicki that he would get the money back one day. In fact, the loss of that money and the unfolding of that particular financial transaction would play out dramatically in coming years.

Meanwhile, Bill and Gina paid DB to live with her and Jimmy when Bill wasn't training or racing in Europe. The summer they got married (in Tahoe), they moved in with Gina's dad, Dennis Ricci, on his ranch in Susanville—330 acres of alfalfa, hay, and oats. Ricci's wife had just left him and he was pretty down at the time—Bill came in, made all the food, took care of the house, and helped him work the ranch. He even castrated pigs.

By the following summer, 1989, Gina's dad had sold the ranch and moved to Palm Springs. For part of that time, Gina and Bill lived in a rental near him in Palm Springs. One night, after too much drinking, they had a huge fight, which Gina sums up by saying, "Bill was difficult." She was concerned about what she calls his "flirtatious behavior"—she would call him in the middle of the night to see if he was really in his hotel room and he wouldn't answer the phone, she would check his pockets and find cards in them. She could never prove anything, but she feels he gave her reason to question his fidelity. "I never really trusted him," Gina says, "and I had this deep feeling that something was wrong."

When Gina woke up the next morning, Bill had taken all his stuff and left. Gina packed up the place they were renting, went to live at Erika's parents' home in Squaw Valley, and decided that she didn't want to be married to Bill anymore. "I was just not gonna do it anymore," Gina says. "I was not gonna be his little…live with my mom, do what you tell me. I just had it." They were apart a few months. Gina spent the time working in a clothing store and passing the test to get her real estate license.

During that separation, and others when Bill and Gina were fighting, DB called Gina's mom. Already Linda's impression of Bill's family from the wedding was that they were "so rude, kind of crude," and that DB's act of coming off sweet was phony. In the course of those calls, Linda says DB would tell her, "It's all your daughter's fault. She's spoiled, she's demanding, she's expecting too much out of Bill. She's pushing his buttons and causing him to act this way." According to DB, Linda says, it was "always, always Gina's fault."

After a little time apart Bill started calling Gina, and sent her a huge bouquet of flowers. "When he was good, he was great; when he was bad, it was awful," she says. "He could be my best friend and my enemy at the same time." Gina made it clear that if they got back together she was not moving in with DB again. She told him that she needed her own space; Bill respond-ed that he would buy her a home. They began house-shopping and settled on a place in Tahoe, on the Truckee River.

Around this time in 1989, during, as ski photographer Jonathan Selkowitz calls it, Bill's "descent" from the Ski Team, Selkowitz ran into Bill while he was in Jackson Hole, Wyoming, for a race. "The legend, there he was," he says. "He had just had a training run, his bib was twisted, his hair a mess, seemed like he hadn't showered in about a week and a half, stuffing tacos into his face."

Selkowitz asked Bill if he had any extra skis to sell. Bill initially said no, then came over and pounded on the roof of Selkowitz's car as he was pulling out of the parking lot and told him to meet him at his hotel. When Selkowitz arrived at Bill's room, Bill showed him a set of skis that were taped together. Selkowitz attempted to untape them, but Bill protested, finally saying, "Listen, bud, these are the fastest skis you're ever going to get your hands on." Selkowitz bought them for $125 and took them home.

"When I untaped them," Selkowitz says, "sure enough, one of them was bent." Even so, he claims that they were, in fact, the fastest skis he ever owned.

During this era the coaches didn't get to know Bill all that well. He was the old man on the team, and rather than ride with the team in the van, he had his own car and usually traveled with Gina or his ski rep (now Andy Luhn, who had taken over Blake's position). By not riding in the van with the other racers, Bill always managed to arrive first at the hotel and demand the best room.

Many of the racers and coaches didn't exactly understand what Gina saw in Bill, but nobody seemed to hold their feelings for Bill against her. "I thought Bill was so lucky," coach Bill Egan says. "She was great for him. She traveled with the team and it was a delight to have her. She went through some adjusting with him. Billy was not easy."

Jim Tracy, who joined the Ski Team in 1987 as an assistant downhill coach, sums it up like this: "Gina was awesome. She was like a tranquilizer for him."

Tracy, who believes that that every athlete has different ways of perceiving and analyzing, uses an individualized approach to coaching. In Bill's case, he says that he tried to be tactful, attempted to give Bill something to think about.

"He was coachable if you knew how to approach it," Tracy says. "If you tried to tell him everything he needed to do he would laugh and ski off. If you tried to pull the reins in on him, it was all over. Billy was Billy." Tracy, in fact, uses the expression "Billy was Billy" repeatedly in an attempt to describe his behavior. He even fits it in to sum up what he felt where the eventual problems in Bill's marriage: "I heard Gina got tired of Billy being Billy."

One example of Bill being himself was a routine that went something like this: Bill would mouth off, someone would tell him to shut up, and then he would mock the person who had tried to quiet him, pissing them off even more. "A lot of guys didn't care for him," Tracy says. "They tolerated him. He wasn't liked all that much." By the end of Bill's Ski Team career, Bill Egan was the head downhill coach. He obviously had an appreciation for Bill's skill. "I never knew anyone who knew the line better than Bill," Egan says. "God, did he have a talent for the line" But looking back on his time with Bill, Egan analyzes more than just his skiing. "He was just so stand-alone-ish," Egan says. "Such a loner, to a fault, where he could only be alone. He didn't have socialization like most people. The usual thing, that other people would do [in a situation]—Billy couldn't grasp that. And sometimes he was mean as a snake."

There was something else about Bill's past that Egan picked up on—how often he had skipped school to ski. "Everywhere he went, I'll bet he played," he says. "What a skier he was. Jesus, what a talent. You don't get that without a lot of skiing, a lot of free skiing."

Bill finished in the top ten five times after the 1984 season, but he never won another race. Bill's friends, former teammates, and former coaches all seem to have a different take on the reason. Many of them simply blame injuries. Several people claim that Bill was trying his hardest but could just no longer perform at the top level, others say that after he won Bill stopped trying so hard.

"He just dropped and dropped and dropped," Nadig says. "It really hurts me. He came, how you say, out of the gutter. We somehow managed to give him an objective, sense to his life. Everything was in his hands, and a few years later, everything was gone. It's sad, it's really sad."

Despite the seeming honesty Bill had revealed about his career to *Sports Illustrated* in 1987, in later years Bill altered his story. In several interviews in the 1990s, he gave a version of the same smooth answer to the press, one that may or may not have masked the truth: "After the 1984 season, I wasn't very motivated. I had achieved everything I wanted in one year. I cruised along and had a good time racing World Cup for five or six years with someone else paying for it. I didn't worry too much about winning anymore. I had more fun than most people, and the guy who has the most fun wins, right?"

Jo Jo had tried to convince Bill to retire at the end of the 1984 season. Picabo Street, silver medalist in the downhill in the '94 Olympics and gold medalist in the Super-G in '98, says she understands Bill's desire to stay on the team after he won. "When I won my gold medal I was very satisfied and a little scared," she says. "What [else] am I gonna do? Your heart is only half into it, but there is a fear of being done. Of not knowing what to do."

Picabo joined the Ski Team in 1989, at age 17, overlapping with Bill for a season. She was 12 when Bill won the Olympics. She didn't have a TV at the time, but she saw a tape of his victory later. What she remembers most about it was how outspoken he was, how he put it out there and had to step up to it. "It was so ballsy and gutsy and impressive," she says. "Over the top." She says that his victory was a learning experience for American skiers. "He did what I wanted to do, and I used what he had just done," she says. "It was against all odds, some self-inflicted. Very inspirational the way he went about it. For sure, absolutely, without ever even meeting him, he was an inspiration."

She recalls meeting Bill the first time at a camp at Mt. Bachelor where the "big boys" were training. A the time she thought, "I'm on the chairlift with Bill Johnson—what should I ask him?" Picabo says that Bill was always especially nice to her—she's not sure why but she thinks it may have been because he recognized how much she loved skiing.

"He was a jolly-go-lucky dude," she says. "He spoke his mind, shot from the hip. That's what I loved the most about him. You know exactly what you are dealing with when you're having a conversation with Bill Johnson."

Not so long after he told the press, "I will never leave ski racing. I love it…I won't quit ski racing until I am forced out," Bill realized that it was, in fact, time to stop. "He was so beat up at that time," Egan says. "There were kids coming on, him hanging on."

In his final season, Bill injured his knee again at Val Gardena. His left knee was still weak, and his left leg was smaller than his right. He was virtually skiing on one leg, which gave him only one good turn. He had difficulty getting enough pressure into turns on his left ski, and he tended to lose that ski. In the past, racers had always skied over the three camel bumps at the end of that course by absorbing the first one, jumping off the second one, and landing on the downhill side of third one. Then, that season, the racers started to jump them all, making up a tremendous amount of time. On race day, Bill realized that he had to ski it that way. The strength wasn't there—he couldn't clear them. He landed right on the uphill side of the jump.

"You're never okay with retiring if you can't go out the way you want to go out," Tracy says. "He tried as long as he could. He wasn't competitive anymore." Bill's relationship with the team was particularly turbulent at the time, he was battling openly with officials, he was in pain, and he wasn't winning. After repeatedly threatening to announce his retirement, perhaps to assess the reaction, Bill left the Ski Team at the end of the '89-'90 season.

Bill had been ski racing for 23 years, competing seriously for the last 13, and spending about 180 days a year on skis. When he retired, he said that he liked the sport still, and he claimed that he was looking forward to choosing his own days to ski. And in a rare moment of insight (at least publicly), in reference to his reputation, he said, "When you've convinced everybody that's who you are, that's who you are."

Long after Bill's retirement, John Norton, later responsible for hiring Bill to be ski ambassador at Crested Butte, had a conversation with Howard Peterson, former president of the U.S. Ski Team. According to Norton, Peterson admitted that his biggest disappointment, his worst misjudgment, during his time at the Ski Team was that the team didn't know how to work it out with Bill. "It came to them too late the awe in which the public held Bill," Norton says. "His Butch Cassidy and the Sundance Kid reputation. These were very straight-laced, proper, New England Yankees running an organization used to pretty straight-laced, small town, American skiers—this brash kid comes out of California and does what no one before him was able to do. They treated him like everybody else. They didn't realize he wasn't like anybody else."

Looking back, Theo Nadig qualifies Bill's success with the comment, "But other athletes not half as successful as him go on in life and do really well." Nadig's view of being a champion is simple: "You win and you move on in life. A sports career is maybe 10 to15 years. Hopefully you have at least 40 or 50 more years to your life." It was never so easy for Bill.

Bill was 29 years old when he retired. He has since spent the rest of his life trying to answer the question of what you do with your life when you retire at age 29. At the time, however, it may have eased his transition to know that Gina was already a few months pregnant. The next stage in Bill's life was clear—he was going to be a family man. Ryan William was born that fall, on September 16th.

CHAPTER EIGHT

"Are you coming? Are you coming?"
– GINA JOHNSON, on a 911 call, October 1991

By the time Bill retired, he and Gina had already bought their house in Tahoe. They paid $189,000 for it in 1989. After feeling, as Gina says, "always off-kilter" with all the traveling and living in Bill's world, she finally felt like she was living in her home, her environment. Although the house did help initially, Gina would actually end up plagued by that feeling for the remainder of her marriage to Bill.

Bill and Gina went in on the house with Andy Luhn. There were two bedrooms and a bathroom in the back of the house on the main floor, and one of them was Andy's bedroom when he was in town. Andy was still working as a ski rep, frequently traveling to Europe and hardly ever there.

The house was in the woods, with 2300 square feet of living space, a spacious, open floor plan, high ceilings, decks, a wood stove. It was right on the Truckee River, with lots of windows to capture the view. The house was on the rustic side, with sort of an upscale, cabiny feel. Bill painted the outside and re-sided the garage; Gina painted the inside of the house and redecorated it exquisitely.

Some of the furniture was older, but slip-covered. The house was fully carpeted, with a steep set of stairs that gave visitors vertigo. At the base of the stairs was a sitting room, with a couch by the back bedrooms and a bookcase along the stair wall crammed with lots of books and some of Bill's trophies. There were very few doors, or even walls, on the ground floor. Adjacent to the sitting room was a family room with another couch and a huge TV. On the shared back wall between the sitting room and the family room were two sets of sliding glass doors—one led to a deck and one led to a separate room with an above-ground hot tub. Toward the front of the house, on the other side of the family room couch, maybe 15 feet from the sliders, was the eating area with a big dining table where Bill usually sat to read the paper and do the crossword puzzle. There wasn't a lot of walking room inside the house, but it was very cozy.

Gina was so comfortable there, with her friends and family around her, that she didn't go to Europe with Bill his final season. Gina says he blamed her for having to quit because he didn't like being without her. She didn't know what Bill's next career would be, but he had always told her that he would make more money when he stopped ski racing. At the time, she was sure that he, and they, would be fine, whatever he decided to do. "He was so talented, he could do absolutely anything he wanted to," she says. She got pregnant that December.

In the following months, Gina bought a collection of belts to wear once she gave birth. She had an easy pregnancy, though she says Bill viewed her condition as his ticket to party. Bill was sometimes out all night or up late playing pool with friends in their garage.

Andy recalls the dynamic a bit differently. "Gina was definitely setting him straight," he says. "She was giving orders and Bill was obeying." On at least one occasion that seems to have been true. Gina knocked on the door one night when a bunch of guys were playing pool. Bill was in the midst of a game he was winning, but fifteen minutes later, he left and went upstairs to Gina. Other times, Gina would hit the garage door opener at 4:30 in the morning to let Bill know that the party was too loud for her to sleep.

Gina delivered Ryan in an hour and fifty minutes, start to finish. Even during her labor Bill managed to shift the attention to himself—by fainting when the baby was coming. "So he had all the nurses," Gina says. "He was passed out on the floor with the nurses, and here I am with the baby and I'm saying 'Are you OK?'"

Initially, they called him "Baby Puke." Gina recalls, "That baby threw up all the time." Ryan was a happy baby, but what everyone remembers most about him what how rambunctious he was, how much energy he had. "He was an ambitious child, he just was go, go, go, go, go," Gina says.

Ryan was walking by nine months old. "He was just such a busy boy," Gina says. "The minute you left something open he was there. He was looking for danger constantly. He was the kind of kid that would open up a thing and empty it. He was just constantly looking for an opening. If there was an opening, he was gone."

By the following fall, 1991, Ryan wasn't talking yet, but he was already making lots of sounds and noises and communicating with his hands. One of his favorite things to do was to soak in the warm bubbles of the hot tub with Gina and Bill. "The baby loved the hot tub. He loved it," Gina says. "He used to go in there a lot."

That fall Bill accepted a job at Crested Butte ski resort in Colorado as a ski ambassador. The family planned to move out there at the start of the ski season. They had sold the house already, and escrow was pending. They were about a month away from moving.

Then, in October, a month after Ryan's first birthday, he slipped into the hot tub by himself and drowned. Everyone was in the house when it happened, each thinking the other one was watching him. Gina would later say it was hard to believe that someone could lose a child in such a quiet manner.

Gina was upstairs packing at the time. She often took Ryan upstairs with her, but this time she left him downstairs with Bill. Bill was doing a crossword puzzle.

Andy was in the house as well. He had been in the hot tub earlier that morning. When he got out, he left the sliding door open, forgetting to secure it with the plank of wood that kept small hands from pulling on the handle. "I was gone all the time," Andy says. "Kids change—crawl, walk, run."

Ryan saw his opportunity. He snuck off to the room with the hot tub, scrambled up the stairs to get to it, then climbed or fell in. There was a cover floating on top of the water to keep the heat in, and he slid beneath it.

When Gina came downstairs she thought the house was a little too quiet. She asked Bill where the baby was, and Bill replied that he thought Ryan was with Gina. Gina said that he was not with her.

"He's not?" Bill said.

And then they all frantically began to search the house. Gina saw the open slider and raced into the hot tub room. Andy still remembers the sound of her screams when she pulled back the cover and found her son. Ryan was blue, not breathing, when she took him out of the water.

She handed him to Bill.

Bill said, "Oh, no," over and over and immediately started to do CPR on his son. Gina called 911, begged them to hurry. Andy went out to the driveway to wait for the ambulance.

"Think of the worst thing you can imagine," Andy says. "It will never go away."

Bill rode with Ryan in the ambulance. Gina went outside and sat down. She was trembling in shock. She remembers the black Lab from next door coming to her and cocking his head up at her as she wept.

At the hospital, doctors got Ryan's heart started and they airlifted him to Reno. "So then it was kind of like I had a little bit of hope, you know?" Gina says.

Bill couldn't stand to be at the hospital; Gina couldn't leave Ryan's side. She waited for every report and every brain scan to come through, looking for an improvement, for any change at all.

Ryan remained on life support for three weeks. The doctors repeatedly ran brain scans and did tests to try to elicit a gag reflex or any kind of bare-minimum response from him, but they were getting nothing at all.

Bill was rarely at the hospital during that time. Gina accepted that he couldn't handle being there. "Bill would go home and he would just hang out with his friends," she says. "He was in the hospital for a while and he just couldn't do it." She stayed with Ryan and researched his condition. She remembers hating one doctor for being so cold, for telling her that it would be best if Ryan died (later, after Ryan was gone, that same doctor waived the entire portion of the hospital bill not covered by insurance).

After three weeks the doctors placed a button in Ryan's stomach to feed him and said that he was ready to be transferred out of intensive care. Gina knew that that was the end. Ryan could have lived in that condition, survived by being fed through his stomach, but Gina never saw it as an option.

"There was just no way I was gonna let my child grow up like that," she says. "This was not Ryan. Ryan was not meant to be lying in a flat bed to grow up."

Gina was grateful, at least, that Ryan wasn't "gone gone," that she was able to prepare herself in some small way. "Before I let him go, I packed his whole room. I went home and I packed all his stuff," Gina says. "I walked into his room and I remember looking in his mirror and it was the most painful thing to see, his little handprint. His stuff is one thing, but to actually see his handprint in the mirror…." She wrote Ryan a letter in his baby book and said good-bye.

Gina spent that night with Bill. At the time she was certain—and she was correct—that Nicholas was conceived two nights before Bill and Gina let Ryan go.

Gina had constantly been by Ryan's side in his hospital bed, but even she couldn't watch him die. Bill wasn't there to help—he had left town to attend a ski event. "Bill really didn't make it any easier," Barry says. It was left to Gina's girlfriend Erika to stay with Ryan when the doctor took his tracheal tube out, then ride with him in the elevator all the way to the bottom of the hospital, where they took his body away.

Ryan's death obviously put an enormous strain on Bill and Gina's marriage. "They had to blame Andy in a way so they could live their lives," Mark Herhusky says, "and they had to blame each other just to cope."

"There was guilt plus pointing fingers," Rochelle says. "Everybody had a hand in it. The door was left open. Gina went upstairs without taking Ryan—she almost always took him. Bill wasn't listening. There were lots of what-ifs from Gina's perspective—'Why didn't I take Ryan with me? Why didn't I make sure Bill was listening?'"

When Gina called her mom to tell her the news, she led with, "Andy left the hot tub room open." At times she has held Bill responsible "because he was *right there*—and just being so wrapped up with his crossword puzzle."

Looking back now, Gina says that over the years she has been through different stages of blaming nobody and everybody for her son's death, including herself. "I blame myself more now than I did at the time," she says, weeping as she talks. "Just because I am his mom and he relied on me to take care of him and I let him down."

Bill says that he remembers Ryan, his life and his death. "He was a great kid but I cannot tell you much about him because he was very small when he died," he says. "That one day he wanted to get in the hot tub by himself." Bill is very shaky on the details of Ryan's death, however, and it is not at all clear that he has an independent recollection of it. Much like someone looking back on childhood pictures and believing they remember the event they see in the photo, it seems more like Bill remembers being told about the tragedy than that he remembers the day itself. His step-mom Mary, an R.N. who specializes in dementia and memory impairment, feels that Bill doesn't have any memory of the loss at all. "And thank God he doesn't," she says. "Thank God he doesn't."

At the time Bill's friends knew that he was devastated by the death of his son, but no one really understood the depth of his pain because he never talked about it, not ever, not to anyone. "It was really not discussed," Jo Jo says. "It happened. Bill called me and just said, 'Bad news, Jo.' He was never good at showing emotions."

Bill's sister Kathryn says that Gina wanted to talk about Ryan all the time, but Bill couldn't talk about him at all. He also didn't want to have any pictures of Ryan up. "Bill didn't deal with death very well," Mary says. "When Ryan was dead, Ryan was dead."

Andy maintained his relationship with Bill and Gina after Ryan's death. "It's not about blame," he says. "It's like blaming life. We were close enough, we had a bond." He says that it was hard to have Bill moving away to Colorado so soon afterward because in the past, he had always been there for Bill to talk to.

Andy remains one of Bill's closest friends today, but he has never met Nick or Tyler. "It's a nightmare," Andy says, "and not just that day, but all the time after." He is still single, and does not have children of his own yet, but he hopes to one day.

Bill and Gina's marriage also somehow survived Ryan's death, although as Barry says, "The marriage was rocked already, but this fucked it hard."

After Ryan was gone, Gina questioned what was holding them together and wondered if it was time to get out. She considered leaving Bill, but there wasn't much time to stop and think. There was a memorial service for Ryan at Our Lady of the Snows in Tahoe, at which Barry played guitar and sung a song he wrote for Ryan called "Ryan, Keep Flyin'." The morning after the funeral Gina and Bill flew to London for a week for an obligation Bill had there, then went to Manhattan, then packed up the house to move to Crested Butte. In the end, Gina realized she needed to be with him.

Gina slept for 18 hours straight in the London hotel, and afterward cried hysterically in the shower. "I cried and cried and cried and Bill just held me," she says. "I needed to be loved. We needed each other. We both needed each other to make it through it."

But Bill's way of getting through Ryan's death was to ignore it. Gina's mom saw how hard it was on Gina for Bill not to want her to grieve. There were times during that trip to London when people who knew that Bill had had a baby but hadn't heard about the accident would ask Gina questions like, "How old is the baby now?" Gina would tear up, and in response, Bill would tell her, "Stop crying, it's done, you can't bring him back. Go up to the room. Don't ruin the night." Gina would go to their room, alone, and call her mom sobbing, needing to talk.

Bill and Gina stayed together for almost another decade after they lost Ryan. "They had so much going on," Rochelle says. "Ryan was only there a year, and then they were off to Europe right away, and then Gina was pregnant right away. It's almost like it was a dream."

CHAPTER NINE

"We didn't see much of the orneriness. We've seen the charm."

**– DR. MOLLY HOEFLICH, Medical Director of the
Acute Rehabilitation Center, Providence Portland
Medical Center, May 2001**

Bill's accident erased some of his memories and left others. He believes that while saving his life, the surgeon literally removed the part of his brain containing memories of certain points of his life. He did not, and still does not, recall most of the 1990s—his father's death, his divorce, his come-back attempt. The crash took almost ten years of his life away.

But somewhere entrenched in Bill's brain, some memories remain. Gina retrieved a locked briefcase with double combination locks from Bill's RV. She had never seen it before, and Bill had obviously purchased it after the divorce, during the time he cannot now recall. When Gina brought it to the hospital, Bill claimed not to recognize it. When she handed it to him, however, he instantly put one hand on each lock, dialed the combinations, and flipped open the case.

In the months after the crash, his concentration, a skill that had come so easily to him, was tattered. His analytic skills were weak. His judgment was impaired.

His physical improvement moved more smoothly. By April 23rd, 2001, just a month after the crash, he was standing with assistance, walking with the help of two physical therapists, and doing strengthening exercises in bed and in the unit's rehab gym. The entire right side of his body was weak, and he moved with a severe limp that seemed to weigh down that side. DB describes it as that side having woken up slower than the other. The medical explanation is that weakness on the right is a common result of a left-side head injury. His face was still contorted, with his left eye nearly shut in what looked like an exaggerated wink. He wore a black baseball hat almost constantly to cover his head wound.

Bill's primary doctor was Dr. Molly Hoeflich, a physiatrist, meaning a specialist in physical medicine and rehabilitation. She says that when Bill arrived, the range for possible improvement was wide open: he could have made a complete recovery or remained semi-conscious permanently.

"Literally anything could have happened," Hoeflich says. She did not expect that Bill was going to recover as far as he did, particularly in terms of his physical progress. "He was profoundly weak on one side, and very confused," she says. "I anticipated significant, noticeable weakness and difficulty using his right side for the rest of his life. For how impaired he was, his physical recovery was remarkable."

On April 26th, doctors inserted a smaller trachea tube into Bill's throat, which allowed him to talk more spontaneously. At that point he was not yet eating solid foods. He received nourishment in the form of a protein shake for breakfast, lunch, and dinner through a tube that went through his abdomen into his stomach. The trachea tube was removed altogether a few days later, and Bill had his first real meal since the crash—ground-up beef with gravy, mashed potatoes with gravy, applesauce, and thickened fruit juice. He ate every bite.

Bill's sense of hearing appeared intact, but the accident had permanently taken his sense of smell, and severely impaired his sense of taste. Early on, he couldn't identify simple pictures of animals—moose, bear, dog, cat, antelope, pig, cow. Images of birds—falcon, duck, goose—eluded him. He couldn't recognize a house, an apple, an orange, cake, coffee, or milk.

His first written word, on April 28th, in shaky capital letters, was "START."

By the following week his feeding tube was removed, and he was upgraded from strained food to regular meals. He kept trying to get up out of bed, but with no equilibrium, he constantly fell over. By early May he began to walk a bit on his own, but he still needed some help to keep his balance. A few times Jimmy had to grab the back of Bill's t-shirt to save him from falling forward. Around this time Bill did some putting on an indoor green, sinking eight-foot shots about 80 percent of the time.

He was using a rubber toy called a Stretchy CatDog so frequently to flex the muscles in his hands that he wore it out. It was no longer available in stores, so Blake Lewis found an employee at Mattel who was willing to sacrifice the one on his desk for Bill.

It was months before Bill really awakened to reality, but pieces of his personality began surfacing right away. He complained about another patient down the hall keeping him up all night. He griped about the food, but couldn't get enough jello and pancakes with sausage.

He was stubborn with his nurses. If they asked him to sit up, he'd lie down; if they asked him to lie down, he'd sit up. He teased them as well, asking the same question over and over, clearly relishing their frustration, winking at his friends to show his pleasure. Entries in his hospital chart repeatedly refer to him as "very impulsive and a high safety risk."

By the end of his stay at the Portland hospital—he remained there until May 29th, 2001, before being moved to a rehab facility—he was routinely, and gleefully, pulling the fire-alarm just to watch the nurses' reaction. Whenever the alarm would sound on the floor, DB would resignedly announce, "It was probably Bill." He also rearranged the furniture in the hallway—or at least shoved it all toward the door.

The hospital restrictions—that he was not, for example, supposed to pull out his catheter or urinate in the wastebasket or escape from the unit—didn't make sense to Bill, and even a brain trauma didn't make him any more likely to listen to authority. Much as he liked to hang out at the nurses' station, he never tired of playing ditch-the-nurse-escort, and would lurch about the hospital wing grinning until he was found. He tried to leave his unit, and the hospital, repeatedly. "He was a little rebellious," Hoeflich says. "He was agitated at first, then very much the joker. His sense of humor actually did come back."

Bill's progress was incremental, but Blake, who saw him every four or five days when he drove to Portland from Washington, saw big improvements between visits. At first the was progress was easy to categorize—measurable skills like walking, using the bathroom. Blake visited frequently both to help Bill and to "give the family a break in the action." Bill knew Blake the first time he saw him, even though the brown curls Blake wore in the '80s had become grey and close-cropped with sideburns, and he had begun wearing stylish wire-rimmed glasses. Bill couldn't speak when Blake first visited, but he eventually recalled Blake's name on his own. To spark Bill's memories, Blake brought lots of photos to illustrate the stories he told Bill. He also brought some of Bill's old ski racing bibs to hang in his hospital room. "I wanted to give him a hard time, give him shit, help him recover," he says.

Bill's former coach Erik Steinberg visited Bill at the end of April. He came from Steamboat Springs, Colorado, where he now works in real estate, specializing in selling hunting properties. Bill recognized Steinberg but he couldn't remember his name. "He said, 'You're my coach, I think,'" Steinberg recalls. "I was fuzzy to him. He knew I was in his life but he couldn't put a name to me." Perhaps offended that Bill recalled Blake's name and not his (which Steinberg claims only happened because Bill recognized Blake's beautiful wife, Dañela, and then associated Blake with her), or, more likely, in an attempt to challenge Bill, Steinberg never did reveal his name, telling Bill that he would remember it on his own soon enough.

"He was the same guy," Steinberg says. "The same guy with a bump to the head and a memory loss." Just as he had in his Ski Team days, Bill showed off for Steinberg—in this case his ability to lift himself two inches off his wheelchair.

Like Blake, Steinberg wanted to give Jimmy a break from watching Bill and from doing "the toilet stuff," so he sent Jimmy home while he stayed with Bill overnight. "He was ugly, irritable, belligerent," Steinberg says. He tried to help Bill change his pants after Bill spilled applesauce on them, and, just like the old days, Bill took a swing at him.

Bill wasn't always so aggressive toward his guests. Sometimes he would doze off while his friends were visiting, just close his eyes while eating. Often he didn't even seem to know his friends were there. He would open his eyes after a nap and, without saying anything, start to play a video game. "His mind was working and he had the hand dexterity," Steinberg said. "He was already playing a video game better than I ever could in my life."

Many of Bill's former ski buddies visited him at the Portland hospital, bringing with them pictures and stories in an attempt to stimulate his memory. Blake and Sam Collins, a former teammate who came from Colorado to see Bill, played cribbage with him, a game they had frequently played on the road together. Bill couldn't, at that point, remember his nurses from day to day, but he was able to play cards virtually the same as he had before his crash. "It came back to him quickly," Blake says. "It was easy for him to count. Cards were very black and white for him." The way Bill made connections in the game, an observer—or an opponent—would not know he had any kind of brain trauma, at least until he got tired. DB recalls watching Bill play two games of cribbage with Sam. Initially Bill was able to count points and place his pegs without a hitch until the last half of the second game, when he had trouble with his concentration and stopped abruptly. "He was counting perfectly and then all of a sudden, he couldn't count any longer," she says. "He couldn't do any more. It was very strange."

Andy Luhn also visited several times from Washington, where he works now in real estate. He had not come to see Bill in the hospital in Montana, feeling that there was nothing he could do to help. "I knew he'd understand," he says. "I thought it was real important to come as soon as he started to change a little bit." Andy didn't mind embarrassing himself trying to get Bill to talk—he would act goofy, try to engage Bill in a food fight, anything to rouse him. When Bill started to wake up, Andy wanted him to hear his voice. To trigger memories, Andy talked about things only the two of them would know.

Andy also tried to initiate his own physical therapy program for Bill, assigning him exercises for balance and strength. He attempted to get Bill to do sit-ups, but Bill declined. Then he tried to get Bill to balance on an exercise ball. Bill looked at him sincerely, and for the first time in their friendship, said, "Andy, I love you, man." Bill paused. Andy, a little stunned, waited to hear what Bill would say next. "But I'm not sittin' on that ball," Bill said.

Alan Lauba was another of Bill's former teammates who came to see him in the Oregon hospital. He had run into Bill just before the Doug Smith downhill the previous January, but prior to that it had been almost a decade since they had gotten together. His sympathy for Bill was laced with frustration that Bill had put himself in such a dangerous situation. Unlike Blake, who felt he reconnected with Bill on his frequent visits, Alan says, "I didn't feel it was my need to go down [repeatedly]. I had said, 'Why are you doing this, you shouldn't be.' I felt sorry for his injury, but not sorry for his decision. He was setting himself up for disaster. Is that what he was looking for?"

Bill lit up when his friends came to visit, and he was usually able to recognize them and eventually reminisce and joke with them. Once they were gone, however, he often didn't remember they had been there.

By May Bill was signing autographs again, but his signature was different, a little loopier. He could read, including the headlines on the bottom of the screen on the news, but he had difficulty with more than six or seven lines of text. When he got to a word he didn't comprehend, he would interject an incorrect one. He had progressed to assembling 100-piece jigsaw puzzles designed for five-year-olds, and he did them without bothering to look at the picture on the box. He had great moments of clarity but then would suddenly slip back into a fog of confusion.

Physically, he was progressing well, and he was able to perform almost everything he was asked to do in physical therapy. Hoeflich placed his physical recovery at the top of the scale relative to other brain-injury patients. The short amount of time before he was up and walking, for example, she calls "much, much better than anticipated." Hoeflich credits the physical progress to his conditioning prior to the crash, saying that because his brain was "keyed-into" physical activity, there were more connections in his brain to get back to it.

Two months after his accident, not atypical of someone who had suffered a traumatic brain injury, Bill still could not tie his shoes or comb his hair. He continued to have problems with cognitive skills such as memory and processing information. He remained vague about most aspects of his life and did not appear at all curious about his situation. According to Hoeflich, some brain trauma patients are confused and curious, but others have such impaired short-term memory that their outlook is only, "Here I am," and they just accept it.

By the end of Bill's stay in Portland, Hoeflich says it was clear he would permanently suffer from significant cognitive deficits—medical terminology that she translates as, "He was not going to be the guy he was." While it would take a few more months to determine the ultimate severity of the damage, Hoeflich stated at the time that Bill's outcome was becoming "increasingly predictable."

She added, "He will improve, but not drastically."

At that point the plan was for Bill to relearn basic functions such as washing his face and brushing his teeth, as well as undergo rigorous physical therapy. His health insurance covered 100 days at a rehab facility, and at the end of May he moved to the Centre for Neuro Skills in Bakersfield, California.

The week before he was discharged from the Portland hospital, Bill held a press conference. His speech was, and still is, slow and quite slurred. A casual observer would likely assume he was intoxicated. The common perception is that the garbling results from his having bitten through his tongue, slitting it lengthwise in the accident. Wilson Higgs, however, the surgeon who repaired Bill's tongue, states that the slurring is the result of the brain trauma. "He speaks like a head-injury patient to me," Higgs says.

In the press conference, Bill demonstrated the progress he had made so far—he was able to joke with DB a bit—as well as the odd bends his thoughts took: "I'm very healthy, and I'm very intuitive. I'm very intuitive about what I need to do to be a part of this show." Asked whether his legendary orneriness contributed to his recovery, he replied "Ornery? Yeah, I'd say so. I'd say so on a calculated basis. The things I bring to this meeting alone are substantial." When Hoeflich commented on Bill's "nice" improvement during his time at the hospital, Bill responded, "She's very courageous with this observation. I'm kind of noble about it, too."

It was at this gathering that Bill publicly announced his intention to ski again. Already this seemed like a less ridiculous notion than when John Creel had talked about it the previous month. It still seemed unlikely, but Creel maintained that he knew Bill could do it, could at least make a couple of turns. "I asked Bill if he needed anything," Creel says. "He said 'I need skis.' I said, 'Well, what else do you need?' And he said, 'I need ski boots.' So he can focus."

The facility in Bakersfield deals exclusively with neural disorders, and it was somewhat of a mental boot camp for Bill. Rehabilitation attendants lived in an apartment with him, retraining him on the routine skills of daily living. His apartment had bedrooms for three patients, with a shared living area. Every day he spent five hours in therapy sessions—concentrated physical, occupational, and speech therapy.

He spent an hour a day in physical therapy, and he also swam, cycled, lifted weights, and did push-ups. Toward the end of his stay, in August, an attendant even took him to a driving range to hit golf balls.

His physical progress was remarkable. In June, for example, during the early stages of swim therapy, he acted like a cat in a pool—he couldn't figure out what to do in the water. He immediately flailed to the side and climbed out. Unsure of what else to do, he simply repeated that procedure about 15 times in a row. When he decided that he liked it, however, he swam several laps doing the sidestroke (he was in too much pain in his right shoulder at first to do any other stroke). By the end of his stay, just over three months later, he was racing his therapist freestyle.

Part of his treatment involved learning to focus on a specific task for a period of 50 minutes at a time, a therapy that initially Bill hated. Like a toddler, he tested the boundaries of his new situation. It was a hard time for him. He didn't understand why he had to stay there, and he didn't like the discipline. There were escape attempts, including one time when he slipped out a window.

He talked daily on the phone with family and friends. Sometimes in these conversations he became disoriented, and the result would be long and frequent pauses. Just as often, however, he was lucid, even witty, and usually cheerful. His grip on reality in Bakersfield was such that he would tell his family that he was "going on maneuvers with the guy that cleans up after me here," or going on a deep-sea fishing trip. (By mid-July the staff did take Bill on some outings, but they were more along the lines of shopping at the grocery store.)

After Bill was in the Bakersfield facility for a week or so, friends wanted to visit, but the administrators limited visits to immediate family. This rule only increased Bill's agitation. He fought with some of the male therapists, a situation DB calls "too many kings in the castle."

Despite his frustrations, Bill's cognitive skills improved slowly but steadily while he was at the rehab facility. He began to communicate more easily. His mathematical skills progressed as well, to about a fourth-grade level. He continued to put together 100-piece puzzles—of crayons and lighthouses. He referred to the pieces as "units of desirement." Ten months after his accident, Bill would achieve a milestone of sorts, completing a 1,000-piece puzzle of a leopard by a creek.

While he continued to suffer from large blocks of memory loss, one memory came back quickly and clearly: "I remember the gold medal and I remember ski racing. I remember that I won."

Bill's concentration could drift quickly, even on a simple task, and he was still frequently and easily confused. Gina and his sons, Nick and Tyler, visited him several times, including on Father's Day weekend. Despite being repeatedly told that he was divorced and that Gina and the boys now lived in Sonoma, California, when it came time to leave the Bakersfield facility Bill still thought he was going home to San Diego with them. "He only," DB says "remembered the romance." It was wrenching for Gina—so much so that she still cries years later while talking about it—to continually explain to Bill that when he left the rehab center he was not coming home with her and their sons.

By September, at the end of his stay, Bill's motions were still a bit herky-jerky, and he continued to favor his right side. His memories of his time at the facility are expectedly blurry. He often talks about having been in a rehab center in Sacramento rather than Bakersfield, which then baffles him, because he also believes that he was near the Mexican border. His one consistent recollection of his time there is of doing a strip-tease for the nurses.

At the end of his 100 days, Bill still had to be directed to most tasks. Once guided, he could usually perform what he was asked to do, but often only with someone's assistance. At the time the staff indicated that Bill was frustrated and occasionally combative, but they also stressed that the rehabilitation pattern of a brain-injury patient is always unpredictable.

When Bill was discharged, on September 6th of 2001, he went to live with DB and Jimmy in their home in Gresham, Oregon. The house is casual and comfortable, set on several acres in a leafy, secluded part of town. Bill moved into the spare bedroom downstairs. Every morning he was greeted by a pink sticky note on his bathroom mirror with "Good Morning!" written on the top, followed by a list reminding him to do various personal grooming tasks such as shaving and putting on deodorant.

When Bill moved home with his mom, she had to install fire extinguishers in every room, just in case. She took money for Bill's room and board, and also "care fees" for herself, out of Bill's Social Security check, in an amount determined by Social Security. "I also, out of my pocket, bought gas, food at restaurants, etc., without compensation," she says.

DB has often described post-accident Bill as childlike, and while living back at home Bill slipped into that role, seeming comfortable about it, telling people that his mom was going to take care of him now. In a way, DB had to raise him all over again. And this time, Bill received the one-on-one attention he had craved as a child.

DB says that during the time Bill lived with her he was consistently sweeter and kinder than he had been prior to the accident. Jimmy agrees that Bill was more good-natured than he used to be. Even so, Bill would frequently snap at DB, appearing enraged. She knew how to handle him, easily talking him down, and his anger would generally subside almost as quickly as it had come on.

Bill was back at the Portland Providence Medical Center, this time for outpatient rehabilitation. He went there four times a week, spending hours memorizing words and doing balance exercises. He felt that his speech therapist challenged him, and he enjoyed his sessions with her most. Not surprisingly, Bill had no recollection of his time there the previous spring. Blake was with Bill once when he ran into a nurse who had spent a lot of time caring for him—"She lived and died for him," Blake says—and Bill's response to her was only, "Do I know you?"

Bill was extremely precise, and constantly calculated the elevation of everything. While he could walk, he still struggled with balance and coordination. He could not run—yet—but he frequently swam, one day completing 20 laps. During one of his outpatient sessions, NBC filmed Bill for a personal piece the network was putting together for the 2002 Winter Olympics. In part of the footage, a therapist patiently explains to Bill that he comes there for therapy because his body got hurt. His considered response was: "Not really. I come here because I don't have anywhere else to go right now." In October, Bill went with Jimmy to Tahoe to pick up some belongings. While he was there, he went golfing with his sons and biking with Gina. They all went on a boat ride on the lake. Bill's old friends Barry and Mark say that while Bill knew he knew them, and remembered that they were associated with Squaw Valley, he didn't necessarily know how he knew them.

That fall, Bill went golfing several times, mountain biking (he fell a few times, but it was a tough trail), and fishing for salmon and steelhead. By Christmas, against the recommendation of his doctors and therapists, Bill stopped attending rehabilitation sessions. "He became very bored with it all," DB says, "and he really wasn't learning many new things." He dropped the occupational therapy first—"It was definitely not challenging," according to DB—and the physical therapy soon after.

"He was becoming stronger," DB says, "but he wasn't happy having to go do the easy exercises they had him to—being a "gold medalist" and all…." Bill agrees that he gave up the rehab because it was too easy. He claims that he was "lined up with a bunch of women" (female therapists) which he felt was fine for "an old guy," but not for him. He planned to return to skis and ski himself into shape, just as he had in the past.

"He was beginning to feel he was fine," Hoeflich says. "I felt he was benefiting from the therapy, but he didn't." Hoeflich wasn't too concerned with Bill stopping the physical therapy—"He went on to do tremendous things on his own"—but for the cognitive recovery, she would have liked to keep him in therapy for another 3 to 6 months. "You stay until you plateau," Hoeflich says, "and he had not plateaued."

When he first moved home, Bill also joined the Cascade Athletic Club to get back in shape, but he more or less stopped going. "We went until he didn't want to anymore," DB says. In any event, DB, indignant that the health club hadn't comped Bill's membership in the first place, didn't renew it.

Post-accident, Bill's sense of entitlement appeared to be intact. "Bill doesn't look at the world differently [since his accident]," Jo Jo says. "He still feels like the world owes him something." That sentiment is strong in DB as well, and certainly responsible for Bill's worldview developing the way it did. Blake is not alone among Bill's friends when he describes the attitude of Bill's family as being "one-sided—what are you going to do for Bill today?" That approach often has the opposite of its intended effect—rather than motivating supporters to give more and try harder, it frequently pushes them away.

It was around the time Bill moved home that Blake pulled back from visiting Bill so often, saying he had to "disconnect for a little while, step out of the scene." He questioned what he called Bill's family's "agenda," wondering whether, for example, they were doing the best thing for him by letting him smoke and drink, occasionally to excess. "I just don't think smoking and drinking go hand in hand with head trauma," Blake says.

Obviously, Bill's doctors agree. They have made it clear that drinking alcohol is not a good idea, and that ideally he should avoid it entirely. For a brain trauma patient, alcohol is a concern on several levels. Where cognitive function is already impaired, alcohol slows it down even more dramatically.

After the year of Bill's accident, he had no follow-up medical supervision or counseling of any kind until early 2005, when he was evaluated by Dr. Mark Lovell, PhD, the director of the sports concussion program at the University of Pittsburgh Medical Center. Lovell is also the director of the NFL and NHL's neuropsychology program, and a consultant for the U.S. Ski Team.

As Lovell says, "A brain injury makes you more sensitive to the effects of alcohol, more disinhibited. Bill is disinhibited enough—throwing alcohol on it tends to make things worse."

Heavy drinking can also lower the seizure threshold of a brain-injured person and put them at a high risk for seizures. In addition, there is the issue of alcohol's affect on long-term progress from a brain injury—an open question among physicians. Lovell points out that after a brain injury, a patient needs to focus on using everything they have left rather than introducing a toxin into their system. "Alcohol would temporarily affect recovery," Hoeflich says. "Long-term, it's hard to say. Theoretically you'd be worried about that, but I can't prove that."

Even without the physical therapy and the workouts at the health club Bill's body remained muscular, but he gained about 25 pounds. He was sad, sometimes, and frustrated, matter-of-factly announcing things like, "To me, I would rather be dead right now, because then I would know a lot."

Sometimes Bill implied that he knew that the accident had changed him, such as asking what the price of stamps was "back when I was alive." But usually, then and now, Bill maintains that his memory loss—which he is always very upfront about—is the only thing different about him since his crash. About a year after his accident he told a reporter: "I've forgotten the last 10 years, period. It's not important to me now. I'm 31, not 41. I don't even know what I'm supposed to feel like, but I feel young."

And when Bill was 31, life was good. Most of his mistakes hadn't been made, his losses hadn't been suffered. When he was 31, he had only recently retired from the U.S. Ski Team, and his fame was still secure. His son hadn't died. His wife hadn't left him. He hadn't felt deceived by his mom. He hadn't tried and failed to make the Ski Team again. He hadn't caught an edge and landed on his head and suffered a traumatic brain injury.

For Bill, being 31 was a lot better than being 41. Ten years prior to his accident, his future stretched before him, and it looked awfully bright—happy marriage, brand-new son, and a job offer in the works at a ski resort that would pay him to ski. But in the course of a few moments on an October day in 1991, that image was shattered when Ryan slipped beneath the water. Although no one close to Bill sees Ryan's death as directly linear to his downfall, certainly from that point on Bill's rosy future continued to slide further away—he lost the job at the ski resort, never to find steady employment again, and Gina ultimately divorced him.

Around the time Gina left him, Bill's self-destructiveness reached its peak. Her departure sent him spiraling further into a desperate cycle of drugs and drinking and rage and reckless behavior that he only partially closed down—and possibly only interrupted—by throwing himself into his comeback attempt. Bill had cleaned up his substance abuse, but his contact with Gina (and his references about her to others) remained bitter and angry. It was the crash itself that finally, as Gina says, "stopped the chaos." Gina denies that Bill was ever really suicidal, but she does admit that near the end, before his accident, she saw for the first time that Bill had stopped caring about anything.

For all it took away, Bill's accident returned him, if only in his mind, to a time when he had it all. Without turning back the clock, he wasn't going to get a chance to redo those years. But since he couldn't get them back, there was only one other way to go. The years could just vanish. The injury to Bill's brain couldn't wipe the years out for anyone else, but for Bill, it could, and did, erase them. In a sense, Bill has gone back in time. For Bill, the bad years are gone. And to answer Alan Lauba's question, in a sense, without even realizing it, maybe that was what Bill was looking for.

CHAPTER TEN

**"I was not in control of our destiny, and our destiny
was falling apart."**

– GINA JOHNSON

S o it was that Gina found herself living in Crested Butte, Colorado, without her family, her friends, her house, or her baby. Her old life had ended. She was a whole new person, living an entirely different life.

She was also—as she had known—pregnant. She spent all her time shopping for baby clothes, focusing on the new life that was coming. "I couldn't replace Ryan," Gina says, "but at least I had something else to live for, to go on to." Nicholas Ryan Johnson was born on July 31st, 1992.

Meanwhile, Bill tried to adjust to a life that did not revolve around World Cup ski racing. He worked as Crested Butte's ski ambassador, but he also continued to travel and compete in professional ski races.

Crested Butte wanted Bill as their ski ambassador because he was one of the most recognizable names in the ski world at the time, and it gave the ski resort credibility, especially internationally. As John Norton, then the vice-president of marketing (now CEO), who hired Bill says, "He had star power. He was a character and Crested Butte was likewise." Gina Kroft, Norton's assistant when Bill was hired, agrees: "Crested Butte was thought of as irreverent and Bill matched that spirit."

The resort initially signed Bill to a five-year contract. The plan, on Crested Butte's part, was for the relationship to be indefinite. In fact, Bill never finished out his initial contract—Crested Butte terminated its agreement with him in 1995.

As a ski ambassador, Bill's duties were to represent Crested Butte Mountain Resort, and that included attending ski trade shows and promotional events, going on ski-along tours, attending meet-the-public events, meeting with press, and skiing with VIPs. The job was not necessarily full-time—Bill had the time, and Crested Butte's blessing, to build houses with Gina's dad on the side.

When Bill and Gina arrived in Crested Butte, they moved into a rental property—the first of many—while Bill and Gina's dad built a house for them. Adding to the general upheaval of living in a strange, and (at that time) relatively isolated place, there weren't many rentals available, so they were forced to take whatever short-term situations they could find. Bill, in partnership with his father-in-law, was simultaneously building a spec house, so it took an extra long time for them to finish Bill and Gina's home. When it was finally completed about two years later, Bill and Gina moved into a 3400-square-foot custom house with a heated driveway at the base of the mountain. Gina had picked out every tile, every faucet. It even had a silhouette of Bill skiing etched into the glass at the front door.

Several people close to Bill, particularly Jo Jo, feel that Bill didn't appreciate what he had in his position at Crested Butte. As an ambassador of skiing, Bill was able to free ski as much as he wanted, show off how good he was, and maintain his celebrity status. There were only so many situations like that in the country, and Bill's friends felt he was lucky to have one of them.

Bill did excel at certain aspects of the job, especially early on. He was perhaps at his best when any of his duties involved meeting with and talking to kids. He was affable with international VIPs—especially the British, whose press embraced him. He was always loyal and gracious to his fans, quick to sign an autograph or pose for a picture.

Norton recalls traveling to a ski show with Bill at the Meadowlands in New Jersey, where the longest line there—around the block—was to see Bill. Several people who knew he would be there brought their copies of *Sports Illustrated* with Bill on the cover for him to sign. "That tickled him," Norton says. A decade later, while Bill was in a coma, he would receive an e-mail from a man named Joe Leone who was at that show. Joe had asked Bill to sign his poster Happy 1st Anniversary to him and his wife Cindy. He still had it on his wall at home, and he wrote Bill to tell him that, along with his hopes for Bill's recovery.

"People were attracted to Bill," Norton says. "Bill can be one of the most charming, attractive people in the world." Bill became a friend to Norton and his family, coming over for dinner with Norton's wife and three daughters, and playing Boggle—a Norton family favorite—with all of them for hours and hours. Norton claims that Bill was the most remarkable player at this obscure game that anyone in the family had ever seen. After his accident, Bill remembered Norton, at least a little, but much to Norton's dismay, he had no recollection of their Boggle battles.

In September of 1994, while he was still living in Colorado, Bill went to a family reunion with his dad and siblings at Lake Powell. Wally was extremely sick with lung cancer at the time, and the trip was a way for his children to see him one more time, all together. Vicki, who was already living in Australia, had asked her dad if he wanted her to come to his funeral or to visit him before he died, and based on his answer, Bill arranged the get-together. "Bill is all about family," Vicki says. "He pretty much financed the trip for everyone. He made sure everyone was there for our dad." The family stayed on a houseboat together, and one night, Bill set off about $2,000 worth of fireworks he had brought, essentially a professional show reflected on the lake for his father.

The following May, Bill stopped in to visit his dad. Kathryn was there as well, and they had a little family gathering. When Wally went to sleep that night, he told his wife Mary that it had been the best day of his life. Bill's dad died, at home, the following day. Years later, after his accident, Bill called Mary in tears. "I don't remember Dad dying," he said. "I don't remember."

Bill started out strongly in his ambassadorship role. Norton left Crested Butte within a year of Bill's arrival, but while he was there Bill's relationship with the resort was positive. "In my entire association with Bill, I never asked him to be somewhere where he didn't show up, never expected graciousness or support when I didn't get it, never had a cross word with him," Norton says. "I counted him as a friend and the guy never let me down."

Bill could not, however, sustain the success. He had a physical altercation with Gina's dad, in which Gina says that Bill attacked her dad from behind, initially hitting him in the back, and then, when he turned around, punching him in the face and breaking his nose. Gina was there when it happened, and after watching in shock, she called the police to come to the house. The fight ended Bill's relationship with his father-in-law as well as the house-building venture—Dennis Ricci wanted nothing more to do with his son-in-law after that incident. And about the time Norton left Crested Butte for Aspen, Bill's relationship with Crested Butte fell apart.

Gina Kroft, who later moved into Norton's position, says, "When Bill is on, he's the best. When he's off, there are situations that you prefer wouldn't happen. Usually involving VIPs."

Norton puts a more positive spin on the situation: "When things did-n't work out between Bill and anyone, it's because Bill was unable, or unwill-ing, to pretend he liked someone when he didn't. It's either a fault or an admirable trait. I respected him for it. Bill didn't suffer fools in the same way the rest of us do."

Certainly he didn't suffer slow skiers, VIPs or not. As an ambassador Bill always skied too fast and often lost his corporate groups. "He'd say, 'Follow me' and they tried," Kroft says. "It was always a conversation piece later that night—there he goes again." Many high-level executives Bill skied with during this time viewed themselves as just as brash and rebellious in their fields as Bill had been in his—or at least wished they were. In any case, some businessmen were drawn to Bill, requesting to ski with him despite his reputation for ditching those he was supposed to be escorting. So while Crested Butte might not have been thrilled with Bill's behavior in leaving guests behind on the hill, it didn't appear to have been a deal-breaker in Bill's association with the resort.

"There were several incidents, not one," Kroft says. "And unfortunate-ly, the incidents generally revolved around alcohol. It wasn't good when Bill drank here." These were off the clock issues—Bill wasn't drinking on the job—but as an ambassador representing a company, Bill had to act a certain way all the time, and he either couldn't, or wouldn't, do it. He was a highly visible person, and when he let his guard down—on one occasion losing his temper and becoming overly aggressive at an airline counter when a flight was delayed—it reflected on the resort as well.

"You can't let the irreverence go too far," Kroft says. "Bill was missing appointments, didn't show up for appearances, he was argumentative, he had an arrogant attitude toward people in the sales department. Part of his personality came out to the wrong people." It was not, she says, a comfort-able situation at the end.

So the Johnson family was back on the road—this time literally. And the family had grown—Gina had given birth to Tyler Dean on April 9th, 1994, in California. Wanting to have her baby in familiar surroundings (just as she had with Nick), Gina had flown home to California a month early to be with her mom. Tyler was delivered via emergency C-section when a nurse discovered that the umbilical cord was wrapped around his neck. There were serious complications that put Gina's life at risk during that delivery as well. Bill had been with Gina when Nick was born, but with the urgency involved in Tyler's birth, he arrived too late. "It was a long way from Crested Butte to California," he says.

After having hated Crested Butte for the first couple years due to its remoteness and unfamiliarity, Gina ended up loving the place. She made friends, she enjoyed skiing with the boys (Nicholas first got on skis at age two), and she completely decorated the house the way she wanted it. Gina hosted beautiful Christmases in Colorado. Bill continued to get free skis and equipment from Atomic long after he retired from the U.S. Ski Team, and one Christmas Atomic sent him 20 pairs of new skis. When Gina's family arrived for the holidays, each of them received skis, poles, and a ski pass for the week. At some point after Bill was no longer racing on the pro circuits, Atomic stopped paying him, but they still sent skis and gear. When the company took Bill off the payroll, he refused to wear their clothes any longer. "He just kept having that attitude that 'I'm Bill Johnson' and they should pay me money," Gina says.

While living in Colorado, Bill and Gina went to Vail with the boys every March for the American Ski Classic. All their expenses were paid—they were put up in condos, provided cars and cell phones and skiing for the week, and given concert tickets and goody bags. Gina loved the event, and it was always held around the time of her birthday. One year the symphony there actually performed the Happy Birthday song in her honor.

With Bill's ambassadorship coming to a premature end, he had a couple of back-up plans. One was to continue professional ski racing, something he had been doing all along while at Crested Butte. Bill would ultimately shut down that path—and that income—due, generally, to the same bad attitude that was responsible for his downfall at Crested Butte. Bill's other idea was to travel the country competing in golf tournaments in an attempt to make the PGA Tour.

To facilitate this, Bill decided to pack up his family and travel the country in a recreational vehicle. They bought a Newmar Mt. Aire, 37½ feet long, fully customized. By all accounts, Gina was not wild about this plan, but with two toddlers to care for, she feared Bill would leave her if she didn't go

Bill in Beaver Creek, Colorado, December 2000.
J. Selkowitz/selkophoto.com

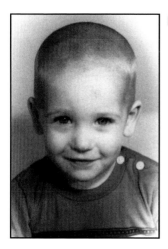

Bill at age one, 1961.

Bill (striped shirt) with his brother, Wally, and sisters, Kathryn and Vicki, in Canoga Park, California, early 1960s.

Bill ski jumping at age 10. His arm was broken so he taped his pole to his glove.

Bill and his dad,
Wally, 1976.

Bill at home in the
early 1970s.

Barry Thys, Andy Luhn, and Bill
leaning on Bill's car in front of
"Hotel California," 1983.

Blake Lewis with Doug Lewis and Bill trying on their racing suits for the first time...and wondering why the candy stripes.

Bill's gold medal run, February 16, 1984.
© 1984 David Madison

Bill on the podium in
Sarajevo.
Bill Eppridge/*Sports Illustrated*

Coach Theo Nadig, Bill, and Blake Lewis at the post-race press conference in Sarajevo where Bill was asked what the gold medal meant to him.

Sports Illustrated,
February 27, 1984.
Tony Tomsic/*Sports Illustrated*

Bill and his mom, DB, at the 1984 World Cup in Aspen, Colorado.

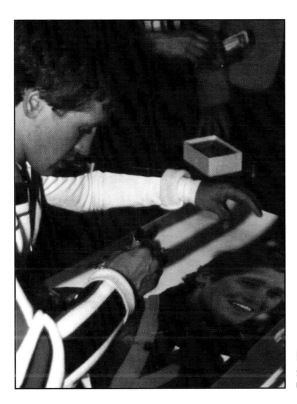

Bill signing autographs,
summer of 1984.
Brian W. Robb

Bill bouncing on a trampoline at a ski poster photo shoot in Crested Butte, Colorado, 1985.

Bill on the road with the U.S. Ski Team, 1985.

Bill's wedding, 1988. L to R, best man Barry Thys, Andy Luhn, Alan Lauba, Bill, guest Mark Herhusky, and Jo Jo Weber.

Bill and Gina on their wedding day in Lake Tahoe, California, 1988.

Bill and Gina celebrating their first Thanksgiving in the Tahoe house, 1989.

Bill, with Ryan on his back, during a trip to Crested Butte, Colorado, 1991.

Ryan William Johnson, 9/16/90–11/11/91.

Bill coaching Nicholas
before a race, 1995.

Bill and Gina with Nick and Tyler on the cabin cruiser
in Oregon, late 1990s.

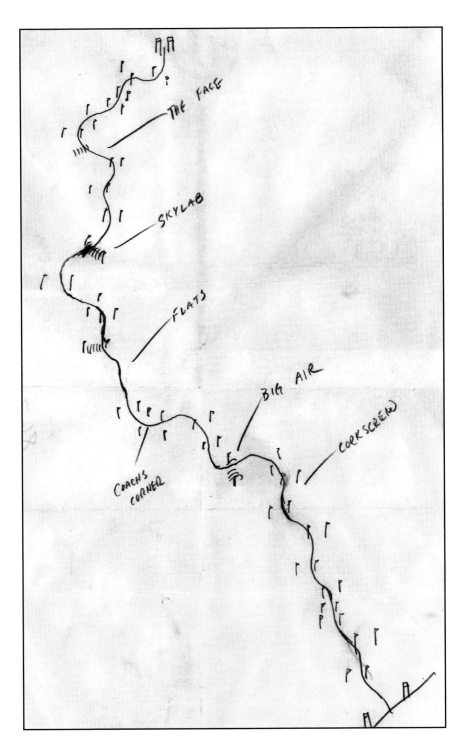

The map Bill drew of the downhill course at Big Mountain
the night before his accident.

Bill's crash,
March 22, 2001.
Eric Einhorn/Mountain Photography

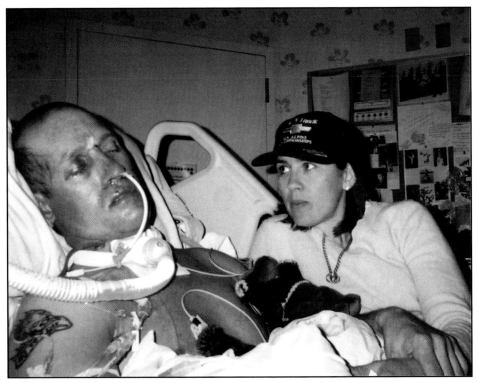

Bill in the hospital with Gina by his side.

Artwork for Bill's hospital room from his sons.

Clockwise from top: Erik Steinberg, Blake Lewis, Bill, Dañela Lewis, and Andy Luhn in the Providence Portland Medical Center, April 2001.

Bill playing golf at an event sponsored by the Brain Injury Association of Connecticut, 2002.

Bill on the slopes with Tyler and Nick at Mt. Hood Meadows,
December 2003.

Bill at home in Zigzag,
September 2004.

along. Jo Jo viewed the RV as Bill's way of keeping his family with him while he traveled, and it did, at least, do that.

The pro golfing idea never became a reality. While Gina was not fully behind it—feeling that if Bill wanted to get there he should do it through his sons instead, she admits that she wasn't sure she could judge what athletic feats an Olympian champion was capable of. As a result, she supported Bill in the endeavor. The family traveled in the RV while Bill trained and competed in several tournaments, mostly in California. By the end of six months or so, he got down to a two handicap. Buddies he would later golf with in San Diego said that Bill probably couldn't have made a living in the sport, but that on a good day he was likely one of the best golfers in town.

Bill's plan to make a living from professional ski racing held more promise, at least in the short term. Since retiring from the Ski Team, he had been competing in various Legends and Return of the Champions races. As an article on the U.S. Ski Team website stated, perhaps a touch derisively, Bill "appeared at countless celebrity ski events."

Almost everyone who knew Bill during this time has a story from the era. He was still trying to live like a star, straining relationships as he went. Erik Steinberg was director of Ski Club Vail then, and he repeatedly asked Bill to give motivational speeches to the kids there. Bill wouldn't do it, wouldn't even return Steinberg's calls.

In February of 1991, at a Tournament of Champions event at Heavenly ski resort in California, Franz Klammer, allegedly skiing for money for the first time, beat Bill in the race. Afterward, ski reporter Robert Frohlich recalls Bill, "pouring out a quart of Evian water, grabbing a bottle of peppermint schnapps from the bartender in the hospitality tent, and siphoning it into the Evian bottle so he could get hammered in the finish corral without anyone's knowledge."

As it existed in the early '90s, the senior ski-racing circuit used a handicapped system that gave older skiers time advantages, resulting in more head-to-head finishes. Bill had been competing in about a half-dozen of these races a year, but he had always been outspoken against the handicapping, feeling it was more a show than a true competition. And if he *was* going to race on the circuit, then he wanted more money. When he didn't get it, Bill's response was to walk away.

"He would rather not do it, not have any money, than to just do it because we needed to pay the bills," Gina says. "He just would not do that. *Would not.*" With appearance fees generally around $5,000 and prize money averaging $7,500 or so for the winner, it had been a quick and easy way for Bill to make money. Needless to say, Gina was against Bill's decision to quit, and she and Bill fought about it, but he simply wasn't going to do something he didn't want to do. "When things don't go his way on his terms, he makes them worse," Gina's sister Rochelle says. "He self-destructs."

DB was still acting as Bill's manager/agent during this period, and Bill's sister Vicki believes that that dynamic caused a great deal of stress in the marriage. "I think Gina's had a hard go," Vicki says. "The money situation was too much for her. If Mom had let go of the purse strings, it would have helped the marriage out a lot. Gina could have handled the finances, but my mother would not allow it. She didn't want to be discovered."

In the early '90s, Bill decided that he would take over his own public relations, such as it was. "Therefore, I didn't follow-up or pursue," DB says. "I believe that Gina wasn't happy with Mama always in the picture, though she never did anything that I know of to encourage or promote Bill. She liked the glitz and cleaning her house more."

In 1993, Bill and Mark Schelde, then at a sports-marketing company called Eclipse (along with Henry Schneidman, Steve Podborski, and Doug Lewis) developed a progressive ski-racing competition called Jeep King of the Mountain. Capitalizing on a time when the Winter Olympics were getting extra exposure with Games in both 1992 and 1994, the concept was to gather top-name ski talent and design compelling, made-for-TV ski races. In terms of professional racing, King of the Mountain—with big prize money, and no-handicap, full-on downhill racing—was more to Bill's liking.

The skiers represented their country in teams of two. The first season, the team captains were Bill for the United States, Franz Klammer for Austria, Pirmin Zurbriggen (who finished 4th to Bill in the downhill in Sarajevo and 1st in 1988 in Calgary) for Switzerland, and Steve Podborski (bronze medalist in the Olympic downhill in 1980 and 8th in Sarajevo) for Canada. For the team representing the U.S., Bill was put together with, once again, Doug Lewis, the other half of the 1984 U.S. Olympic downhill team. And this time, as Schelde says, "Billy had to root for Doug because it meant money in his pocket."

The King of the Mountain rules were made up by the racers themselves, and they were all consensus-driven. Bill, never known for his team skills, had trouble working in a group. As Rochelle explains it, "Bill didn't really try to make sure that people liked him. So most people didn't."

Worse, Bill was bound to have problems not just with group dynamics, but with group decision-making. The way Bill saw it, from his I-want-what-I-want perspective, when things weren't going his way, things weren't fair. There was a meeting, for example, to decide whether the skiers would be allowed to use back protectors—an apparatus akin to an armadillo that straps on a skier's back. Ski Federation rules do not allow aerodynamic aids, and the device added an airfoil in the back, so everyone in the group but Bill decided against them. "He had real trouble with not getting what he wanted," Podborski says. "He sat there and stewed. You could tell he wanted to drill somebody, but there were too many of us."

The idea behind the Jeep series was to give the power to the athletes to design the courses they wanted to ski, something that had never been done before. To that end, Schelde gathered the four captains on the top of a run at Aspen Highlands on a weekend in January of 1994. There was six inches of new snow obscuring a clear course down the mountain. Schelde, not a ski racer himself, admits he was "winging it." He handed Bill a gate and told him to start skiing down the mountain. Schelde's instructions to Bill were to watch the other captains gesturing to the left or right, and when at least two of the three of them raised their hand, "sink the gate." That went smoothly enough, so when the skiers all met at the first gate Schelde handed the next one to Klammer with the same instructions, and they moved down the course that way.

At some point Podborski, laughing, turned to Schelde and said, "You Americans don't understand. Having the four of us side-slip the course and set the gates is kind of like having Joe Montana mow the grass before a game."

"These were arch-enemies," Schelde says, "working in unison. And they were all *giggling* all the way down the mountain."

When he was with the King of the Mountain circuit, Bill put in a lot of time doing site surveys on the mountains, strategizing with the camera and production crews, laying out the best possible courses. He excelled at this, and he was paid a bit extra to do the work. Bill was heavily involved from the beginning, and Schelde believes that his help in developing the program was instrumental to its success.

"The guy was brilliant," Schelde says. "He saw the big picture, but he could also focus on the small details." By the second season, other professional ski circuits began to form, all competing for top talent and trying to buy athletes away from King of the Mountain. Bill remained loyal throughout—refusing to even talk to other racing circuits—and Schelde credits him with being honorable and never wavering in his commitment.

In his King of the Mountain days, Bill's skiing remained very strong in some areas. He still had a fantastic touch with softer snow, but he didn't try to stay in top condition. Woody Woodruff knew Bill from the Tournament of Champions (where Woodruff was the athlete liaison), and he worked with Bill again as the director of operations for the Jeep series. "Billy at his best was such a joy," Woodruff says. "But he was frustrated not being on top of his game. He didn't work as hard as other athletes. He always thought he was the best, and he thought he just would *be* the best because he was Bill Johnson."

"At that point, I was skiing better," Doug says. "Bill was a party guy—he wasn't as fast. I had to help him. It was a change in dynamics."

But Bill had been better than Doug in 1984, and he never let anyone forget it. Whenever Bill was introduced to sponsors on the racing circuit, he would hold his hand out to shake hands and say, "Hi, Bill Johnson, gold medalist."

"It was very sincere," Schelde says. "He said it in an innocent, honest way, like it was his middle name. But it was odd."

Working with Bill to get the Jeep series started, Podborski describes, almost verbatim, the same sense of unease that former high school classmates had felt toward Bill twenty years earlier and that teammates of Bill had experienced ever since. "You never knew what you were going to get with Bill," he says.

Franz Klammer had the same concerns about Bill. "One thing with Billy, he was sometimes hard to calculate," Klammer says. "He was the nicest person possible and the next second a different person, turning—it is hard for me to explain in English—he is turning, turns around, not so nice."

Bill also exuded the same sense of physical threat to these racers that he had toward classmates and teammates in the past. Asked if anyone ever played jokes on Bill, Podborski responds: "Someone probably did it once. I didn't. He'd drill you."

One time Podborski was in the starting gate, with Bill set to ski down next to him a half-second later. As soon as Podborski left the gate, Bill yelled,

"My clock isn't working." As Podborski explains, "If I turn to look I'm a fool; if I don't I'm a jerk. I couldn't win either way." He did look back—not a good thing for his race time, or probably, for his safety—only to see Bill laughing. The other racers never knew if stunts like that were malicious or meant to be jokes. Podborski has his opinion: "He was never a buddy enough for a practical joke."

Bill was competitive, obviously, but so were all the other top skiers in the world. Even within them, Bill couldn't play any sport unless he could win. He couldn't stand to be beaten in anything. In a pick-up game of football among the racers at the end of the day, for example, Bill just walked off if he wasn't winning.

"I'm hard-pressed to find a nice thing that Bill did for other people, but he never did anything nice for himself, either," Podborski says. "The world was a tough place for Bill—he was always fighting everything." For the most part, Podborski kept his distance, left Bill alone. "It was like living too near an ongoing train wreck," he says. "If you got too close, you'd get sucked in."

Meanwhile, Woodruff was constantly confronted by Bill's failure to at least temper who he was to match the situation he was in. "Public appearances—you either get it or you don't," Woodruff says. "Bill didn't get it."

It wasn't that Bill wasn't skilled, for example, at public speaking—when he wanted to, he knew how to command and charm an audience. It was more that he often didn't care to try. "If he didn't like you," Schelde say, "he had no time for you." And what was worse, from a ski promoter's perspective, is that Bill's destructive side was virtually unpredictable. "Sometimes you had no idea what he was gonna say," Schelde says. "You couldn't trust him."

When he won a gold medal, by default Bill was a role model, a heroic figure even, and he clearly understood that, but he couldn't live his life in a way that matched that image. The reason doesn't seem to be that he just didn't want to. Bill has been quoted in the press as saying, "Everybody wanted me to be an All-American, and I wish I was, but I'm not." Some people in Bill's life have speculated that he was only interested in the pure joy of ski racing and didn't care about the money or the endorsements or the self-promotion afterward. More likely, he cared greatly, but he had always succeeded—against advice, contrary to convention—by doing things his own way. It was how he had gotten as far as he had. He didn't know any other way to be, and he didn't see a reason to change.

Bill certainly didn't alter his approach to skiing with VIPs while he was on the pro circuit—Schelde had the same issues with Bill that Bill's employers at Crested Butte had. The Sunday morning, from nine until noon, after a Jeep race was generally set up for the racers to ski with sponsors, and Schelde had to endure Bill "going Mach 5 through the run, ripping through the trees," then appearing surprised that he had lost all his people. Bill was fun to ski with, but no one ever knew what to expect—Bill being brash, or sensitive, or both at the same time. "It might have been an act inside himself," Schelde says. "He never winked at me, but he might have winked at himself." It was due to Bill's failure to appear at the Ski with Sponsors mornings—or to be difficult when he did show up—that a rule was implemented to withhold the racers' payments until after lunch on Sundays.

In 1994, Tommy Moe became the second American male to win the Olympic gold medal in downhill skiing, beating Kjetil Andre Aamodt of Norway by .04 of a second. Tommy thinks that Bill may have had a sense that Tommy would win at the Olympics—when Tommy met him in 1986, Bill's first words to him were, "Oh, so Tommy Moe, are you golden or what?" The effect of Tommy's victory on the pro racing circuit in the following years was significant—the in-fighting among competing pro ski tours got uglier, and the sponsors wanted younger racers, especially Tommy. It wasn't apparent where Bill fit in, although there clearly would have been a way to keep Bill on, even if Tommy joined the circuit—a U.S. ticket with two gold medalists would have been a marketing dream. Snowboarding was also getting popular at the time, putting the future of pro ski racing in jeopardy. Bill's response was to act out. "He was confrontational with people who were not helping Billy," Schelde says. "He was abusive to everybody across the board."

"A lot of people gave him lots of chances," Doug says. "The team. The sponsors. He burned all these bridges and there was no one left."

Woodruff believes that some of Bill's anger may have been fueled by alcohol, but he saw bigger problems. "He was belligerent, not really respectful," he says. "Getting in fights. I wasn't in a position to judge him or tell him how to live his life. Those close to him let him live his life. He's a star. It's funny. They wouldn't say anything."

Living through this time with Bill, Gina had virtually the same perspective as those outside the family. "It was hard to watch," she says.

At some point, while speaking to a representative from Visa about a position with the company, Bill had a confrontation with the woman who interviewed him, essentially asking her who she thought she was. "I thought, 'What the heck are you doing, do you realize what you're doing?'" Gina says. "I would try to tell him. I would try to say things. And it got worse. It just got worse. As every event went through, I just knew at some point he was going to get irritated with somebody and cause a scene and it was gonna end."

Those around Bill knew that Gina was getting the brunt of Bill's frustration. "It wasn't a partnership, they weren't a team," Rochelle says. "He didn't care what she had to say. She was along for the ride."

In addition, Gina had had just about enough of living in the RV with two young boys and an Alaskan malamute. One time they drove it to Vegas where Bill stayed out all night. As in life, in Vegas Bill could lose big or win big. The next morning he wouldn't talk to Gina about what had happened, but she later found out that he was sulking at having lost $10,000 in a night, money they certainly could not afford to lose. "He could just put it on the edge like that," Gina says.

"Their relationship was good at first, but shaky afterward," Bill's old teammate Alan Lauba says. "There was lots of fighting at friends' houses. And then they were living in that motor home—I don't think it was that smooth." It was around this point that Gina insisted on living in a home without wheels. Bill told her she wasn't the girl he married, and she agreed—she wasn't 21 anymore, and she had two kids. They were visiting San Diego at the time—the summer of 1996—and they decided to settle there. As Jo Jo says, "Gina's interests came first on occasion."

Meanwhile, on the ski tour, the situation began to break down. Bill's former teammate Debbie Armstrong recalls several incidences of Bill embarrassing sponsors, including one at a Tournament of Champions fundraiser at the Telluride Theater in Telluride, Colorado. "Bill was sitting in the back with his wife, totally drunk, getting loud, uncontrollable. His wife was embarrassed. I didn't like how he was with his wife—rude," she says. "He was turning into a bit of a joke."

Bill ultimately worked his way out of the events, and in so doing, dwindled his sole source of income down to nothing. Woodruff, who calls Bill "one of my favorite people when he wants to be," didn't see a choice. "He was just sort of troubled," he says. "I couldn't justify it anymore, I couldn't do it to the sponsors anymore—it was too much of a liability. He was too much of a risk at these parties."

The last straw, in 1997, was in Vail. Bill was not invited back to the Jeep series after that event. The press later coyly called the end of the relationship "a disagreement with sponsors." Woodruff recalls that Bill got in a fistfight with a security guard; Doug Lewis believes it was a valet. Tommy Moe thinks it was a bellboy. In any event, Schelde says that Bill showed up that evening drunk and angry, yelling obscenities, and the organizers were so nervous about Bill creating a scene at the dinner that they locked him out of it.

Other people, including Erik Steinberg and some ski reporters covering Bill at the time, claim that Bill also threw a punch at one of the directors of the racing circuit. Bill's mom says that Bill's dispute with King of the Mountain had to do with profit sharing that was not benefiting Bill. His sense of entitlement, and hers, is clear from her version of Bill's final event: "Bill finally confronted them at the last event he was in and literally walked out on them and their event right in the middle of it which made [them] mad," she says. "But it was totally justified."

"Bill made his own bed," Armstrong says. "Every turn, he brought it on himself. He tapped out all of his options. He clearly was just spiraling out of control." In fact, Bill was merely at the beginning of a long spin downward that would span the next several years.

Other world-class skiers that Bill had competed with witnessed him self-destruct, and they were frustrated and saddened by it. "Bill had a chance to become anything he wanted," Podborski says. "He had a chance to transcend his upbringing, and for a while he did. He was one of the finest skiers in the world. If he was more sympathetic, he could have been a god."

"Bill had every opportunity to turn his life around," Phil Mahre says. "He slammed every door he opened because of his attitude. He could have been the American *dream*. He let it drift away. It's a tragedy in the long run." Everyone around Bill at the time recognized that he was mired in his glory days, and they feared where he was headed because of it. "The medal was never as big as Bill needed it to be," Woodruff says.

Podborski, who believes that "you own what you become," felt that Bill couldn't envision a brighter future, couldn't see any solutions. "He could never find a way out of there," he says. "I wasn't sure if he wouldn't leave where he was because he was happy there, or if he couldn't leave there because he couldn't find his way out."

CHAPTER ELEVEN

"There's just a lot with Bill. Even when there's nothing going on, there's a lot with Bill."

– DAVID WATT

Bill and Gina kept the RV when they bought their house in San Diego. Their first year there Bill was still getting paid to ski, but even then they were having trouble paying the mortgages on both the house and the RV. They also had a problem finding a place to put the RV—the homeowner's association in the community where they lived had rules against it, and, in any event, the driveway wasn't big enough. They parked it on the other side of their house, on a bigger road, and Bill constantly moved it up and down the street.

Despite the financial pressure, what Bill mostly did in San Diego was play golf—not competitively, but for fun. Bob Sankey, who was a golf pro for years (he now sells swimming pools), met Bill at the first tee at a golf course. "He said he was Bill Johnson, and I said, 'Like the skier?'" Bob says. "He said, 'I *am* the skier.'"

Bob had just retired from a job teaching golf, and he had lots of time to play golf and "bang around" with Bill. His kids were about the ages of Nick and Tyler, so the families became friends, with Bill becoming "Uncle Bill" to Bob's kids. At that time Bill's own kids called him by his first name. (Nick and Tyler also referred to their mom as "Gina.")

If not exactly a doting father, Bill clearly loved his sons. Jo Jo believes Bill was a poor disciplinarian, but he explains that Bill once told him, "After losing a child, do you think I can scold?" Britta Sullaway, a neighbor four or five houses down, recalls that Bill was often working at a computer in an office he had set up in the garage while Nick and Tyler played ball in the driveway and rode their bikes.

Gina's sister Rochelle remembers Bill during this time as a fun dad who was definitely proud of his kids and especially wanted to do "boy things" with them. Bill taught his sons how to ski, and how to get out of the starting gates, but he never wanted a future in ski racing for them. It wasn't due to a fear of the danger, but because there was more money in golfing. He also didn't want them to be out in the cold. Bill still hated cold weather, and he was happy enough to live in San Diego for that reason. Gina, on the other hand, a self-described "mountain girl" who grew up around skiing and married an Olympic skier, wasn't entirely comfortable living away from the base of a mountain.

Bob Sankey went to some pro races with Bill to watch him ski, and he was there when Bill's relationship with professional skiing came to an abrupt end. "He had hit rock bottom," he says. "He had to start working." But Bill was never successful, not ever in his life, at making a place for himself outside ski racing. At almost 40 years old, he had essentially the same conversation with Jo Jo that he had had at age 20, about never having worked a day in his life, and the comment obviously played a lot better back then. "He said, 'Damn it, I was somebody. I shouldn't have to go back to that,'" Jo Jo says.

In a where-are-they-now article in *Sports Illustrated* in February of 1998, Bill stated that he was considering a career in the stock market or the construction business. In fact, rather than get a steady job in either of those industries, Bill took on some odd jobs as a carpenter and played around day-trading. He sold his Portland apartment building and put the proceeds into the stock market, only to trade the money away.

Mark Schelde had always thought that Bill would make a ruthless, successful stockbroker, and he encouraged him to work for a brokerage firm. He believes that Bill didn't pursue that path because he didn't see an easy point of entry into the field. Schelde knows that he bought some books to study for the securities exam, but he says that Bill wouldn't have had a problem passing the test with or without the books. He suspects that Bill must have been a closet reader, for him to know so much and never appear to read anything. "He gobbled up information from somewhere," he says.

At first glance, Bill certainly didn't present as the near genius that everyone who got to know him realized he was. "He was a very crass guy," Bob says. "He always had to be right. Everyone that met him at first didn't like him. But to know Bill is to love Bill."

Bob's wife Heidi liked Bill as well, despite the fact that he "had an edge to him." She witnessed a lot of arguing and problems in the marriage, fights over money and the kids, sometimes both at once—one argument occurred when Gina bought the boys a bunch of new clothes and Bill didn't think they could afford it. Bill's family believes that Gina's taste ran to the expensive—in her own clothes and accessories as well as her home furnishings. Bill's brother Wally describes Bill and Gina's houses as "decorated to the hilt."

"Gina wanted him to be wealthier than he was," Heidi says. "I got the sense that Gina thought she was getting more of a glamorous lifestyle than what she ended up with. I had that feeling. At a Jeep event, how she handled herself—she liked the limelight. She thought she was getting something different, but it didn't work out that way."

Gina has described herself as "the perfect trophy wife," and Bill used that phrase himself after their divorce, telling Creel, "With a trophy wife, when the money runs out, so does she." That doesn't, however, seem exactly fair to Gina, given the level of volatility in the marriage. Even those who claim that Gina lost interest in Bill at the time the money ran out can't say that it was necessarily *because* the money ran out. And the reality is—whether she preferred a different lifestyle or not—Gina stayed with Bill long after those days were over. Years after the money stopped coming in, Gina was still trying to make the marriage work.

Schelde says, "Billy had to be a nightmare to be around in '98, '99, in the winter," and he has it right. For the first time since he was six, Bill's winter season was not built around competitive ski racing at some level. He did not adjust at all well. From the beginning of their relationship Bill had used the phrase "Welcome to Gina's world," and now, feeling that Gina was being too demanding, he began to say it more frequently and more viciously. Friends and family recall a lot of fighting and screaming during this era. Nick and Tyler saw their dad lock their mom out of the house in her pajamas a couple times, and knew that she had to call the police to get back in. "I can't remember a lot of happy, happy times," Rochelle says, "Bill was all about himself, all for himself."

Once Bill stopped skiing he seemed to have no idea what else to do, and he reacted by doing virtually nothing at all. Gina's family knew that Bill clearly had the ability to achieve goals when he focused on something, and they kept waiting for that skill to shine again. "We knew he had it in him," Rochelle says, "but he was his own worst enemy." Bill seemed to want a new direction to just happen, to come to him naturally, like his athletic ability. He could have continued to make a living in the ski industry—doing television commentary, coaching, running ski camps—but he didn't seem content with, or even interested in, a traditional lifestyle. He liked being on the move. His restlessness was such that he was never really able to feel at home anywhere.

As it turns out, the question of what Bill should do when his fifteen minutes were over was ultimately less important than what he would do in an attempt to get them back. In the end, Bill was willing to die trying.

As a result of the financial instability, Bill's home life was coming undone. To try to stem the crisis, Gina got a job as an assistant at a realtor's office. Rochelle felt that Bill had never treated many people, including her sister, with respect. When Gina started working, Bill, who had told his wife that he would always take care of her, began to lose respect for himself.

During this time, Bill was hanging out—drinking, taking drugs, going to strip clubs—with Bob and a friend of his, David Watt, who went by "Kawika," his Hawaiian nickname meaning beloved. There was a little sports bar at the end of the street, called Stuft Pizza then, and they often went there to drink. "I wondered what was going to happen," David says. "Bill wasn't participating in family life. We were party boys. We were drinking, drinking all night. He was with us *a lot.*"

Looking back on this time in Bill's life, Mark Herhusky, a friend of his since his Ski Team days, sums it up by saying, "Bill would go out for a gallon of milk and come back two days later without the milk." Not surprisingly, David recalls that Gina never seemed particularly happy to see Bill's friends, especially in the early morning hours when, on a couple occasions, she came looking for Bill.

It was during this time that David, born and raised in Hawaii and comfortable on a surfboard since kindergarten, introduced Bill to surfing. At 6'2", 240, and in top shape, David was an excellent surfer. He was close to many of the professional surfers who lived in the area, and he welcomed Bill into his circle. "Bill started off very, very bad," David says. "But his balls were just huge. He didn't have any fear for elements I respect." They began to spend even more time together, mostly on the beach, hanging around with David's surfer buddies. "He was a flawless athlete," David says. He adds the next part seriously, not as a joke: "The only thing wrong with Bill Johnson was his personality."

With Bill constantly vanishing, Gina was doing the best she could to try to hold things together for the boys. "He didn't say thank you very much," Gina says. "He didn't give other people credit, for his skiing, for anything, and he definitely didn't give me credit."

Bill's judgment was such at this time that he would take drugs even in the presence of his mother-in-law. Britta Sullaway, the neighbor from down the street, says that Gina once told her that she was "consumed with what she was going through, and didn't want to drag people in."

In the end, Bill and Gina's relationship was based on such intense highs and lows that it began to mirror those extremes. During the course of their marriage, Bill's friends say that they had physical altercations that involved, at a minimum, some shoving-type behavior on Bill's part. Gina focuses on the emotional abuse. Around the time of their divorce, for example, Bill taunted her that he had had five affairs. Gina had suspected him for a while, and tends to believe it. On at least one occasion a woman called Gina to tell her that Bill had been at her house the night before drunk, taking drugs, and hitting on her.

Some of Bill's friends allude to his infidelity, particularly when he and Gina were living at the house in Tahoe. "He's good at making something go south," Erik Steinberg says. "There were scam, shams, and swindles going on there."

Jo Jo witnessed the abusive dynamic firsthand on a visit to Bill and Gina in San Diego. Gina, who had always been a gourmet cook (once at a Thanksgiving dinner she hosted for Bill's family she prepared every single dish listed in a magazine of holiday selections), was preparing a lavish dinner. She played a country CD in the background. Bill told her that Jo Jo didn't want to listen to that kind of music. Despite Jo Jo's repeated protests that he liked it, Bill stormed over to the stereo, took Gina's CD out, and smashed it in front of her. He then put on some AC/DC and turned up the volume while Gina sat there shaking. Jo Jo told the couple at that point that they had to end the relationship before somebody got hurt.

Even Bill's friends, who knew Bill didn't want the divorce, didn't blame Gina for leaving him. "Bill was angry a lot, trying to find a way to support his family. He would take his anger out on Gina," Bob says. "Gina had had enough. She told me, 'He verbally abuses me so much, I can't take it.' She hung in there for a long time, gave him a lot of chances." David saw the situation from Gina's perspective as well: "I don't know how much more Gina could take. I believe in standing by your man, but he was verbally abusive, very abrasive. How much more could she take?"

Although Bill's mother claims that she "always enjoyed Gina," she says that she "was no lily" and "caused a lot of it." DB believes that both Bill and Gina had a spending problem—"one as bad as the other"—and looking back she wonders how they could have survived as long as they did. "Gina thinks she's the good guy, he's the bad guy," DB says. "It was both their faults. Their tempers and their spending got in the way."

In an extremely uncharacteristic move, Bill told both his mom and Kathryn how devastated he was about his marital problems. "He was no longer able to be his own person, he was being molded into her way of thinking," DB says. "But she couldn't remake the man." Bill said that he was doing everything Gina asked him to do and she was still pushing him away.

"Bill did not know how to be the person I needed him to be," Gina says. "He got a job, got clean, stopped partying, started going to [marriage] counseling. But I had lost respect for him by then. And in the past, he had tried and it never worked. And the money was falling apart. We were selling things off to make it. I thought this was the only window to get out."

"Things didn't change enough for Gina to get past what she was feeling," Heidi says. "And then nothing was ever going to be enough."

Already estranged from Gina in late 1999, Bill had a dispute with his mother that friends say left him feeling betrayed by her. Bill apparently felt that everything in his life had fallen apart and now his mom dumped on him, too. Bill's old friend Tom Mahoney says Bill told him, "Forget her. She used me." Happening simultaneously with Gina leaving him, it was just too much for Bill. He reacted by completely cutting off contact with his mother. "Bill refused to ever speak to her again, that's it," Vicki says. "He was done."

"If he wouldn't have hit his head," John Creel, Bill's coach during his comeback, says, "he still wouldn't be talking to her."

The argument was triggered by the death of Bill's grandmother. She died in October of 1999, leaving everything to her daughter, DB, and cutting her son, Bill Morris, out of her will as she had said she would when Morris lost Bill's investment. Bill claimed that his mom owed him the money—$70,000 at the time, more like $100,000 with the finance charges Bill accumulated on the debt—that she had invested for him in her brother's get-rich-quick scheme years ago. His position was that his mom was responsible for that investment, and now that she had an inheritance and was in a position to give him that money, she should do so. Her perspective was that her brother's investment was simply a risky gamble that Bill had lost. She reminded him that she also lost $10,000 of her own money, although she later recovered some or all of that from her brother.

In the last conversation that Bill had with his mom prior to his accident, he told her that she was responsible for all the bad things that had happened in his life: his divorce, his being broke, Ryan's death. It is unclear whether Bill was just looking for a scapegoat for his troubles or whether he really viewed the initial loss of that money as the source of all his problems. Issues surrounding money surely caused stress in his marriage, but $70,000 likely wouldn't have been enough to permanently offset that pressure. As for being broke, Bill ended up more than $70,000 in debt at the time of his crash, so that money wasn't likely to have turned his life around.

The comment about Ryan, coming from a man who had never before blamed anyone, including himself, for his son's death, is the most interesting accusation. The only way Bill could have meant to connect the two events is that his investment occurred around the time he and Gina were looking to buy their first home. The house they bought was the one in Tahoe, where Ryan later drowned. According to Gina (who does not connect these events, but who can follow Bill's thought processes), with another $70,000 to use as a down payment, they might have bought a different, more expensive house. Or they might not have bought the house with Andy, who then may not have been present in their house that day, possibly shifting the events that played out. The comment does seem to indicate an uncharacteristic belief in fate that Bill had only expressed once before, when he seemed to know that he was destined to win the gold medal.

In any event, as a result of this dispute and his failure to recover money that he thought he had coming to him, Bill shut his mother out of his life. "His mom sand-bagged him," Tom says. "She bought a new house. She put his money in her pocket."

The next time Bill spoke to his mom was a year and a half later, when he awoke from his coma, seemingly with no memory of his fight with her. According to Blake Lewis, in the early phases of his awakening, Bill did come out with ugly bursts of words in connection with his mom. Words like "money" and "hate."

"It was still pretty fresh in there somewhere," Blake says.

Bill seems to have forgotten that he remembered, however—to this day, he has expressed no further recollection of a dispute with his mom, financial or otherwise. He does not recall being estranged from her, does not even remember being angry with her: "I've never been mad at her or anyone in my whole life." And so Bill and his mom are, in the end, together once again. Vicki, who believes in karma, feels that by wanting Bill back in her life without having to give him the money, in an eerie sort of way – much like the wishes made on the monkey's paw in the W.W. Jacobs short story—her mom got what she wished for.

Toward the end of his marriage (although he didn't know it then), Bill left Gina a note on the computer and was gone for three weeks before coming back. If, as he claimed at the time, his intent was to make her miss him, the strategy backfired. "The way he thought was so complicated," Gina says. "What he meant and what he did were so different." The first week she was devastated, the second week she made a plan, and by the third week she didn't want him back. She did get back with him, but only to continue an on-again-off-again relationship until she finally left for good at the end of 1999. "The man I fell in love with could do anything," Gina says. "He was successful, powerful. He could make our world work." But things were not working, and Gina, who still loved Bill, who still loves him to this day, had to say good-bye to him. They sold the house in San Diego at the end of 1999. Gina moved to her uncle's farm in Sonoma. She filed for divorce in January of 2000, and it was final in August of 2000.

After Gina left, Bill lived with the Sankey family for a couple months, with his RV parked in front of their house, then with David Watt at the beach. His partying increased dramatically. "Who he was was gone," David says. "Marriage, finances. Everything he'd ever identified with was gone."

According to Steinberg, "There were all these demons in Bill's head. He felt he didn't get enough respect inside his head." Even Jo Jo had to take a break from Bill during this period—there was about a 10-month span in which they didn't talk. "It's an explosive combination," Jo Jo says, "a world-class athlete and depression."

Alcohol, always a problem for Bill, was particularly prevalent in his life at that time. His drug use, mostly cocaine, seems to have been more a symptom of deeper troubles than the cause of them. "[The drug use] was-n't a problem," Bob says. "He used certain drugs socially. He was escaping a little bit, getting away from reality."

On the question of drugs, David says, "Well, how do you stay up all night and drink? It was a little phase in our life. We went to a lot of areas that we probably shouldn't have." Bill told his friend Mark Herhusky that he could get the stuff so cheap, he couldn't not do it. Ironically, David views Bill's drug use as having been under control in part because Bill was spending so little money on it. Bill's friends in San Diego claim that, to some extent, the drugs and drinking helped him cope with his bitterness. "And he was bitter," David says. "Damn bitter."

David also believes that Bill was so strong-minded that he could not be addicted to anything. "His mind was always so totally in control of that," he says. "If he didn't want a drink, he didn't have one." That theory is actu-ally somewhat supported by the fact that during his comeback, especially in the days prior to a race, Bill did cut way back on his drinking.

Strong-minded as Bill was, however, David knows there was an excep-tion. "Nothing could hook him," he says. "Except Gina. Gina is heroin to him."

Already wounded by the divorce of his parents when he was an ado-lescent, Bill simply could not deal with his own marriage falling apart. Bob Sankey says that Bill "loved Gina to death, but he just had a different way of showing it."

"He truly, truly loved that lady and wanted her so bad," David says. David assessed the future of Bill and Gina's relationship as follows: "Could he have gotten Gina back? I think so, if he was a kinder, gentler person. So no."

Bill had always liked to gamble, both literally and figuratively, and at this time in his life his recklessness raged out of control. He was not suicidal, but he was not afraid of hurting himself either. He surfed at midnight and rode his motorcycle at night in the rain.

In the midst of a raging storm one night, Bill and David stayed up late drinking. David then went to his girlfriend's place and came back home around five in the morning. David's house in Oceanside was about 12 feet from the water and, with the high tide and enormous waves, water was splashing up all over it. In the twilight, David saw Bill jumping from rock to rock with his surfboard. As he watched, Bill jumped into the water and was sucked out 50 feet every three seconds. "If I had said, 'Don't do it,' he was gonna do it more," David says. David saw Bill try to catch a huge wave and get tossed. There was no one else in the water. "The conditions were barely survivable, even if you were a water man," David says. "I ran in the house and shut the doors and the curtains so I wouldn't see it." Bill came in the house 45 minutes later and said, "It's not good out there."

Other days Bill would be at the computer in the early morning hours, smoking a cigarette, gambling the last of his money away day-trading. In an attempt to raise funds, Bill tried to set up various extreme ski appearances—a "Ski with Bill" event somewhere in South America, and the Arctic Man race in Alaska. Billed on its website as "truly the Ultimate Adrenaline Rush for spectators and competitors alike," the Arctic Man combines downhill skiing and snowmobiling, with the skier towed by a snowmobile for part of the race. Bill never did participate in these events, and apparently he didn't earn any money elsewhere either. According to DB, when the divorce was final, Bill and Gina each walked away with $20,000. At the time of his accident, less than a year later, Bill was $110,000 in debt.

"You couldn't pick a darker time," David says. David had a complex relationship with Bill. It was an odd mix of idolizing him—"He was greater than most men"—and recognizing Bill's very worst side—"He would say he was doing fine, but he was spiraling, spiraling down. I could see it in everything he did. He was truly, truly trying to fit in someplace. He was desperately searching for something."

But despite how far down he fell, Bill retained the ability to make someone care about him, make someone feel special about themselves and their relationship with him. When Bill lived with David, David thought of him like a brother—they were inseparable, with David constantly defending Bill to others. "He wasn't a normal person and he never believed that he was," David says. "He didn't belong in mediocrity." Rather than alienating David, Bill's arrogance had the opposite effect. "I was determined that that man come out shining again," he says.

David noticed the same quirk in Bill that his teammates and competitors had picked up on: he simply did not display stress. "Look at Bill's face on the *SI* cover," David says. "That's the same face he had when he took out the trash. It's just a walk down the driveway." It's a quality that contributed to Bill's greatness as a ski racer, but his extraordinary level of calm in the face of adversity was not always healthy. During Bill's comeback, John Creel recalls being with Bill in a restaurant when he received a call from Gina telling him that the divorce was final and discussing visitation with their sons—Bill said, "Okay," hung up the phone, and went back to his meal.

It may be, as most people who know Bill believe, that he actually didn't feel pressure, or it may be that he just wouldn't show it. He did, certainly, feel pain. David says that Bill was destroyed that he wasn't a star anymore. He sums up Bill's state of mind like this: "You don't like Bill Johnson anymore? I won't shower—how do you like that?"

At some point, even David eventually discovered what most people close to Bill knew: Bill tended to wear people down. In an attempt to save himself, David kicked Bill out of his house. Bill's response was to park his RV in David's driveway. "He was as close to crying as I had ever seen him," David says. "He said 'You're not mad at me, are you? Because you're my best friend.'" David let him back in, the friendship tighter than ever.

To this day, David (who now owns an excavation company that digs swimming pools) feels enormous guilt for pushing Bill into his comeback. Despite the fact that David has plenty of first-hand experience that Bill was the last person who would do something he didn't want to do, he still believes that in urging Bill to get his life together, he was somehow responsible for the crash.

"I told him to get off his ass and get back into the game, asked him what he was doing with his life," David says. "His comeback can be pinpointed to my living room." David says they had the same three-second conversation night after night, and all of a sudden Bill was on a training bike.

And the way David believed in Bill, it is clear why Bill would have been motivated, hearing things like, "This epic thing that you're gonna do to this world, turn it on its ear, you're gonna do it." David's faith in Bill was such that he truly believes that if Bill had gotten to the starting gate at the 2002 Olympics he would have won. He is realistic about the qualifying process, and he concedes that Bill might not have made it through the requirements, but he says, "Get him there at game day, there's nobody that could have beat him. He's a winner and he would have won."

The reasons behind Bill's comeback seem simple, inevitable, to David. "That's who he really, really was," he says. "He needed to be that person." Perhaps personalizing the issue more than he should have, David seemed genuinely devoted to helping Bill earn back the respect David felt he deserved. "I wanted him to be everything he could be," he says. "So everyone who doubted him, pushed him to the side, called him an asshole, would have a tear in their eye and say that that son of a bitch is America's greatest. I wanted them to hate themselves."

David cares about Bill so much, in fact, and has felt so much blame about how his comeback ended, that he has not been able to see Bill since his accident. Hearing about Bill's crash tore him apart. David called Bill afterward: Bill recalled surfing, but not David. When Bill was in San Diego for a visit a couple years after his accident, Bob showed pictures of David to Bill. Frustrated, Bill told Bob that it looked like Bob knew more about his life than he did, but he still didn't remember David, and David can't handle that. "I don't want to see what was and what is," he says. "I don't think I can look at him. How could you not know me? I love you, I miss you, you were the most important part of my life for a while, and I was of yours. How could you not remember me? How could you not?"

Bill never specifically discussed the danger involved in a ski-racing comeback. He did, however, say something to David that has disturbed David ever since. "It makes me shake to think about it," Bill said. "It makes me shake to think about it."

"I guess we all know our destiny," David says. "Somehow we all know." Crying now, he continues: "I would love to say that Bill didn't say it made him shake to think about it. It was spooky to me. He knew something bad would happen. I was driving it home."

But the truth, of course, is that Bill did what he did for Bill, not because somebody talked him into it. For Bill, it was always about Bill. What mattered is what Bill wanted. And above all, what Bill wanted was to be Bill Johnson again.

CHAPTER TWELVE

"The only thing on my mind is skiing right now and in fact I am skiing in my mind right now."

– BILL JOHNSON, Fall of 2001

Contrary to all medical predictions and perhaps all common sense, Bill was back on skis only eight months after the crash that almost killed him. Off the slopes, he was having problems with his focus, his memory, but one thing was clear on the mountain at Timberline on the last day of November in 2001—Bill's body remembered how to ski.

John Creel, Bill's coach during his comeback, had noticed that he seemed a little restless with his routine at the gym, and Creel wanted to give him a reason to stick with his physical therapy. And, of course, Bill wanted to ski.

The night before, Bill's mom told him he had to wear a helmet. He told her no, he didn't want to, and besides, he was Bill Johnson. The next morning, Bill showed up at the breakfast table fully dressed for skiing, including the helmet.

Creel was there that day, along with DB and some local reporters DB had contacted. Some skiers and snowboarders recognized Bill with his trademark red Atomic skis and stopped to watch or wish him well. He started on the bunny hill, letting gravity pull him along on a slight grade. After some snowplowing and a couple of shaky runs, Bill got on the chairlift. By the end of the morning, he was able to get to the bottom faster than nearly everybody. His only fall happened about a fourth of the way down the mountain when he lost his balance and fell onto the snow while waiting for everyone to catch up to him. Refusing offers of assistance, he helped himself up.

It was clear that Bill was taking it easy, with gentle turns at a safe speed. But as DB says, "He still could out-ski everybody. He went over all the ice like it wasn't even there. No fear whatsoever."

With year-round skiing on Mt. Hood, Bill told Creel that he planned to come out 200 days in the next year. "He kind of sets his goals rather high," Creel says. After lunch Bill wanted to get back on his skis, but Creel discouraged him, suggesting it would be better to quit while they were ahead the first day out. By that point Bill was feeling the cold, but despite the chill, he was visibly thrilled to be on the slopes again: "It's so nice out here. It's so sweet."

Bill was skiing again, but his accident had taken away any chance of him racing competitively. Still, his goal in attempting a comeback was to participate in the Salt Lake City Olympics, and in a sense, he got his wish. Creel and Harold Burbank, a former ski racer who knew Bill back at Mt. Hood Meadows, wrote letters and called contacts lobbying for Bill to carry the torch in the Opening Ceremony.

"I promised Bill he would make it to the Olympics and he did," Creel says. "We just went down a different road."

The U.S. Olympic Committee flew Bill and DB to Salt Lake City early to practice for whatever role Bill might have. None of the athletes knew what was going to happen until the night before the Opening Ceremony.

When they went to the rehearsal at midnight, Bill found out that he was scheduled to carry the torch in the Olympics stadium with Phil Mahre. The plan was that they would receive the torch from figure skaters Peggy Fleming and Scott Hamilton and pass it to speed skaters Bonnie Blair and Dan Jansen. With music playing in the stadium, Bill and Phil practiced handing off the torch. The producer told them the timing wasn't right, and asked them first to walk faster, then said they had to jog.

In response, Bill pulled the producer aside and said, "You don't jog to music." Bill started running the show, telling the organizers how it was going to be, how he was going to work it. He pointed out that since he and Phil were passing the torch to Bonnie and Dan, both speed skaters, the producer could just have the two of them skate a little faster.

In the Opening Ceremony the next day, Bill and Phil ended up walking into the stadium with the torch. In response to Bill's refusal to jog, the producers adjusted the spot so that he and Phil didn't have as far a distance to cover.

"It's tough to see where he's at right now," Phil says. "He's not the person he was before the accident, but he has a brashness about him still."

Bill ended up watching the Olympic downhill from a seat in the grandstand. When the Americans failed to medal, he simply said, "Not this time." When the race was over, Bill signed autographs, shook hands, and posed for photographs with fans. After televising the downhill, NBC aired a segment about Bill, focusing on his recovery. It was narrated by Jim McKay, host of the 1984 Olympics.

Despite all the adulation Bill received at the 2002 Games, he still managed, post-accident, to continue his self-destructive—and bridge-burning—streak. In Salt Lake, Bill's former coach Erik Steinberg contacted a friend of his at Visa to potentially develop some brain injury sponsorships for Bill.

"Trying to save Bill is a waste of time, but you gotta help him," Steinberg says. "Do you get a thank-you from him ever? No. Does it matter? No."

At one point after his accident Bill asked Steinberg, who worked with neon at the time, to make him a neon sign with his winning Olympic time on it. Steinberg custom-made it for Bill, a several-thousand-dollar item, and sent it to him. The shipping costs alone were a couple hundred dollars. Steinberg says he wasn't doing it for a thank-you, and he never received one from Bill, not even an acknowledgement that it arrived safely.

Nonetheless, Steinberg arranged a reception for Bill at the Visa House in Salt Lake. The staff there donated an original Leroy Neiman picture to be auctioned off, with the proceeds going to Bill.

According to Steinberg, Bill showed up "hammered, unwashed, and unrepentant."

The invitations had said "mountain semi-formal," and many of the guests were wearing suits and ties. Bill showed up in jeans, an unironed sports shirt, untied cross-training shoes, and a ball cap.

Bill Marolt gave a speech about Bill's historic Olympic win. "Bill couldn't muster a thank-you and didn't even take off his ball cap during the ceremony," Steinberg says. "I was furious with DB for letting Bill show up like that. I left early and drove back to my hotel in Park City madder than a hornet. It pains me to even think of it." Afterward, Visa declined to pursue sponsorship opportunities with Bill.

Bill and his mom both reverted to pre-accident form. The result was, once again, lost opportunities.

At a charity golf tournament, Blake recalls that Bill got "hammered" at a reception that night. "That part of his personality hasn't gotten away from him," Blake says.

As in the past, the offers have all but stopped coming, and various events in which Bill has participated have not asked him back. After two years, Big Mountain resort in Montana, where Bill crashed, decided to discontinue the ski/golf tournament it had held in his honor. The Special Olympics, which for three years had included Bill in an event on Mt. Bachelor in Oregon, did not invite him in 2005.

DB has slipped into her role as Bill's manager again, asking for stipends and appearance fees to augment Bill's disability payments. In one case, the organization responded that it did not pay stipends, but pointed out that it has contributed to various charities, such as the reforestation of Sarajevo, on behalf of an athlete. For Bill and DB, the charity for which they wanted the appearance fee was Bill himself.

When Bill was invited to the 50th anniversary of the Oneida Silversmith race at Snow Ridge, where he had won in 1980, Brooke Bobela, the organizer, offered to pay travel expenses for both Bill and DB so that Bill could attend. Even though, as Bobela says, the small resort was "scraping together pennies" to put on the celebration, DB still asked for an appearance fee for Bill. Bobela went back to local sponsors for more funds, and Bill received his fee.

Some of Bill's friends believe that DB has chased away opportunities for Bill due to her own control issues. Shortly after Bill's accident, he had a chance to sign with SFX, the sports agency that represents Bode Miller, but DB turned them down. About a year after the crash, Bob Sankey offered to organize a charity golf tournament in San Diego with all proceeds to Bill, but Bob says, "Bill's mother wouldn't let it happen." People close to Bill have been approached by various sponsors saying they would like to help Bill but were only willing to do it if DB wasn't involved, and as Creel says, "She has a way of being involved."

In the first years following his crash, Bill was particularly in demand, enjoying a bit of celebrity again. He attended functions ranging from the Spirit of America Fourth of July Parade in Portland to the Netherlands Peace Mission in Sarajevo.

He also attended numerous ski events. Blake saw Bill on the slopes the first season after his accident and maintains that his style looked the same as it always had. "He was making the same mistakes he made when he was skiing before," he says. "That's his skiing."

Bill skied nearly twenty times the first season after his accident, including a couple of slalom runs in a celebrity Return of the Champions race during the U.S. Alpine Championships at Squaw Valley in March of 2002. It was a pseudo-competitive race, Bill's first since the crash, and he skied cautiously but smoothly.

At that event Bill was placed once again on a team with Doug Lewis. Doug says Bill seemed to remember him "about half the time," and Bill did recall Doug's name. "I could see glances of Bill in there," Doug says. "Is he gone? Is he still in there? A couple statements were the same get-you-off-your-guard-with-one-comment-Bill. There's Bill in there somewhere."

At the Squaw Valley event, ski photographer Jonathan Selkowitz was with the crowd of skiers as it poured out of an awards ceremony into a casino. Bill was already seated at a blackjack table, with an ashtray full of cigarette butts, looking like he had been there for a while. "He was smoking, drinking rum and cokes," Selkowitz says. "He looked like the same old Bill." Just then Picabo Street, who had known Bill for over a decade, began talking to him. Bill didn't remember that he knew her, but suddenly, like any eight-year-old discovering a celebrity, Bill said, "Hey, you're Picabo Street!" A second later, he caught the attention of the cocktail waitress and ordered another rum and coke.

"He moves slow, talks slow, everything is slow now," Picabo says. "He used to do everything pretty fast. But he's still a smart-ass. He still teases me because he got a gold and I got a silver [in the downhill]. That's very refreshing for me. I was worried it was a memory he would lose."

Exactly one year after his accident, Bill returned to the scene. The local newspaper, The *Whitefish Pilot*, placed his return 8th on its list of top stories of 2002. He came back to Montana to thank the emergency personnel who treated him and also to see if revisiting the place he crashed would trigger some memories.

"What happened to me was really incredible," Bill told the press at Big Mountain, a grandiose comment that managed to shift responsibility for his accident away from himself. He was a semblance of Bill Johnson again, at least for a couple days, and as always, Bill loved the attention. People not only knew who Bill was, they came up to him to pat him on the back, shake his hand, get his autograph. People in chairlifts cheered as he passed underneath.

"It's impossible not to be recognized," Bill said. "It's just those people, they love to treat me like I'm somebody else right now. And apparently I am."

Bill had no memory of his last race, and initially he did not remember the course, announcing he had never skied in Montana. Riding the chairlift with ski reporter Keith Liggett, Bill said, "I know this mountain, but it was somewhere else." He described how the downhill course used to be, pointing out specific changes, such as where the trail was cut to take out a flat section, where trees were cleared and turns created. Then he shook his head and said, "But I never raced here. It must be somewhere else."

The following day, while again riding up the lift, Bill recalled that he had in fact raced there, and stated (correctly) that he had won in 1982 and 1989. He also knew the place where the start house had previously been erected—it wasn't there at the time of his accident, but it existed back in the '80s when Bill had raced there.

"He's real different," Liggett says, "but parts of his personality are still there. He still doesn't truck a lot of stupidity."

While Bill was back in Montana, he talked about another comeback in the future and how important winning a second gold medal still was to him, saying, "It's my life." The following month, in a *NBC Nightly News* segment narrated by Tom Brokaw, Bill retained that sentiment but lost the plan to ski race again, saying only, "Skiing is very important to my life. It is my life. It's a good memory."

The starters from both of Bill's races at Big Mountain stopped by to see him: Kent Taylor from the Doug Smith race earlier in his comeback, who comments that Bill was "not altogether back," and Park Frizelle, from Bill's final race, who says, "He was nowhere near the same."

Bill skied well. At one point DB caught up with him and told him he was skiing very fast, to which Bill replied, "Thanks. You're skiing very slow."

One day there was a little ceremony at the top of the run in Bill's honor. He was participating, even signed one of his race bibs, but he was getting impatient. He turned to Mike Maronick, a friend from the days of his comeback, and told him he wanted to ski down. Mike let him lead, and Bill took the path down the exact slope of the downhill course. At the Corkscrew section, Mike stopped Bill and they looked at the wreck site together. And then, as retribution to the ski gods, they dropped their pants and took a leak right on it.

After a long day, Bill held a press conference. He said he was happy to be there and, even though he obviously didn't remember anyone, he thanked them for saving his life. He was tired, and it was a stumbling, if heartfelt, speech. Near the end a reporter came in and, unaware that Bill had already answered the question, asked him what he was doing back at Big Mountain. Bill hesitated and looked over at Dr. Charman, who had been the first doctor to reach Bill after his crash. Bill may not actually have winked, but he might as well have. He pulled his t-shirt down to display the surgical scar on his neck and blurted out "Revenue enhancement." With DB trying to make him stop, Bill, clearly enjoying himself, went off on an involved story about Charman attacking him and how Bill wanted more people to come to Big Mountain and get hurt because the doctor needed the business so he wouldn't have to attack people on the mountain. Bill pointed at his throat (actually, Charman was not the doctor who performed that procedure) and said, "Look what he did to me." The crowd loved it.

Around this time Bill's friends describe his alcohol intake in terms of "drinking wine with his Cheerios." Bill says only that he loves merlot, "because I know that women love it." Members of the group present in Montana recall two things that struck them as odd about the evenings there—first, that Bill was drinking five or six beers at a time, and second, that DB seemed unfazed by Bill's behavior.

Although Bill himself generally doesn't believe he has a brain injury (not an uncommon phenomenon), since his accident he has acted as a spokesperson for various brain-injuries associations. He participated in banquets and golf and ski tournaments for brain injury associations in Oregon, Wisconsin, and Connecticut. At some of those he gave short speeches or answered questions with a little prompting and refocusing.

Sometimes Bill's responses were confusing, rambling. At a ski reunion in 2005, when he was asked what his motivation to keep going after his crash was, Bill responded: "I skied nine months after. I don't remember leaving Montana, traveling to Sacramento. I don't remember being flown to Oregon, airport code PDX. No memory of moving out of San Diego. No memories of the '90s at all. I remember losing one baby in Tahoe." Bill was interrupted then and redirected, to which he responded: "I've got a story I'm telling."

In December of 2002, Bill attended the Hartford Ski Spectacular in Breckenridge, Colorado, a weeklong winter sports festival for people with physical disabilities. Carefully reading from a card that had been prepared for him, Bill stated that he was there to help people focus on their abilities, not their disabilities. The festival didn't go so well for Bill or for the organizers of the event. On an intermediate run, Bill fell over while trying to extract a pole from under his ski and broke his left femur (the long bone that connects the hip to the knee). He wasn't covered by insurance at the time, so the charity had to pick up the tab for the entire hospital bill.

While in the hospital in Colorado, Bill grew agitated waiting for someone to bring coffee and got of bed, against doctor's orders, to get it. When hospital security guards stopped him, he took a swing at one. DB contacted Jon Franklin, Bill's former agent at IMG, to sort out the situation. When Franklin arrived at the hospital, he found Bill on the psych ward, strapped down to a table.

Other events since the accident have turned out positively. In February of 2003, Michael Morris, then the managing director of Bank One, asked Bill to speak to a conference of 150 real estate clients of the bank at Snowbird, Utah. Morris says that stories he had heard about Bill's life had touched a nerve with him. He wanted to get some capital to Bill, he had the budget to do it, giving Bill a $10,000 stipend for his appearance. Bill traveled with a brain-injury specialist to keep him on message.

At the conference, Morris played the segment that had aired during the '02 Olympics about Bill, then just told Bill to tell his life story. Bill talked for 20 or 30 minutes, much of the time about his boys—how much he loved them, how they had gone to the dark side and were snowboarders now. The Q and A went smoothly enough. Other than a further tirade about snowboarders, Bill mostly stayed focused. At one point, he pulled school pictures of Nick and Tyler from his wallet—little photos, about two by three inches—and held them up to the whole group. "Here are my sons," Bill said. Even in the front row, nobody could see the pictures. "It was the cutest thing," Morris says. Bill received a standing ovation.

For two years in a row Bill has appeared at the Bill Johnson Vertical Challenge at Cranmore ski resort in New Hampshire, an event that raises funds for the Brain Injury Association of New Hampshire. Bill, who refused to wear a helmet the first year he was at the event, wore one the second year at the request of the association's representative, who convinced him that it didn't look good for their cause for him to be seen without one.

When he's asked—or allowed—to be Bill Johnson, Olympic champion, Bill is at his best. At Cranmore, Bill was charming while signing postcards of himself skiing (confirming the spelling of people's names and telling them to be careful while the ink from his Sharpie dried on his autographs) and posing for pictures ("I'll be in the middle").

With his cash, Bill was careless, leaving all the bills from his pocket on the crowded table at the ski resort when he went outside. He did, however, make sure that his gold medal was safe while he was gone, turning to the woman manning the table where it was displayed, pointing to it, and telling her, "Watch it." From his tone, it sounded like he meant it.

In 2004, Tommy Moe – who calls Bill "a maverick, a pioneer, in alpine racing"— ran into Bill at a Legends event in Alaska. He describes Bill, affectionately, as hanging out at the start area "with a pot belly, smoking a cigarette in a downhill suit."

Even so, Bill remains fast on skis. In 2004 he also participated in a Speed Trap event at Skibowl on Mt. Hood, with all proceeds benefiting him. All the skiers were timed, and Bill was the fastest with a speed of 69.9 mph. John Creel was the second fastest at 69.4 mph.

Later that season, Bill skied with Creel at Big Mountain at an event called the Powder 8's. Despite poor lighting they made it down, and as a team, finished tenth. Creel says Bill's performance was a "truly inspirational thing," adding, "Bill was pissed off we weren't first."

Bill's doctors do not think that his eyesight was affected by his head injury. In retrospect, Creel says that Bill's vision may have been a problem before. During his comeback, Creel would give Bill little makeshift, can-you-read-that tests with license plates, and he says, "It wasn't spot-on. I had real concerns about it. I think he probably needed glasses. Vanity may have played a role."

Bill had passed the DMV's oral testing to get his driver's license back just a year after his accident, then had to have his eyes checked twice and get glasses for the first time in his life to pass the eye test. On the ride home from the eye doctor he looked from side to side announcing, "I can see, I can see!"

He passed the driving test in 2003 and has been driving since, so much so that his monthly gas bills often top $800. He drives a teal 2000 F350 Ford truck, and his 1984 pickup. He has driven to Seattle to visit Andy Luhn and to Sonoma (10 hours away), to see his sons. Andy had told Bill to visit anytime and—in typical fashion—with no notice, Bill called Andy when he was three or four miles away from his house and asked which exit he should take.

"A lot of things are diminished," Andy says, "but some things just aren't." When they play cards, Bill still beats Andy, and by the same score. One time when Bill visited, Andy got him a compass and they went out to the airport to pinpoint where planes were landing on the runway.

Bill has retained skills connected to analytical, mechanical, and mathematical processing. In March of 2004 he stayed with his friend Mike Maronick in Whitefish, and they took a side trip to Big Sky, Montana. Bill asked how many miles they had to travel. When Mike told him, Bill calculated within seconds an average speed of 77 mph and announced how many minutes the ride would take.

He also timed everything with a watch. Mike says Bill was very programmed, adding, "I've never seen a more routine guy since Dustin Hoffman [in *Rain Man*]."

Bill was moody throughout the visit, and he became enraged a few times—mostly, Mike says, from frustration when he didn't understand someone or when he was tired or out of his routine. "He was stubborn, very impatient," Mike says. "He would blow up, get mad at me, use me like a punching bag."

On the golf course with Mike, Bill picked the right clubs, determined where the ball needed to go, kept track of his own score, and pulled his own cart. He displayed a competitiveness that Mike says was "off the chart," refusing to even speak to anyone and turning a friendly game into a battle. "The more he rehabs," Mike says, "the more the unruly Bill comes out. It's almost like we liked him better two years ago."

Mike did notice a lot of innocence in Bill. He seemed happiest when he had something constructive to do. He installed Mike's new DVD player, fixed his computer hook-ups, attached Mike's boat trailer to his truck, and helped Mike get his boat out of storage.

During the visit, Bill didn't want to field a lot of questions from people, and he seemed to want to avoid Big Mountain. When they went there for a ski-patrol gathering, Mike immediately felt Bill's discomfort. At the event, Bill skied the race and then became anxious, wanting to leave the mountain quickly.

"He seemed a little down, especially when a lot of the attention wasn't on him," Mike says. "He lit up when admirers honored his presence and was always quick to pose for a picture or sign something. It is important that he receive encouragement and compliments—he does have his agenda, that is for sure."

Bill spent some quiet time on the beach, watching the ice melt and following the progress of two ducks on the water. Before he left, he went onto Mike's deck and stared intently at the ducks, as if he were saying good-bye. The female approached Bill as closely as Mike had ever seen a duck approach someone without food. "Mike, shhhhh, watch her…she is reading my mind," Bill said. "I can't read hers but she knows what I'm thinking."

In the fall of 2004, Bill went to Tahoe with Gina and the boys to visit his old friends Barry and Mark. He wasn't the same Bill they used to know, but Barry says there were still "sparkles in there."

"Maybe it's an expression or a look that he has, goofy, and it's Bill," Mark says. Mostly, Mark and his wife Stacey saw Bill as frustrated, so angry at times that veins popped out of his head. They say that the way he would lash out at them without warning was almost scary.

The visit became especially uncomfortable when they all went boating. Mark says Bill became aggressive when one of his sons didn't want to get in the water. When things went Bill's way, however—when his son got in the lake and up on a board as Bill had wanted—Mark recalls Bill "just had the biggest smile."

During the trip Mark noticed that Bill still excelled at math, leading him to describe Bill as "a mad numbers guy." Bill was always exactly on time and very structured—"I eat breakfast at six. Lunch is at noon."

Bill also retained his old sense of privilege. When they were planning to go golfing one day, Bill said, "Call ahead and tell them it's Bill Johnson and we'll all be golfing for free."

Bill also traveled to Washington to visit his brother Wally. Early one morning, while Wally was sleeping upstairs in his bedroom and Bill was downstairs, Wally heard Bill moving around. When Wally came down, Bill seemed completely disoriented, and surprised to see his brother there. "What are you doing here?" Bill asked. Wally said, "I live here. Do you know who I am?"

"You're my brother," Bill responded, and then, gesturing upstairs, said,

"I'm going golfing with that guy up there."

Creel's view of Bill's recovery is to "give him as much as he can handle, like cramming for an exam." He has often taken Bill fishing for steelhead on the Deschutes River at Creel's house in Maupin, Oregon. Maupin, population 460, is a tiny place that looks like a model train set town. Creel calls the town "epic."

The medical records from Bill's accident mostly reflect his address as "unknown," but Maupin is listed on one form, because Bill parked his RV at Creel's place during much of his comeback. At the time of his crash, Bill was over $100,000 in debt, $57,000 of which was the loan on that RV and the rest of which was credit cards bills. He kept getting new cards to pay off the ones he already had. Those debts still exist, but for the most part the creditors have stopped calling.

A lot of people do things for free for Bill and his family. The attorney who handled Bill's disability claim. The attorney who is handling Bill's criminal cases. Meanwhile, Bill's funds are set up in a conservator account, where they are protected.

After the accident, DB took over his comeback website to provide updates on his condition. She also asked for donations, giving the contact information for a local Gresham bank under the title "Bill could use your support." Despite the claim on the website that "Although he has a pretty good health insurance policy, it doesn't cover everything, and the bills are already starting to roll in," in fact DB now says, "Everything was covered. Bill had insurance through the ski team as well as the Blue Cross/Blue Shield that he had to have in order to race. There was truly no burden." The donations were used, DB says, for Bill "to do things, such as go out to eat, buy anything, clothing, etc."

The U.S. Ski Team did not hold any fundraisers or even set up a fund for Bill, but Bill's friends did. Blake Lewis, Andy Luhn, and Erik Steinberg set up the Bill Johnson Foundation. Between word of mouth and an ad in *Ski* magazine, the foundations raised about $15,000, mostly from the ski community. The intent was that the funds would be used for any retraining into society that Bill might require—education, courses, instruction of any kind. Instead, Blake says that DB kept calling asking for money for things like attorney bills and taxes. "That's not what it was for," Blake says. "I felt like I got burned. We finally said 'Fine' and gave it all to her."

Bill also received some help from an unlikely source—Franz Klammer gave him $10,000 from his foundation in Austria. "We go back a long way together, skied together," Klammer says. "It was the clear thing to give him some support."

In the beginning, Klammer's foundation started with his brother Klaus, who was a ski racer as well. In 1977, Klaus was the Austrian junior downhill champion. Two weeks later, he was paralyzed in a crash during a race. He ended up going to college and receiving a degree in economics. Klaus now works as an accountant, and although he is still in a wheelchair, with the aid of a specially designed apparatus he is back on skis.

Since his accident Bill has been skiing several times with his sons, who view the experience not as skiing with a gold medalist but just as skiing with Dad. Gina points out that with Bill a little slower on skis now, he doesn't have to wait so long for everyone at the bottom. "My dad is a very good skier," Tyler says, "but he's not as good as he was before. He's kinda taking it a little slow because he doesn't want to get in a big crash and die. Because if he does that again he won't survive. It's amazing that he survived the first time."

Tyler, age 11, does snowboard, but he prefers skiing. Sounding a bit like his dad did when he was a kid, Tyler has this to say about his own ski skills: "I already know everything about skiing—how to balance, how to jump. I know everything on skis. All I do is go straight down the hill and dodge everything."

Tyler recently had an anger problem at school, hitting kids and getting detention. With Gina working four days a week, she says that he was starved for attention. Not having regrets about how she raises her boys is important to Gina. "Now I'm there for him all the time," she says, "and he's sweet, loving."

Nick—who likes to snowboard more than ski—enjoys building things, and last summer on a visit to Bill's house the two of them put in a lawn and assembled Bill's pool table.

Bill attended one of Tyler's baseball games last summer, and afterward all his teammates crowded around Bill asking him to autograph their caps. During the game, there was a tense moment when other parents got upset with Bill for lighting a cigarette. When Gina asked Bill to put it out, he said there was no sign prohibiting it and refused to believe there was a no-smoking policy at the field.

Bill's belligerence has had bigger repercussions than angry glances at a ballpark. On his 43rd birthday, he was arrested for assaulting a public safety officer and resisting arrest at the airport while returning home with Jimmy from a ski/golf benefit in Montana. DB met them curbside and asked Bill, who at this point hadn't yet driven since his accident, to stay with the car while she joined Jimmy inside to check on missing luggage. Bill was waiting in the back seat when airport security asked him to move the car. Bill tried to tell them that he was unable to drive due to his brain injury, but the officer wrote a ticket.

Bill got out of the car, pushed the officer out of his way, took the ticket off the windshield, and tore it up. The officer called for backup. Police arrived on the scene and a physical altercation ensued. Believing that Bill was intoxicated, likely due to his slurred speech, the officers pinned him to the ground, lying on his recently broken leg and grinding his watch into the ground. DB says that Bill "wriggled somewhat only because they were not getting off of him;" the cops say that they weren't going to get off him because he wouldn't stay still. "The cops put into their report that Bill used profanities, but he never did," DB says. "He called them stupid, which they were."

The reasons behind the arrest are many: Bill's legendary temper still intact post-accident, probably a bias on the part of the police who made incorrect assumptions about Bill. But it all circles back to the sense of entitlement that runs so strongly in at least one branch of the Johnson family. Whether or not Bill could drive, whether or not Bill has a brain injury, the car was parked illegally and it wasn't being moved. Bill clearly felt that he didn't deserve a ticket, that the rules shouldn't apply to him. And by not sending Jimmy out to move the car and remaining inside so long, DB apparently felt the same way. "I had to fill out lots of paperwork to get the bags forwarded to the house so that we could leave," she says. "Time was passing, but I wasn't thinking about the time or that anything was wrong outside."

Bill's has grown more impulsive since his accident. For example, in the midst of a conversation with someone about a friend's background, he will immediately start dialing that friend's number to confirm his nationality. While waiting to see a doctor, he will go to the receptionist's desk and ring the bell repeatedly. Often it's not so harmless.

In December of 2004, Bill had dinner at a sushi bar, became fascinated with its fish tank, and headed to A to Z Pets to buy one of his own. He picked an $800 tank, and the store gave him enough water and chemicals to make the tank ready for saltwater fish. He felt he needed more water and, not wanting to go back to the store, he drove over two hours out to the ocean in the rain to collect two buckets of water, ignoring storm warnings and heavy winds. He took along Buddy, his new white toy poodle. While balancing the buckets of water, Bill let go of Buddy's leash. He was unable to find the puppy in the storm, and he went home without him. The next morning Bill got a call that Buddy had been hit by a car. The dog died later that morning.

Bill's lack of impulse control can be outright dangerous, like the time he got in an argument with his friend Dave Ligatich, whom he had known since they were kids. When Dave asked Bill to lower his voice in front of Dave's kids, Bill hit Dave over the head several times with the mug of coffee he was holding. Dave received multiple stitches as a result and got a restraining order against Bill, mostly, he claims, to get him help for his anger.

Shortly after this episode, on February 11th, 2005, while the criminal charges from the airport incident were still pending, Bill got into trouble again. He was pulled over around four o'clock in the afternoon by Troutdale police as well as the Multnomah County sheriff's office. According to the police version of events, Bill was not speeding or driving erratically in any way. The police say they stopped Bill for a seatbelt violation, but the real reason turned out to be a tip from an employee of an eyeglass clinic, who called the police to report that a visibly intoxicated man had just driven away from the store. Bill had been in the eye clinic, trying to purchase eyeglasses for a drunk hitchhiker he had picked up, but he had not been drinking. The clinic employees, just like the officers who stopped Bill, believed he was drunk due to his confusion and his slow, slurred speech. Although police arrested Bill for being under the influence of intoxicants, he in fact blew a .00 on the breathalyzer exam, and his urine test was negative for controlled substances. That charge is no longer pending against him.

When the police stopped Bill, he did not understand what he had done wrong, and feeling like he was being hassled for no reason, he quickly became agitated. According to police, Bill threw his keys at Multnomah County Sheriff's Deputy Jeff Cordes, then reached out the window, grabbed the deputy's shirt, and punched him several times in the face. The police report describes Bill as being in a blind rage, and Cordes and Troutdale Sergeant James Leake used Tasers to subdue him. According to Leake's report, after Bill was handcuffed he began yelling, "Do you know who I am?" When

Leake answered Bill's question in the negative, Bill then allegedly told him, "You don't know shit," and kicked him in the groin. Neither officer suffered serious injuries in the incident.

As Bill explains the events: "I got pulled over for not wearing my seat belt then terrible things did happen – don't understand it all but it is okay." Creel refers to the incident as "Billy pullin' a Billy."

Bill was charged with two counts of assault on a police officer and two counts of resisting arrest. The case is still pending, as is the one involving the incident at the airport. The charges are misdemeanors, not felonies, and there is no mandatory jail sentence associated with them. Bill's criminal attorney, Gerald Doblie, believes that Bill is unable to aid or assist in his own defense, and he plans to have Bill evaluated to determine whether he is legally competent to stand trial. Even if he is declared competent, and even if he were to be found guilty at trial, it is unlikely that he is facing any jail time.

His behavior did, at a minimum, result in a lost opportunity for him. A branch of the U.S. Olympic Committee relating to disabled athletes had been considering Bill as a spokesperson, but apparently after this arrest the organization was no longer interested. As Bill's old friend Tim Patterson says, "Every time you thought Billy could get it together, he dove deeper."

Since his wreck, Bill's thought processes have been interrupted by obscure and random digressions. When he has difficulty reasoning he will often merely repeat questions to the person asking them. For example, when he is asked, "Why not?" Bill's response is most often, "Why?" He is either being incredibly astute and philosophical (which is not impossible), or he is simply parroting information from the question. Bill often repeats other phrases verbatim as well (for example, "You got guts," elicits "I do got guts"), and it is not possible to determine whether he is being consciously funny or just at a loss for an answer.

Bill says that when he becomes president, he will lower the age for buying alcohol to six years old—"If you want to buy alcohol, buy it." Between that plan and legalizing drugs, he figures he has a good chance of getting elected in 2009.

"He is very one-dimensional," Blake says. "He focuses on a single target. Common sense is not part of his daily life. It's black or it's black."

"Bill doesn't really think there is anything wrong with him," Dr. Lovell, who evaluated Bill in 2005, says. "This denial of deficits is very common, but it makes it doubly hard to help someone."

Mostly Bill maintains that aside from some memory problems, he's the same guy he was before, telling *People* magazine, for example, "It was an accident. I'm just hurt. I've been hurt before." But every now and then Bill will say something revealing on the other extreme, such as, "I don't have a brain. I don't think very well."

Blake thinks that Bill is aware enough to know that he's not who he wants to be, and that's why he's angry so much of the time.

An IQ test Bill was given in 2004 fits the medical analysis. His scores in the various sub-categories varied wildly, in a very unusual pattern. In the area of perceptual organization, Bill's IQ was 128, putting him in the 97th percentile. His clearest strengths were on tasks requiring visual processing and organization—block design, matrix reasoning, and picture completion. The examiner concluded that Bill's retention of some strong visual skills could contribute to a lack of insight, leading him to believe nothing else has changed.

In that same testing, Bill was also noted to have mood swings, word-finding difficulties, perseveration (a tendency to obsess on irrelevant information), and trouble concentrating. The examiner commented that Bill "frequently becomes tangential, and rarely provided clear, logical information." In addition, Bill's abstract reasoning abilities were particularly weak. For example, he was unable to explain the meaning of common proverbs, and he could not identify what a chair and a table have in common.

Lovell states that a patient's improvement after a brain trauma generally levels off and is essentially complete after two or three years at most. "Any spontaneous recovery in terms of Bill's brain recovery was over a long time ago," he says. "Once the swelling goes down, the wiring goes back to where it's going to be."

In recent testing, Lovell found that Bill showed "delusional thought processes that were often grandiose in nature." For example, Bill believed he could develop a nuclear-powered apparatus that would remove people's heads. In his report, Lovell noted that these delusions were "fixed" and that Bill became agitated when any of his beliefs were questioned.

Lovell says that Bill's amnesia is very dramatic, one of the longest spans of lost time he has ever heard of. "You typically see minutes or hours [of memory loss], days are uncommon. You almost never see years," he says.

In addition, Lovell states that the way memory is distributed in the brain, to have long periods of time blocked out is unusual, even striking.

Bill has repeatedly told the press, as well as his friends, that he only recalls the happy times. The idea that Bill only remembers what he wants to remember is not grounded in science, but Lovell admits that there could be a psychological aspect: "Some of it may be not particularly pleasant memories, so maybe some element is Bill doesn't want to think about those things." And while he cannot prove it, Lovell says it is also possible that Bill may be exaggerating somewhat. "Bill does get a rise out of people when he says he can't remember getting divorced," he says. "And Bill is certainly somebody sensitive to what gets a rise out of people."

CHAPTER THIRTEEN

"Well, I beat all the guys that crashed."
– BILL JOHNSON, DECEMBER 2000

In February of 2000, a month after Gina filed for divorce, Bill went to a party by himself in San Diego. He was supposed to go with David Watt, who was waiting for his jeans to dry. Aggravated at being held up, Bill stormed out of David's place, peeled out of the driveway in his RV, then came back five minutes later demanding that they leave immediately. David put on his jeans damp and got in his car to follow Bill, but Bill went 110 mph on the freeway and David ended up losing him. Consequently, Bill arrived alone.

Bill heard about the party through his friend Mark Herhusky in Tahoe—Mark's wife Stacey was friends with Andrea, the woman throwing it. Andrea's sister was dating a tattoo artist from Miami Beach named Bill Conner. Conner had flown out to California for the party and was set up in a little trailer doing tattoos, mostly "paws and other little ones for the ladies," charging half of what he would back at Tattoo Circus. It was sort of a white-trash, hoedown theme. The house was going to be torn down, so guests spray-painted a "sacred" corndog on the wall with horns and wings and praying hands.

Everybody had more than a few drinks, including Bill. He took his gold medal out and flaunted it. Later, when Andrea bent down to pick up her beer, Bill reached over and grabbed her butt. The incident was witnessed by five Marines, one of whom was Andrea's fiancé (now her husband), and it did not go over well. They responded by pummeling Bill and ultimately escorting him out of the party with some bruises and a gash on his head. The next day, Bill accused David of not being there for backup.

But earlier in the evening, Bill wandered into Conner's trailer. He told him about his RV and showed it to him when Conner asked to check it out. As they talked, Bill told him how he was training to get back into ski racing, then said he wanted a tattoo. They collaborated on the skull with flames coming out of it, but the words were Bill's alone. Conner drew it out—putting the phrase "Ski to Die" in a banner—and Bill approved the design.

Bill says he got the tattoo on impulse, and the fact that the drinks were flowing that night somewhat supports his position. But he had at least a little time to think it through. Conner said he would do the tattoo for $60, but Bill didn't have the cash on him, so Connor waited over a half hour while Bill drove to an ATM and came back with the money. It took Conner about 40 minutes to ink the tattoo on Bill's right bicep. He hadn't done one like that before, and he claims he wouldn't do another one like it now. It was a custom job for Bill.

At the time, Bill was unemployed and, as the saying goes, of no fixed address. A month after he got his tattoo, he got into a brawl at the Mangy Moose Saloon in Jackson Hole, Wyoming. He allegedly punched a woman and bit a man on the arm, and after leaving the bar and walking along the highway, he was arrested for public intoxication and interfering with an officer. He was given a hearing date and released from jail the next morning. A warrant for his arrest was issued when he failed to appear in court. The warrant was still outstanding at the time of his accident a year later, at which point Bill's friend Tim Patterson settled the matter, legally.

After spending the next several months essentially tooling around the west in his '84 pickup, in the summer of 2000 Bill showed up unannounced at "Hotel California," Barry Thys's parents' house in Tahoe. He was back to his roots, back to where it all began. Nina and Buck Thys had always supported Bill in the past, and they welcomed him into their home then as well. He lived with them and worked with Barry, an electrical contractor, wiring houses. Barry owned his own company, and Bill, who already had a California contractor's license from years before, billed customers separately. Wanting to start his business name with an "A" to be listed early in the phone book, Bill named his company "A Gold Medal Construction."

Bill had a steady job working eight-hour days, and he was making good money (from $40 to $80 dollars an hour). Barry, who was having fun working with Bill, says that Bill was enjoying it as well. Bill wasn't drinking, he had good friends (Barry and Mark) nearby, and he was working out. For the first time in 12 years, Bill was in good enough shape that he didn't need to wear his back brace. Gina's sister Rochelle recalls Gina telling her at the time that Bill really seemed to be getting it together.

Then one day in the early fall, as suddenly as Bill had arrived, Barry says, "He just bailed, he just up and left." Never one for long hellos or good-byes, Bill simply collected his last paycheck and left town.

For reasons that he cannot now recall, Bill walked away from what seemed, from all accounts, to have been a beneficial situation. Since he can't remember that time, he can't explain his departure. Earlier in the summer he had mentioned returning to ski racing, but there were no definite plans as far as Barry and Mark knew, and they figured it was more or less a passing thought. Bill's friends don't know if he had planned to leave all along and the weightlifting and swimming had actually been an off-season training program, or whether something specific caused him to go. They just know that they were surprised, and disappointed, that he left.

The explanation could be as simple as in the end, the only thing that made sense to Bill was ski racing. He had gotten so far away from where he wanted to be that he couldn't think how to go forward without trying to go back. He wanted to recapture lost glory, sure, but it was more complicated than that. He missed the adulation, he missed the thrill, he probably even missed the structure of competition, but mostly he missed the start-to-finish way his dream had become a reality when he was 23. Receiving the gold medal made Bill feel like a winner. At age 40, after living a life that redefines the expression "extremes of fortune," Bill wanted that feeling back.

When Bill asked John Creel to coach him in his comeback, Creel asked Bill what he wanted from him.

"Hope," Bill said.

Ski reporter Robert Frohlich interviewed Bill during his comeback season, and Bill told him that after "spending the first part of the millennium in a stupor," returning to ski racing "gave me a goal."

Whether Bill's goal of winning another gold medal was a positive thing or not is a matter of perspective. However misguided people may have believed Bill's comeback attempt to be and how tragically it turned out, by giving him a purpose, in a sense it saved him.

Creel says that given how damaged Bill saw himself at that point, his life virtually depended on a return to ski racing. "Where he was at—it's kinda like well, if I crash and I live, or if I don't crash and I win, it's all good," Creel says. "You can get to a point where you're kinda up against the wall. I don't think a lot of people understand how up against a wall a person can get."

Viewed from another angle, Bill cleaned himself up from the drinking and the drugs only to focus on something that turned out to be a whole lot more self-destructive in the end.

When Bill left Tahoe, he headed to the Hoodland Fire Department in Oregon where Creel worked as a lieutenant. Creel had skied with Bill at Mt. Hood Meadows in the '70s. They weren't close back then. Creel says, "I don't know if we were *friends*. We raced each other. Bill was rippin' across the hill this way and I was rippin' across the hill that way." Creel claims, however, that he and Bill were both part of the "ski-racing brotherhood."

Bill had first showed up at Creel's fire station the previous summer, in '99, walked into the truck bay with an ice cream cone dripping down his shirt and talked to Creel about coaching him in a comeback. Creel told Bill to get in shape. When Bill showed up at the firehouse a year later in the best shape of his life, Creel decided he was serious about it.

At 6'2", 215 pounds, Creel is a paradigm for extreme sports. He is a former professional skier, a former professional foosball player, a waterfall kayaker, and the first person to ski the crater of Mount St. Helens after it erupted. His early life was all about skiing. After racing he worked as a coach, then a ski instructor, then did stints on a ski patrol team and as a ski rep for Yamaha. He then finished his degree in fire science and started as a volunteer fireman in 1983. Now 49, married with a daughter and a son, Creel plans to retire from the fire department in another five years, though he seems much too young for that. He is vital, imposing. If the Kramer character from *Seinfeld* were more athletic and a little mellower, that would be Creel. He talks in essentially his own language, sort of an amalgam of wise philosopher mixed with West Coast cool dude. "When you go fast," Creel says, "time slows down."

In addition to approaching Creel, Bill asked Blake to be his ski rep for his comeback. Blake, now a partner in a graphic design firm in Redmond, Washington, turned down Bill's request, telling him he didn't even know what a scraper looked like anymore.

Bill had always had technicians to take care of his skis on the Ski Team as well as the pro circuit, and he wasn't so familiar with how to prepare them himself. Petr Kakes, a former speed skier from Czechoslovakia who now works as director of the ski school at Skibowl, helped him out. Petr first met Bill back in the '80s when Bill called him – in an affectionate sort of way, according to Petr—"a fucking Commie." Petr retaliated by calling him "Billy Boy," which Bill hated. After his accident, Bill no longer remembered Petr from those days, leading Petr to say, almost slyly, "I'm not the Commie anymore, but he's still Billy Boy."

Bill did not contact the U.S. Ski Team about his comeback, at least not for advice. Asked if Bill had talked to him beforehand, Bill Egan, head coach of the team at the time, says, "No, no, no, no, absolutely not."

After so many years away, the Ski Team obviously wasn't going to just put Bill back on the team. Even if it had, simply being a member of the team wouldn't have qualified him to compete in top-level or World Cup races. There is an international ranking system, a mathematical formulation governing a skier's ability to enter certain levels of races. When Bill first returned to the sport, he did not even meet the entry standards for most of the lower-level races. According to Tom Kelly, spokesperson for the Ski Team (no relation to the former Ski Team slalom coach), the team jump-started Bill by allowing him to compete in races where he could start "building a points profile."

Making the U.S. team would have involved subjective, and probably political, criteria, but even if Bill were willing to compete in World Cup races on his own, he first had to work his way through various regional circuits.

At the time, the Ski Team was careful not to publicly endorse Bill's comeback either way. "He's on his own," Kelly said. "We're just providing the opportunity."

Even now Kelly won't officially say whether the Ski Team thought Bill's return to ski racing was a good idea, stating only, "whether it was wise or not wise is immaterial." As cold as it sounds, Kelly's point makes sense, at least from a business perspective. The U.S. team is in the business of taking the fastest skiers, whoever they may be.

Most people in the ski community now claim the Ski Team was openly unhappy about Bill's comeback. The team was never enamored with him even in his prime, when he was the top downhill skier in the world, and now they saw him as back to divert attention once again.

"The Ski Team was afraid Bill would do what he had a tendency of doing—succeeding," Jo Jo Weber says. "Heads would have rolled. [The team] was scared shitless that Bill would be the center of attention."

These days, the coaches and Ski Team officials from the '00-'01 season put a positive spin on Bill's comeback. No one thought he would be one of the fastest racers in the country, but they insist over and over that they would have taken him on the team if he had been. But it seems odd, defensive somehow, for a coach to even bother saying that if someone was one of the best skiers in the nation the skier would be, in fact, included on the national team. The sentiment is repeated so frequently and so earnestly that it almost seems as if the team is protesting too much—really, we would have taken him, really we would have.

Looking back now on Bill's chances at the time, Bill Marolt, now president and CEO of the Ski Team, manages to answer the question without using Bill's name: "If somebody can do it, meet the criteria, we'll name him. Has to be what it is."

In general, the Ski Team's position on Bill's comeback was that it was great Bill was trying to do it, but it wasn't going to happen. There were a few candid comments mixed in, such as Bill Egan telling the press it was "a bit sad that at his stage in life, he's looking at the U.S. Ski Team as a valid career option." Although Egan calls Bill's comeback "nonsense," he claims that it did not especially surprise him.

Egan at least thought that Bill was going about it the right way, telling a reporter, "You can look pretty ridiculous trying to do what Bill was trying to do. He did not look ridiculous."

Most people affiliated with the Ski Team express their position on Bill's comeback with politically correct banalities. For example, Marolt uses the word "challenge" three times: "At his age, it was gonna be a challenge. It was a big challenge that he took on. All you can do is encourage. It was a big challenge. He put a lot on his plate."

According to Bill's former coach Erik Steinberg, in reality Marolt was anything but encouraging about the idea, and in fact tried to get Steinberg to talk Bill out of it. "Marolt was as livid as I was," Steinberg says. "He thought it was absolute folly. Insanity. Off the charts. He said 'This is frickin' insane. Talk to him. Give him a reason why he shouldn't.'"

Steinberg says that Marolt's feelings mostly had to do with the vision of the 1984 Olympic team. "Marolt didn't want to soil the image of that grand era, didn't want smudges on that great time," he says.

Talking about him now, Marolt puts a happy face on his impression of Bill. "He wasn't always agreeable, but I just liked his spark," he says. "He had a personality that sparked. A little bit of a rebel, and that's okay with me. Other people probably call him a lot of a rebel, and that's okay with me, too."

Marolt's true feelings about Bill, however, appear to run pretty deep. According to Steinberg, after Bill's accident Marolt was "really pissed" that Steinberg had gone to the hospital to visit him. "Connie, [Marolt's] wife, told me what she really thought about me supporting Bill," Steinberg says. "She laid into me, saying, 'You really disappointed [Marolt] on this.' I was one of [Marolt's] guys. I was supposed to be loyal to him, tow the party line. I was just trying to do the right thing—the guy was down and out. But loyalty is everything with Bill Marolt."

Steinberg did try to convince Bill not to ski race again. He told him not to even think about it. He stressed to Bill that at 40 years old he had "lost a couple of twitches in his nervous system" in a sport where even young racers were skirting between death and winning. "It's one thing to do a comeback and be embarrassed," Steinberg said to Bill. "It's a whole other thing to go out and get your ass killed. You're going to get yourself killed."

Some people were probably supportive enough of Bill's comeback at the time, but knowing that it ended badly, no longer think it was such a great idea. Steinberg does not appear to be one of those people. He genuinely seems to have thought it was a terrible, reckless idea from the very start and conveyed that straight-out to Bill. When Bill asked Steinberg if he could help him get some equipment, Steinberg turned him down flat. "I'm not going to get you skis so you can go faster when you hit the tree," Steinberg said to Bill. "I'm not supporting your comeback, period. You're out of your frickin' mind."

Aside from the obvious concerns connected to ski racing with a 40-year-old body and aging reflexes, there was also the issue of the technological advances in the equipment. The changes in the gear were less significant in downhill skiing than the more technical alpine events, but even so, the new skis were radically different from the skis Bill won on in 1984. The red sleds had stiff tails and tips and no side cut at all. Current skis were shorter and parabolic—narrow in the middle with wide tips—which enhanced the turning ability. Even the skis Bill received from Atomic a few years before, when he was on the pro racing circuit, were obsolete by the '00-'01 season.

In an interview during his comeback, Bill acknowledged the equipment changes but dismissed their impact, stating, "Basically downhill remains a sport for someone with no fear."

Bill started training and competing on three-year-old skis, but he wasn't necessarily comfortable with them. At one point he went back to the Thys's house in Tahoe looking for some of his skis from the '80s, telling Buck Thys that he was thinking of sticking with familiar skis. "He wrestled with it—if he should learn how to perfect the new skis and totally abandon the idea of the old-school skis," Buck says.

In addition to not being used to new skis, there was also the problem of *getting* some. This was not merely a financial consideration. The skis that companies provide to the top racers they endorse are not commercially available. Bill believed that the past head of Atomic, who had retired, would have done anything for him, but the new management at Atomic didn't seem inclined to sponsor Bill again.

He did receive a new pair of skis from Atomic, from an Atomic representative in Canada, after he saw Bill race in Whistler the first week of March, 2001. On his website, on which he posted his progress throughout his comeback, the entry for March 5th read, "Go figure, I've been begging for skis all year. And guess who comes through, the Canadians." It was those skis that Bill would crash on just over two weeks later.

Bill's website was www.billjohnson1984gold.com. The first page prominently announced "The Comeback of the Millennium!" Bill provided updates and attempted to solicit funds to keep racing. The text began "America's First Gold Medalist in Downhill Skiing is going back to the Olympics, find out how you can help get him there."

Bill wrote in detail about an elaborate plan to raise money for his training expenses. His idea was to raffle off the collection of race bibs that he had saved from 1980 on. For $1,000 a chance, Bill explained that when the season was over he would draw—"unless you would personally like to draw"—a bib from his bag of bibs and sign it for the winner. Under this plan, as Bill envisioned it, "Everyone will be in the running for the prized Olympic bib (#6)."

Bill's training expenses did not include funds for a coach. Bill never paid Creel for helping him out. Creel never expected it and, except for some jokes about what he would do for Creel once he hit it big again, Bill never offered.

At the bottom of Bill's home page there was a quote in bold, extra-large letters: "LIVE - your life to the fullest, LOVE - with all your heart, it's worth the risk, LAUGH - like you never laughed before and remember there may be no tomorrow, so dance…."

In addition to being corny, in retrospect the saying is a little creepy, given that there very nearly was "no tomorrow" for Bill after his accident. Still, it does sort of sum up Bill's life.

Whether he knew it or not, Bill lived by the theory that it is better in life to regret doing something than to regret *not* doing it. Almost everybody, in the course of their lives, has made compromises, small or big, in what they wanted for themselves, in what they would accept. Bill is one of the few individuals who can look back over his years and honestly point to so few things he regrets not doing.

He did not seem discouraged that his return to ski racing began with what, for a former champion, was essentially baby steps. His entry on his website after being ranked in the top 600 downhill racers in the world states, "It's a learning process that's taking longer then [sic] I thought it would. But, I will do it!"

On his website, the only reason Bill gave for his comeback was, "I have returned to what I know best."

About a month before Bill's accident, Tom Kelly, the Ski Team spokesperson, talked to the press about the comeback. In addition to some comments that really said nothing, such as, "It's a long shot for sure," and "Time is not on his side," Kelly also said, "Some people think Johnson's crazy, and there are a lot of mixed feelings."

"Mixed feelings" is putting it mildly. Except for people associated with the Ski Team—who for the most part make bland, semi-positive comments like, "If he could do it, more power to him"—the topic of Bill's comeback, especially with the benefit of knowing how it would end, brings out extreme reactions from just about everyone.

The feelings people have about what Bill was doing break down roughly along the lines of how successful they thought it was going to be. The issue of *should* he do it was tied up in *could* he do it. Those who felt Bill had no chance of winning any race, much less the Olympics, generally believed that his comeback attempt was sad, pathetic, desperate. Almost nobody really thought that Bill could win another gold medal, but the people who saw it as a possibility, who thought that you could never count Bill out once he set his mind to something, for the most part viewed his quest as noble, brave, inspiring.

Many people, including Bode Miller, who knew Bill from the ski world, advised him not to do it. Initially, from what he had heard about Bill from other skiers and coaches, Bode didn't have such a favorable opinion of Bill, saying he thought that he was "super, super cocky and never took stuff that seriously." There was also the time, back in the early '80s, when one of Bode's friends was stretching and Bill jumped on his back.

After Bode got to know Bill for himself, however, he says that Bill was "pretty solid to me." Bode told him directly that he thought the comeback was not a good idea. "I can recognize the desire," Bode says. "But it's risky and dangerous. Once he decided to do it, it was his own decision. You have to listen to people around you. Bill was motivated by a desire to prove people wrong."

Bill was never about being told what not to do, and he refused to hear what he couldn't do. When he was driving, Gina says, "If you told him to slow down, he'd drive a little faster."

Andy Luhn says that all it would have taken to convince Bill to try it was ten people telling him he was crazy. Then again, at that point in his life Bill might have been more interested in proving something to himself than to other people. Either way, he wasn't going to back down from it once he made up his mind. Nobody was going to talk him out of it.

Bill's former teammate Mike Brown thinks that Bill's failure to listen to others contributed to his downfall, not necessarily in terms of his comeback, but over the course of his life. "It's too bad someone couldn't sit him down and work out this antagonistic caricature that he'd turned himself into," Brown says. "He needed help, but he wouldn't get it."

Most of Bill's family members believed that his return to racing was good therapy for him, whether he won or not. Bill's mom, to whom Bill hadn't spoken in over a year at that point, felt that Bill "was lost, just a lost soul flailing around." When she heard about his comeback, DB thought it might be "a healing thing."

Brother Wally felt it gave Bill new life. "Golf, construction—that wasn't Bill," he says. "He was back on the slopes, back doing what he wanted to do." Although Kathryn wished that Bill hadn't won a gold medal in the first place, given where he was in his life she also supported his comeback.

Other members of the family, like Bill's step-mom Mary, simply told him to be careful.

Many people thought Bill should not tarnish his legacy. On the issue of whether an athlete, a champion, has an obligation to preserve his image for posterity, some of Bill's former teammates say definitely not. "Did people get on Michael Jordan?" Andy asks. "It's the same mentality." Mike Brown says, "If someone wants to keep doing something, I don't see why they have to stop."

Most athletes staging comebacks much later in their lives do wind up their careers, at least in the record books, with a whimper. It would not be the case with Bill. Given the inherent dangers associated with downhill racing, he was putting more than just his reputation at risk. His career would end not pathetically, but tragically.

Picabo Street says she understands why Bill wanted to do it. "Being an athlete is a very structured life," she says. "You don't have to think a lot. It's relaxing, comforting. The real world is real chaotic. It's random—the gas pump won't work, the baby won't stop crying—so many variables. [As an athlete] you can really narrow the variables down."

Now the mother of a one-year-old son, Picabo is familiar with the randomness of a baby's tears. But back in 2001, she was attempting a comeback herself. Only out a couple seasons, she was also struggling with the new equipment. She says she was shocked by what Bill was doing. "He got the itch, wanted the rush, that adrenaline rush again," she says. "I never asked him what personal thing he was running away from."

A lot of people in Bill's life thought there was no reason for him *not* to do it. He didn't have much going on, didn't have anything else to do, didn't even *know* what else to do. Creel certainly fell into this category. "What's the guy's options?" he says. "He just said 'Heck with it, man, I'm just gonna go and ski race one more time.' Why not? At that point, *why not*?"

With Bill so dangerously depressed, Creel felt a return to racing would be a way for him to be around people, socialize, have fun. "Win, lose, or draw, he would be doing what he liked to do," he says.

Creel seemed to view the comeback as a win-win. "No matter what happened, whether he crashed, did the Van Gogh thing where he cuts his ear off and his paintings become valuable, or he wins—either way, he comes out okay," Creel says. It's an interesting analogy, Bill to Van Gogh. They actually share the same birthday, 107 years apart. After living an anguished, tortured life, in the end, at age 37, Vincent Van Gogh stopped the pain by killing himself.

Creel believed in Bill as well, feeling that with enough time to train and race he had a chance to win again. He refers to him as "the guy that broke through, that showed them you can win." He thought that on the right day, on the right course, Bill could have "slipped right in there and snatched it." According to Creel, Bill was still the fastest glider, the most aerodynamic, and he could win under the right conditions: "Take the glider, put him in a glide scenario, with soft snow…."

Looking back now, Creel says, "I thought we'd make an impact. Things would happen."

Some members of the ski community felt that enough was enough. Bill had had his time, everybody else had moved on. There were other, younger skiers to focus on. Some went further than that, believing the comeback was disrespectful to the sport. Casey Puckett, who at age 28 would finish second in the Kandahar Cup (the race in which Bill crashed), told a reporter, "You've got to be kidding me. In a way, I felt it showed no respect for the rest of us."

Debbie Armstrong, who also won gold in Sarajevo, thought that Bill's comeback "showed a lack of respect" as well, in that at his age he didn't appreciate what he was getting into. She feels that the "unnatural, superhuman" amount of strength a skier needs is the type that takes years to develop, day in and day out, every day, not something that can be decided on a whim a year before. She calls the comeback "insane and suicidal."

Bill's old coach Andreas Rausch does not think that Bill was capable of achieving his goal in one year, but he does believe that Bill could have qualified for the Olympic team at that age if he had started earlier. Rausch claims that if Bill had begun competing three years beforehand, or possibly even in 1999, he "probably would have had no problem" competing in Salt Lake.

The age difference between Bill and the other skiers was starkly contrasted in at least two instances in the Kandahar Cup alone. One young racer was the son of a skier Bill had competed against as a kid in Idaho, and Kim Taylor, who knew Bill from high school (her brother, Chris England, raced with him), also had a son in the race.

"Bill was kind of in la-la land," Kim says. "My son and his group were just laughing at Bill. He didn't belong with them."

Ironically, and perhaps not lost on Bill, these were the same type of comments he had heard in the lead-up to the 1984 Olympics. And he was used to being laughed at.

Bill's former teammate Alan Lauba thought Bill's return to racing was crazy, and he made that clear to Bill. Alan was at Big Mountain for the Doug Smith Memorial race in January, coaching a team of young racers from Crystal Mountain in Washington. He noticed Bill's name on the start list, then saw him in the finish area after a training run "acting like a downhiller again, like we were young kids." Alan told Bill that it wasn't his time, that it didn't make any sense in terms of his family, that skiing is a dangerous sport to begin with, even at 20 years old.

"Bill's success came from risk-taking," Alan says. "It may ruin his life, but he may win. Gambling, ski racing, whatever. Huge risks for personal gain was always Bill's game."

At dinner that night, Bill told Alan about his drug and alcohol problems, saying he had been drinking a case of beer a day but had cleaned himself up. Perhaps to prove his point, when Alan ordered a beer with dinner, Bill did not.

Alan feels that although Bill had gotten himself into shape, he still had old-fashioned technique on new equipment. Alan couldn't believe that Bill was "acting like he was going to ski really well."

"He was fooling himself," Alan says. "He was not in the real world in his brain. There were 17-year-old kids skiing as fast as he was."

Bill told Alan that the reason for his comeback was simply that he loved ski racing. Alan's analysis is a little more complex. "Downhill was the best place of comfort for him," he says. "It brought him back to where he had been. He didn't have a different place to go."

A few of Bill's former teammates, including Alan, say Bill's return to racing wouldn't have been a bad idea if his intent was to gain attention from it, market himself to celebrity events, dig himself out a little bit along the way. But Bill believed he could do it. His comeback wasn't a publicity stunt.

"If he was doing it for competing alone," Alan says, "there was something wrong with him."

Yet there are plenty of people who say there was a chance Bill could have succeeded, mostly those who in the past had witnessed firsthand the phenomenon of Bill single-mindedly chasing and achieving a goal against all odds. People who claim that when Bill really focused on something, there was no stopping him. The dedication Bill showed toward his comeback reminded some people what he could do when he wanted something badly enough. It had, after all, happened before.

"It would have had to be just right," Andy Luhn says. "But a guy like that, you never put it past him." Mark Schelde, who worked with Bill on the King of the Mountain tour, says, "If there was somebody who could have ever done it, I would have bet on Bill."

Jo Jo says that he didn't believe Bill could do it, but points out that he didn't believe Bill could do it the first time, either—sort of a backhanded way of endorsing the possibility. On *Primetime* (after Bill's accident), Bob Beattie, referring to Bill's chances of success, said, "There was just that little flicker that said 'Remember the old days?' Maybe he *could* do it again."

Blake Lewis gives a surprisingly emotional response for a former technician. His answer is not tied to equipment advances or ski preparation, but more to a gut feeling. "I thought he was crazy, but when Bill put his mind to something—it's in there somewhere," he says. "Maybe he could do it. The likelihood, probably not. But yeah, I guess he could. He had beaten the odds before. He had shown the naysayers before."

Blake points to Olympic swimmers who returned to their sport years later and competed in the Olympics again after completely relearning their technique. "With Bill, you have to say there's always the possibility," Blake says. "He was so determined. Why couldn't he make it back? It's Bill. It could happen with Bill."

Confident as well as determined, Bill started his comeback at the end of 2000, racing on the NorAm circuit in the United States and Canada, the top level of racing in North America but the equivalent internationally of the minor leagues in baseball.

Creel felt Bill had been training well, and his body had muscle memory for his former ability. He says that it was "pretty uncanny" to watch Bill's feet on the slopes—he could ski over pretty much anything, taking all the bumps out of the hill. The obvious concern was that the skills necessary to react at 70 mph—timing, strength, power, agility, quickness—all tend to diminish with age.

Franz Klammer had a unique perspective on Bill's comeback: "At the age of 40 you cannot compete," but not because of the physical aspects. He says that competing in downhill at the highest level is not like pick-up basketball, just a thing that you do. "Physically, you can prepare yourself," he says. "Mentally, you're not there anymore. You need guts and no fear."

At least on the surface, the mental aspects of Bill's approach seemed to be as sharp as ever. "His ability to focus is higher than the norm," Creel says. "When it's time to go, there is no hesitation."

Bill's first race of the season was not a downhill, but a Super-G, on the NorAm Super Series circuit in Beaver Creek, Colorado, the first week of December. According to Creel, Bill was racing in a Super-G to "quicken his feet up." He finished 51st out of 63 racers.

Bill competed in several more Super-Gs and a few giant slalom races throughout the season. Creel wanted him to have as much experiencing turning as possible. In the '80s, there were fewer turns on the downhill courses. Racers essentially pointed their skis straight down the hill. When the equipment advanced to skis that carved more easily, the courses changed as well. Since the skiers were faster in between the turns, the power built up in the skis required course designers to add some big, arcing turns to slow the racers down.

The modifications in the skis and the runs also forced racers to change their technique. Racers approached the sport with a different mentality than in the past. Before, the skier controlled what the skis did. Now, the skier essentially set the skis up to do their job. On the new skis, racers had to do less, apply less pressure, to complete a turn. If, on the new skis, a skier made the adjustments that had been necessary to make a turn in the past, the skis would spin out of control. A racer had to carefully pick the points on a course to turn. By 2001, downhill racing had become much more of a power sport, but also much more precise.

In Beaver Creek, Bill raced in two more NorAm races—another Super-G, where he placed 46th, and a giant slalom race in which he finished 33rd. Sam Collins, Bill's former teammate and also his ski tech on the King of the Mountain circuit, waxed his skis for him. Sam told Bill he had a lot of catching up to do. In response, Bill was good-natured, matter-of-fact. "I can do it," he said.

Bill competed in the Beaver Creek races in the same candy-striped race suit he had worn in Sarajevo. In one of the races, he started, as he says, DFL (dead fucking last)—99th in a field of 99 skiers. Even so, his presence there generated excitement. After the first 20 skiers or so, the results of a ski race are usually pretty well decided. But with Bill there, skiing at the back of the pack, people stayed around just to watch him race.

Bill's story did inspire people. He elicited a certain vicarious response from people who had taken a straighter path, who weren't willing to make the trade-off to sleep in their cars to follow their dream. They admired Bill for going after what he wanted in a way they never had done but possibly always wished they had. This reaction is encapsulated in a letter he later received from Sugarloaf, Maine, which begins: "I'm a 47-year-old insurance executive, somebody whose ski career didn't progress as far as yours.... I have been watching your comeback with great interest and envy...."

Skiers early in their careers were also motivated by Bill, legions of anonymous kids who saw Bill's victory as opening the door for downhill racing in America. It wasn't just Bill's win, but the way he did it. Young skiers remembered the attitude. One wrote to Bill to tell him that his confidence inspired her.

On March 24, 2001, two days after the accident, while he lay comatose in a Montana hospital, Katie Enright sent him the following letter, addressed to "Mr. Johnson:"

"....I don't know if you remember me. I rode up the chairlift with you once while we were both training in Mt. Hood.... I was very homesick and trying not to cry when you asked me who I was and were [sic] was I from.... By the time we got off the lift, you had me laughing.... But the thing that has stuck with me the entire year was the advice you gave me. I told you I was on the Nevada Union High School Ski Team. You asked how good was I and I said I was awful. I wanted to get to States my senior year though, even if I didn't win them. You told me that was the wrong goal. I had to go to states this year and win states my senior year. I had to practice hard and race to win, every time.... "[At a race the next season] right before I took out of the starting gate I remembered what you said, to race hard and always win the race. My time was the best time I've had in my entire racing career. And I finished with a smile."

In the moments after one of his first races in his comeback season, Bill was less focused on inspiring America's youth than he was on catching his breath. The Beaver Creek race had been over for about ten minutes or so, but Bill was still breathing hard. He was in the finish area, out of his skis, his suit down around his waist. Jonathan Selkowitz had taken pictures of the race and was at the bottom of the mountain gathering up his photo equipment. Bill looked right into his camera, pulled his t-shirt up to show off his tattoo, flexed his muscle, and said, "Hey, here's your cover shot."

While he was in Beaver Creek, Bill stayed with Stephen Connolly, who worked in the winter sports division of IMG and was representing Bill under the loosest of arrangements. Connolly's wife, Dawn, was sick with the flu at the time. Bill knocked on her door every morning before he left asking if there was something he could get her, and he checked with her in the evenings to see if she needed anything.

Nothing was happening with endorsements, but Connolly figured that by acting as Bill's pseudo-agent he couldn't lose. If Bill didn't go anywhere, Connolly was just a guy who tried to help out, and if Bill made it to the Olympics again Connolly says it would have been "the biggest comeback in the history of sport and I would have been the face in the corner of the picture."

After Beaver Creek, Bill traveled to Jackson Hole, Wyoming, where he competed in two giant slalom races and a Super-G, finishing 45th, 60th, and 35th. In early January Bill competed in two downhill NorAm races in Lake Louise, Canada, finishing 40th and 49th.

Later that month, Bill went to Big Mountain, Montana, for the Doug Smith Memorial Races and placed 14th and 19th in the downhills and 15th in the Super-G.

Bill needed a place to stay in Montana, and a mutual friend hooked him up with Mike Maronick, a sales associate at a pharmaceutical company. Mike had an extra condo in Whitefish that he let Bill use. As was his habit, and his skill, Bill bonded quickly with this new person in his life. "We connected right away," Mike says. Mike saw Bill as dedicated, training hard, and not drinking, except for one night when Bill drank way too much and took a swing at Mike.

Mike says Bill loved training in Whitefish. The locals seemed to accept him and the ski shops let him use their facilities to grind his skis. Bill used to drop into Kathy Sullivan's Mountain Photography shop now and then to chat with Kathy, who always called him a renegade. "Everyone around here got very attached to him," Kathy says. Both Mike and Kathy say that Bill talked to them about settling in Whitefish permanently.

A couple months after meeting Bill, Kathy was on the mountain taking photos of the Kandahar Cup. She snapped one of Bill crouched in the air on his new red Atomic skis, green ski pole flying, seconds before he fell.

In February of 2001, a month before the Kandahar Cup, Bill competed in a NorAm race at Snowbasin in Utah, the Olympic venue for 2002. One of the ironies of Bill's comeback is that even if, as his biggest supporters believed, Bill could have won gold again if the course and the conditions were just right, Creel himself admits that "the mountain in Utah would not have been Bill's mountain anyway."

Bill was in the top 25 racers in the training runs, but he crashed in the race, flying 150 feet in the air, then tumbling. His only injury was a deep knee bruise. According to Creel, that wreck was the result of a lip on the course pointing up, a defect that was repaired for later racers. Afterward, Creel asked Bill, "Well, are you done?" Bill looked at Creel like he was insane and just said, "No." Creel said, "I support what you think you need to do." But privately, Creel said a little prayer.

"He was trying to ski race," he says, "and there was a lot of clutter."

Much of the clutter involved the ex-wife and sons Bill had left behind in California. When he was in Montana earlier in the season, he had asked Mike Maronick how far Whitefish was from Northern California. Mike responded that he didn't know, maybe a thousand miles.

"That's not far enough away from my ex-wife," Bill said.

Mike says that Bill talked about his boys a lot, missed them like crazy. Bill's mom says, "It just broke Bill's heart to be separated from those boys. Just completely broke his heart."

Bill might have missed his boys, but he stayed away. Nick and Tyler hadn't seen their dad for six months when they visited him in his hospital bed. Gina told them, "Daddy's ski racing, Daddy's training for the Olympics."

Gina thinks that she and the boys were "a package." If Bill couldn't see her, it was too painful for him to see them and hear about her and whom she was dating. He ignored the legal process of the divorce, attending only one hearing, on custody.

Bill didn't do a lot of dating during his comeback. When he was in Big Mountain in January he saw a girl named Darci Berreth in a restaurant called Great Northern. He didn't actually meet her, but he did pull up his shirt and flash her. The next day he saw her again, eating at Trubie's restaurant. She was sitting with a male friend (not a boyfriend, but Bill didn't know that), and he came over anyway and joined them at their table. He told Darci he had won a gold medal and asked her to check with the bartender if she didn't believe him.

Darci did have a serious boyfriend and wasn't interested in Bill, but they had a playful sort of relationship over the next couple months. "I was just a hot girl he wanted," Darci says. They e-mailed each other, hung out a bit. She was working on the mountain at the time at a property management company, and Bill would come into her office without warning, throw himself down at her desk, and use her computer.

Darci says that although Bill was fun and "party happy," it was clear he was at a low point in his life. She knew he was struggling with his divorce and wasn't in contact with his children. "He was in a bitter stage, bad-mouthing his wife," she says. "I got the feeling she left him. He was a not-in-a-good-place kind of guy."

Bill might have seemed spiteful about his divorce to new people he met, but he told Creel that he wished Gina would come watch one of his races. When he first raised the idea of a comeback with Gina, she told him he was being selfish, that this was the time he needed to give to his kids. She said the boys needed a father and Bill shouldn't be putting his life in danger. Mostly she told him she didn't want him to get hurt.

Bill's return to racing was about more than getting Gina back, but the idea of Gina was certainly driving him. The way Bill looked at the world, his gold medal was the best thing in his life. He believed that the medal, and everything that went with it, was responsible for getting Gina in the first place. In Bill's mind, if he could win again, everything good would come back, including Gina. And it had worked the first time. The gold medal made him lovable for the first time in his life, and in a sense it won his parents back.

He told Gina that if he won another gold medal he would have status and money again, and he would be the person she fell in love with. Gina says that Bill would have had a better chance of winning her back by holding down a steady job, finding a house, paying child support, anything to show her he could be a business person, a family person. She claims that if Bill had been stable enough to keep his job, stay clean, and establish a home in Tahoe, she would have been there with the boys "in a heartbeat."

"He was doing absolutely the wrong thing to get me back as far as I could see," Gina says. "He did absolutely the exact opposite of what I needed him to do. I needed him to grow up. I wanted him to get *over* the fact that he'd won a gold medal, not win another one."

Maybe Bill simply wasn't capable of doing what Gina said she needed him to do, or maybe he didn't believe her. She was dating one of his old ski reps at the time, and possibly he felt, despite what she said, that regaining fame and fortune was his best shot.

Jo Jo, who refers to Gina as "perfect, a saint," says, "If Gina had a flaw, it was that she really missed that rock-star lifestyle…but who wouldn't?"

Bill must have known that a return to racing was no way to get Gina back, but if he made it, if he really pulled it off, this time he would have those millions he had envisioned back in Sarajevo. Gina was not concerned only with money, but if financial and career pressures were suddenly removed from the relationship, maybe they could have gotten back to where they once had been.

During the course of the season, Bill entered as many races as he could afford. To work on his speed, he also competed in some City League races around Mt. Hood against some world-class speed skiers.

In the first week of March, Bill finished 31st in a NorAm race at Whistler. It was his best result of the year (as it was a more competitive field than at the Doug Smith), and it impressed the Canadian rep for Atomic enough that he had a pair of skis flown in for Bill the next day.

Looking back, Tom Kelly, the Ski Team spokesperson, carefully describes Bill's pre-accident success as follows: "He had a ways to go, but he was improving. He had pretty decent progress. Reasonable forward momentum."

Daron Rahlves (who would finish first in both the Kandahar Cup and the U.S. Nationals that season), felt that Bill had been removed from the sport for so long that he had "no chance, no way to step back in." Even so, Daron says that he respected Bill for what he was doing, just as he admired Bill's contribution to racing in the past. "Bill definitely brought the U.S. into the limelight a little bit," he says. "He brought cockiness to it, a lot of energy, and just fire. Some kind of edge. The Europeans were reserved and serious. Bill was a ballsy downhiller. That's what I always felt he represented."

Daron welcomed the recognition and media attention Bill was again bringing to ski racing with his comeback. "A lot of people looked at it as a joke," he says. "You can take your own opinion on that. I thought it was great for the sport."

Many people, including Daron, were looking past the comeback, hoping Bill would move through this phase and get his life together. When Bill called Mark Schelde in the early stages of his return, Schelde told him: "Get it out of your system, Billy. Because you gotta get on, try to move on. You gotta move on."

Daron says he knows how proud Bill was of his medal, but he felt that Bill was "trying to cling on a little." He adds, "A trophy is a trophy. They're meant to sit up on the shelf. I'm happy to be successful, but it's all what comes next."

Bill's gold medal did not sit on a shelf. When reporter Robert Frohlich asked Bill where he kept it, he responded, "The gold medal travels with me everywhere I go."

After Whistler, the medal went with Bill to Boise, Idaho, where he made a special trip to Sun Valley Ski Tools. The shop is frequented by World Cup skiers and renowned for the quality of its tools. Jim Vermillion, the owner, says that Bill stopped in to let him know of his plans to be the next Olympic gold medalist. Bill told him that he was looking for sponsors and asked Vermillion if he could help him out.

"That kind of courage, I couldn't say no," Vermillion says. He agreed to be Bill's "sponsor," although that meant simply giving Bill wax, tuning equipment, and ski prep with no expectation of anything in return. The arrangement was fine with Vermillion. "He was a guy with a dream that he couldn't let go," he says. "If he wanted to try something like that, I wanted to give him a shot."

Vermillion feels that Bill had the talent, and the confidence, to pull it off. "Something inside of me tells me he would have given them a run for their money," he says. "It would have been fun to see."

After Bill left Vermillion's shop, he headed for Montana.

CHAPTER FOURTEEN

"I'm throwin' down tomorrow. I need this race."

– BILL JOHNSON, to John Creel, March 21st, 2001

A few days before the U.S. Alpine Championships in 2001, Daron Rahlves sat Bill down at Big Mountain and asked him why he was ski racing again.

"It's not the money," Bill said. "It's not the fame. It's all for the chicks."

Bill came to Montana in the middle of March that year ranked 404th in the FIS world downhill standings and 56th in the U.S. He was in town to compete in two downhill races: the Kandahar Cup on Thursday, March 22rd, and the U.S. Championship the following day. Both races were being held on the Ursa Major downhill course.

Contrary to how it was reported in hundreds of newspaper and magazine articles afterward, Bill's crash occurred not in a training run, but in an FIS downhill race. The idea that Bill's accident happened while he was training belittles what he was doing on that mountain. He crashed because he was risking everything he had to win a race.

John Creel equates the phrase "Ski to Die" with a faith that is spiritual, almost religious. As he explains it, you risk it all and you don't cringe, because you're either going to win or they're going to carry you out, and either way you've come to terms with it. Bill is not religious in any traditional sense, but he does have faith. He was able to cast aside fear because the strength he drew on was his belief that what was going to happen was meant to be.

The Kandahar Cup mattered for points. A strong finish would have dropped Bill's world ranking significantly, helping him just as much as a good result in Nationals the next day. But even more importantly, the race was essential in terms of visibility. Since the U.S. Championships were being held that weekend, all the Ski Team coaches, as well as the national media, were watching.

Even among supporters of the comeback, competing in a race at that level early in his training seemed to be dangerously accelerating the process. But Bill didn't have a lot of time. Those two races were close to the end of the season, and the results would affect how he was positioned for summer training and fall race circuits. The Salt Lake Olympics were less than a year away. If Bill was going to impress the U.S. Ski Team coaches, he had to do it there and he had to do it then.

Bill was skiing well in the training runs, especially his last one. Paul Mahre, Bill's former teammate on the Ski Team (and Phil and Steve's younger brother), was the program director at Big Mountain and the Chief of Race for that week's races. Paul says that in the training runs, Bill's times put him generally among the top 20 to 35 racers.

Bill figured that to force the Ski Team coaches to at least consider him, he had to finish in the top ten. Although the coaches feel Bill was dramatically underestimating the strength of the field, Bill believed he could finish among the top seven skiers.

In Creel's opinion, for Bill to do that he would have to be smoother and hold his line better—in short, ski "twice as hard and twice as fast" as he had in previous races that season. In earlier races, Creel claims that Bill had been only giving 85 to 90 percent. In this race, Creel says that Bill made up his mind to "scorch it," and there was no point trying to convince him otherwise.

To make up time, Bill decided, as had been his style in the past, to go as fast as he could in the most dangerous section. On the Big Mountain downhill, Creel and Bill, riding on the chairlift together the day before the race, had easily identified that area as a series of three narrow turns called Corkscrew. Creel was concerned with the three layers of red fencing in that spot, pointing out that none of it was A-fencing, the strongest in terms of protecting a falling racer. From the chairlift, looking down at Corkscrew from above, Creel told Bill, "The color's wrong, the corner's wrong, it's in the shade." That night, Bill sketched out a map of the downhill run from memory.

The race strategy took into account the psychological benefit of Bill finishing at the top of the pack, in terms of the other racers as well as Bill himself. If Bill had a good result in the Kandahar Cup, Creel thought it was possible that Bill would be on the minds of the other racers heading into Nationals, and if they saw him as a threat, they might try harder and make mistakes. With regard to Bill's state of mind, he had always found a way to pump himself up with his own success.

Bill Egan, then the head coach of the Ski Team, ran into Bill at Big Mountain a day or two before the Kandahar Cup. Egan says that Bill was excited and "very up." Bill told Egan that he was coming right along and was going to do great in the race. It was small talk mostly, but Bill did bring up the issue of training with the team in the summer.

Looking back now, with the benefit of how Egan was approaching the situation at the time, it seems that Bill would have had to do even better than he had calculated to have a shot at the U.S. team. While Egan calls the chance of Bill looking like one of the better racers in America "remote," he says that if Bill had had a "really good finish" in the two races that weekend, he could have put himself in a position to make the team. Egan first defines a really good finish as one in the top five, then clarifies his position to state that if Bill had "made the podium" (meaning been in the top three) in the Big Mountain races, as well as in subsequent races in North America, he would have been named to the team.

"We knew he was racing," Egan says, "but we weren't making plans to have him." In terms of including Bill in the summer camps for the development team, he says, "We wouldn't have wasted the money."

Meanwhile, Bill was finding it more and more difficult to finance his comeback on his own. Months earlier, to raise some cash, he had planned to put the skis from his gold medal run up for auction on eBay. Creel called Bill's mom and told her about it, and she offered to buy the skis. Creel told her Bill needed $5,000 to keep training. DB countered with $4,000 and the condition that Bill sign a document stating the skis were hers. The red sleds now reside at DB's house in Gresham.

In Park City, a few weeks before his accident, Bill was working on selling another, less significant pair of skis. Bill had gotten together with Tom Mahoney, a friend of his since the early '80s, and told Tom he needed to raise some money. Tom was heading back to California and offered to bring a pair of Bill's training skis with him to sell. Bill signed a pair of skis and gave them to Tom.

Bill and Tom also discussed the old helmet Bill was racing in. Tom told Bill that he should be wearing a full-face helmet, and offered one to him. Tom had suffered a head injury himself, spent eight days in a coma as a result of a fall off a balcony in 1984, and it had made him sensitive to safety issues. Bill told Tom that he wasn't comfortable with a full-face helmet and that in any case, he wanted to race in the "lucky helmet" he wore when he won gold.

Creel couldn't convince Bill to wear a helmet with a face mask either. "Bill said 'This helmet's faster—it's been in a wind tunnel,'" Creel says. As a result, Bill raced with the especially dangerous combination of new skis and an old helmet.

After Bill's crash, opinions differed on whether a different helmet would have changed the outcome. Some skiers say it would have made a "night and day" difference, but others, including Creel, say it would not have, not in this type of fall. Later, doctors at Kalispell Regional Medical Center would declare that while a helmet can mitigate an impact directly to a brain, in Bill's case his brain rotated inside his skull, and no helmet could have protected against that.

The U.S. Ski Team certainly was concerned about the helmet. Perhaps fearing a lawsuit (which neither Bill nor his family ever pursued against anybody in connection with his accident), representatives of the team came to the hospital and tried to confiscate Bill's helmet while he lay in a coma.

The sale of Bill's training skis was successful. Tom, at Big Mountain to do some freelance video work with ESPN's crew, saw Bill the day before his crash and told him he had sold them to a guy in Silicon Valley. Tom said he had $600 for him, but he didn't get a chance to give it to him before the race.

Months later, while Bill was recovering, Tom visited him with six $100 bills in his pocket. Although Bill is steadfast about recalling nothing from the years leading up to his crash, Tom has no doubt that Bill has a memory of their conversation from the very day before. "He definitely remembered," Tom says. "When I saw him he said, 'Don't you have something for me?'" Tom pulled the money out and asked Bill if that was what he meant. Bill said yes and gave him a big hug.

The day before his accident, Bill also ran into Kent Taylor, who had been the starter for the Doug Smith downhill race a few months before. They had a cup of coffee together, and Taylor remembers laughing at how Bill described the progress he was making in his comeback. "I've knocked off all the 16- and 17-year-olds," Bill said, "and now I'm focusing on the 18-year-olds."

Taylor recalls that although Bill filled out his racing suit, looking more like an adult male than a kid in it, there was a lot of excitement in Whitefish that he was there racing. He says he doubts Bill ever had to pay for a meal while he was in town.

That same day, March 21st, Bill had lunch with two other race officials—Andy Anderson and Parke Frizelle. Anderson was set to be the start referee for the Kandahar Cup, a position that entails communicating with the race officials down the course and directing the slip crews checking the run. Frizelle was scheduled as the starter, responsible for sending the racers down and staying in contact with the finish line.

Early that afternoon, after the day's training, Anderson and Frizelle were walking through the parking lot at the same time as Bill. Bill got his gold medal from under the seat in his pickup and showed it to them both, even posed for pictures wearing it.

Most of the skiers set to race the next day were either babies when Bill won his gold medal or not even born yet. Frizelle says that the younger racers thought Bill was crazy and some were legitimately concerned about him.

"Bill will always be respected for what he did," Frizelle says. "But they didn't respect what he was doing."

Anderson remembers the meal with Bill, saying, "It's not every day an Olympic champion invites you to lunch." They ate outside on the terrace at a place called Moguls. Anderson and Frizelle both had beers with their hamburgers, but Bill didn't drink. He was friendly, and confident about the race the following day. "He talked like he could do it," Anderson says.

Bill talked about athletes in other sports making comebacks in their late 30's, even early 40's, and he pointed out that Roger Clemens was still pitching (at that point, at age 38). He didn't seem to draw a distinction between ski racing and the relative danger of other sports, saying only, "Other guys have done it at my age."

Bill also told Anderson and Frizelle about the Atomic rep giving him a new pair of skis. Frizelle says that Bill was really proud about the skis.

One of the last things Bill did on the day before his accident was give away his U.S. Ski Team jacket. Mike Maronick had hoped to watch Bill compete in the Kandahar Cup, but he had to go out of town on a business meeting that morning. The night before, Bill gave the coat to Mike as a thank-you for all he had done for him, saying, "I know you like it. I want you to have it. It's yours."

Mike says he didn't, and still doesn't, see this as any kind of premonition on Bill's part, but the timing in relation to Bill's accident is bizarrely coincidental, almost like someone giving away their prized possessions when they know they're dying.

The morning of March 22nd, 2001, was sunny and cold, and Bill and Creel were up early testing skis. They were having what Creel refers to as a "waxing dispute." Creel had punched the weather conditions into a computer—cold snow, wet snow—and prepared Bill's new Atomic skis with a cold grind. Figuring that the mountain was cold at the top and warmer at the bottom, Creel waxed the skis for the bottom.

The new Atomics had the stiffest flex of any pair of skis Bill had. They were shorter skis than he was used to, and they had a bigger side cut—narrower in the center, faster in the turns. He had only been training on them for two weeks.

Picabo Street was in Whitefish to compete in Nationals as well as the women's Kandahar Cup, and she also was adjusting to the new parabolic skis. "You are on for the ride on those skis in a bad way," she says, "They have a mind of their own."

Creel had prepared the new Atomics, but Bill, not taking any chances, had prepared a separate set. Earlier in the season, Creel had once purposely waxed Bill's skis "slow," and Bill was furious with him. At Big Mountain, Bill insisted that Creel prove the ones he waxed were faster, so they went up on a hill together and tried both pairs. Bill set his pair down and stepped on. When the skis stopped, he jumped off. He then ran back up the hill and did the same thing with the new skis Creel prepared. That pair went 40 yards farther. Bill decided to go with those.

Bill had been saving a new downhill suit to wear for the first time in the Kandahar Cup. The suit cost approximately $1200, and had been given to him by Descente. It had a black-and-grey design on a white background. Later, in the emergency room, Dr. Keith Lara would cut it off Bill's body.

That morning, Bill had planned to hook up with Jonathan Selkowitz. He wanted the photographer to take a portrait of him in his new downhill suit and new skis to give to his sponsors as a way of thanking them. They were supposed to meet before the run, but Selkowitz was running a little late and they misconnected.

Picabo describes the mood of that race day as "turmoilish." She says she was mostly concentrating on not doing anything stupid during her run. "There were funky conditions there," she says. "I felt weird. It was spring, edgy at Nationals. I was holdin' my breath, nervous."

When Picabo saw Bill getting into his new race suit that morning, naked from the waist up, she noticed what great shape he was in. When she thinks of Bill now, Picabo claims to still have that picture in her mind.

She says she was worried about Bill, not for his safety, but for "how he was going to accomplish his mission." She was concerned not because he wasn't taking his comeback seriously enough but because he was taking it *so* seriously. He was not loose as she was used to seeing him. "It was a different approach, all of that seriousness," she says. "He was trying to focus in, be crisp, precise. It was not him, in a sense, and it didn't work for him. His intensity was foreign to me—it came naturally before."

At the race, Bill didn't have "a staff or six or seven" as Creel claims some of the other skiers did, so Creel asked a few of the coaches if they would help Bill out. He says that Bill feeling "invited in" was the highlight of his time there.

Jim Tracy, who had coached Bill at the end of his career on the U.S. team and was in Montana as head coach for the women's team, spoke to Bill in the lodge twenty minutes before he went down the mountain. Tracy says they talked about nothing for five minutes. His main recollection is that Bill seemed happy. "He was out skiing," Tracy says. "He loved it."

No question, Bill loved to race. Earlier that month, on March 13th, he had filled out a little e-mail questionnaire about himself and forwarded it around to his friends. The questions (and Bill's answers) were mostly random: What is your favorite fast food restaurant? ("Mac's Steak House, the rainbow room, better known as McDonald's"); Piercings? ("Soon"); What is your favorite sport to watch? ("N/A, don't like to watch"); Have you ever loved somebody so much it made you cry? ("Yes"). In the midst of it was this question: On a scale of 1 to 10, how much do you love your job? Bill's answer was "10."

After their conversation, Tracy wished Bill luck as he headed for the start area. He says that if Bill had done well that day maybe the U.S. team would have taken him somewhere, but he repeats the word "maybe" three times. According to Tracy, Bill knew how important the race was, with all the coaches and the TV cameras around. "If he wanted to show them something, that was the place to do it," Tracy says.

Earlier that morning, knowing that Bill would be skiing from flat light into bright light, Creel changed the lens in Bill's goggles three times, at one point saying to Bill, "You can't see, can you?" Creel claims that Bill was skiing faster than his retina could adjust.

A young skier named Erik Jitloff, running 20th in the race, just a few minutes before Bill, crashed during his run. Erik's mom claims that his crash was due to the flat light conditions at the time he was racing. He was riding to the hospital (his injuries required surgery, but were not life-threatening) at the same time Bill was being airlifted there.

Up in the start house, Bill was singing to stay loose. "He was joking," Creel says, "but it was serious business. We weren't playing tiddlywinks. We weren't messing around."

In talking with Creel, Bill used an expression from his old racing days, "spinning the wheel," to describe how he planned to ski the race. He was sparring a bit with Creel as well, snapping at him to "Just do what the other guys are doing."

"When Bill gets nervous, he gets pissy," Creel says. "I certainly wouldn't want to be married to him. He wants to work up the juices, go verbally back and forth so he goes out a little bit harder."

Bill obviously didn't have a coach posted down the hill to warn him about deteriorating conditions, so Creel asked the race officials for an update instead. One of them told him, "There's a ripple on Corkscrew, but most guys are driving through it."

On the map Bill drew of the run, Corkscrew, near the bottom of the course, was the last place he marked. Approaching the area cautiously, or taking a higher line, would have lowered the danger but increased the time. "I didn't even have to talk to Bill," Creel says. "I knew what he was thinking. Today was the day to risk."

Creel started to prepare Bill's equipment. He describes his role like a "sherpa" getting a gladiator ready to fight, bringing him his sword. One at a time, like swatting flies away, Creel dusted the snow off the face of Bill's skis. Then Bill lifted up each leg, like a horse, and Creel wiggled each boot to make sure it clicked in correctly, then checked the bindings.

Creel had just finished with Bill's skis when Bill turned to him and said, "Brush my skis off."

"Bill, I just did that," Creel said. Creel believes that one of Bill's primary strengths as a racer was his ability to center himself, to concentrate and regulate his intensity. He sees Bill's comment as a sign that Bill was already focusing elsewhere, to the first gate, down the course.

But only seconds before he was going to hurl himself off a mountain, Bill wasn't aware of what was going on around him. He may have been so hyper-focused that he wasn't paying attention at all. In an eerie sort of way, he was already gone.

As Bill moved into his place in the starting gate next to Frizelle, Creel told him he would see him at the truck.

Frizelle is extremely conscious of being the last guy to talk to Bill before his accident. Although the conversation was brief, he recounts it almost reverently. He says that normally he wouldn't talk to a racer right before they left the starting gate, but in this case they had just had lunch together the previous day. As Bill got set to race, Frizelle commented on how he looked in his new downhill suit and admired his new skis.

The last thing Frizelle said to Bill was, "Are you ready for the day?"

"Yeah," Bill said. "I am."

CHAPTER FIFTEEN

"I saw my hero bleeding on the snow."
– DR. CHARLES CHARMAN

As the assigned haz mat guy, Chris Burke had to stay behind to pick up all the debris from the mountain. The pieces of gauze were rapidly staining the snow red, and bloody rubber gloves and the packaging from a plastic air tube littered the slope. Burke scooped up the trash, leaving a clean path for the next racer, then skied down to the helicopter to check on Bill's status.

Burke, 43, has been a member of Big Mountain's ski patrol team (whose motto, "You fall. We haul," is printed on the back of their ball caps and rescue blankets) since 1999. He came to Montana over 20 years ago when, luckily for him, he discovered he had an allergy to jet printer spray and took a leave of absence from his job analyzing statistics in Philadelphia. He now spends his summers working in the backcountry at Glacier National Park and the rest of the year with the ski patrol, with one day off in-between seasons.

Burke stepped on skis for the first time in Whitefish after getting a good deal on "rental crappy skis." These days, his skill is such that he has never had to buy dessert for the other 21 ski patrol members in the monthly most-falls competition. Wholesome and steady, with a trim brown goatee, Burke loves coming to work, and he seems genuinely concerned by the idea that "Some people hate what they do and where they're going."

On March 22nd, 2001, Burke was staged to watch the downhill racers jump a perilous section of the run known as Launchpad. The vertical drop for the downhill course is 2110 feet. Launchpad was maybe two-thirds of the way down the run.

It was a clear, still morning, conditions that later allowed the helicopter pilot to land without delay. The course warmed up later in the day, but at

9:51, the temperature was hovering right around freezing.

Kent Taylor, who had had coffee with Bill the day before, was slipping the course, skiing down after every ten skiers or so to test it. His opinion was that while the weather conditions were perfect, the course itself was a sheet of ice, and he was shocked at how fast he took the first turn.

When Bill came down the mountain, the number 34 emblazoned on his racing bib, Burke recalls thinking to himself how smooth his form looked.

"He'd just made a landing off this jump—he nailed it. He looked like he knew what he was doing," he says.

Burke, along with just about everyone in Whitefish, had heard about Bill's plan to make the Olympic team. He had also heard some of the younger skiers complain that Bill was disrespecting them by attempting it, but Burke saw it differently. "Some of the younger generation were flailing like little girls at that jump, they backed off, they were petrified of it," he says. "Bill wasn't scared of anything."

After landing the jump on Launchpad, Bill dropped down a roller and momentarily passed out of Burke's view. Corkscrew, where Bill was headed, narrowed into a fall-away turn. It was the place on the course where Bill had been warned about a ripple, the point where most racers decided to slow down, ease through it. Asked later if the curve was dangerous, Taylor, who had slipped that section, responded, "If you got low it was." Creel knew that Bill intended to go through the section "hot"—and low—to try to make up time.

Corkscrew was the last turn on the course. After that, it was a straight shot down to the finish line.

Burke started to turn his attention upward to watch for the next skier when he caught sight of Bill pinwheeling through two sets of red restraining fences. The fences were stripping gear off Bill as he tumbled—first his poles, then his gloves, caught in the safety netting. There were bloodstains in a trail all the way to the last fence.

By the second bounce, Bill's body was limp.

Even before the gate officials below started screaming, "Help him, he needs help," Burke had grabbed a sled and begun skiing toward Bill. He reached him within, he estimates, 15 seconds.

In the ensuing half-hour, several other ski patrol members, doctors, and emergency personnel would work together in a stunning display of efficiency to get Bill down the mountain and on his way to the emergency room. For the first full minute after his accident, however, Burke was alone with Bill on the mountain.

Bill was lying motionless, face-up in the snow, blood coming from his ear. He had massive injuries to his head and face. His mouth was a tangle of blood and tissue. From beneath his helmet, his forehead was swelling. His pupils were not reacting to light. He was unconscious, making gurgling noises from his throat, and his hands and arms were twitching.

"He was out," Burke says. "I knew it was pretty bad."

Franz Klammer once said that nobody wins the Olympic downhill without being prepared to lose it all. Bill was that kind of prepared. Corkscrew is a right turn to a left to a right across the slope, and Bill was coming into the second turn when he caught the inside edge of his right ski and got thrown off balance. The skis did, it turns out, have a mind of their own. Bill's legs separated, then spread-eagled, and he was thrown forward between his legs. He slammed face-first into hard snow and ice.

That impact, at the rate of speed Bill was traveling, caused his brain to rotate inside his skull. By the time his body came to a stop, tissue in his brain had torn and bled, and his brain began to swell, ultimately putting immense pressure on his brain stem.

Race officials, assuming that Bill would have been slowing down coming into that section of the course, publicly estimated his speed at approximately 50 mph when he crashed. Dr. Charles Charman, who treated Bill on the mountain, calls it more like 70. The hospital records reflect a high-velocity skiing accident at a speed of "up to 82 mph."

From where coach Bill Egan was positioned on the mountain, he saw Bill's fall, but not his landing. "He was in a vulnerable position. He happened to lose his balance at absolutely the wrong turn," Egan says. "He had no possibility of stopping himself. The blink of an eye and he was no longer in control."

No one but Egan heard Bill say anything during or after his crash, and in fact several people recount how unnaturally quiet it was on the mountain while the accident played out in agonizingly slow motion. Even so, Egan is certain.

"He screamed at the top of his lungs—as loud as he could," Egan says. "He was very, very aware for a moment what had happened. It was not garbled. It was very loud and very strong and it was very distinctly Bill's voice. He said, 'Help me.' And that was the last thing he said."

Despite skepticism that it was even medically possible for Bill to yell, Egan insists he heard him cry out for help. "I'll never forget it," he says. "I heard it. I've told other people and they've said no, no, it couldn't have been. I know what I heard. I know it was him."

Bill's old friend Tom Mahoney was also on the course that day. He was at the top of the turn, about 50 yards above Corkscrew. He recalls thinking that the light was pretty bad in that corridor. One racer had already fallen in the area earlier (and another racer, further back in the start order than Bill, would crash there later that morning). Tom remembers thinking that Bill was going into the gate too straight, his ski too flat, and then he says, "It looked like a wishbone in a turkey breast, when you make a wish and break it in half. Each ski went out like that. He was spread-legged like a frog, and then he splattered into the snow full force, face-first."

Jonathan Selkowitz had posted himself on the skiers' left-hand side of the hill and was taking pictures of the racers coming off the jump there. Bill's crash was about 80 yards below him. As Selkowitz watched Bill ski down, he noticed his right ski start to catch and slip away from him. He saw Bill almost pull his skis together before they split totally apart, then saw his head smash down between them. "It was so spectacular and went for so long, such an incredibly long fall….," he says. "He looked like a sack of potatoes as he slid through the fences."

The heartbreaking fact that at the last moment Bill nearly succeeding in getting his skis back together is reminiscent of his skis splitting apart during his wild run in Wengen, where it all started for him. On that course, Bill's career could easily have ended before it really began. But in that race, seventeen years before, with more familiar skis, stronger legs, and quicker reflexes, Bill was able to pull his skis back in.

As the loudspeaker blared "34 down," number 35 skied off the course, number 36 held in the starting gate, and all activity in the race was suspended. Burke sent the following transmission to dispatch at the top of the mountain: "Unit 62, 62 dispatch, I need ALERT, oxygen, assistance, and a backboard."

There are certain spots on Big Mountain that are dead zones for radio reception, and the place where Bill landed happened to be one of them. Ski patrol members in the post at the top of Big Mountain only picked up a garbled reception. They weren't even sure who made the radio call. They were, however, able to make out one word, and incredibly, that word was "ALERT." Without waiting for any further clarification, they instantly called the Advanced Lifesupport Emergency Rescue Team—the rescue helicopter.

Minutes later, up at the top of the mountain, Frizelle saw the helicopter flying through the clouds. He obviously knew who racer 34 was, and he was in contact via headset with the people at the finish line about the situation. He didn't communicate what he saw and heard to anyone in the start house, however, because he didn't want the other racers to know. As Frizelle says, "It's not good karma to say Johnson's down and they're bringing in help."

From all accounts, Bill's transport off the mountain was flawless. The U.S. Ski Team has referred to it as "front to back, the best medical response anywhere." The various teams of medical personnel are quick to compliment each other, unsolicited. While some such comments might naturally be tossed around to foreclose liability, it is clear that these come from pride in a job seamlessly performed. There is no question that there were dozens of ways—communication problems, small delays here and there—that Bill could have died on that mountain. Everyone involved in the rescue that day agrees that the cooperation and speed of the operation saved him.

In giving tribute to the rescue effort, Dr. Charman also openly credits Dr. Ken McFarland with saving Bill's life twice—once at the scene of the accident and again, at the base of the mountain, where his desperate and blind insertion of a breathing tube was pivotal to Bill's survival. Later that morning, the decisive action of Dr. Keith Lara in the ER and the painstaking efforts of Dr. Rob Hollis in the operating room would save Bill two more times.

Charman, a volunteer doctor on the course that day, was summoned to the crash site by Billy Brown, another member of the ski patrol. From his vantage point on the mountain, Brown sent a radio transmission stating: "We need a doctor here right away." From the edge of panic in his voice, it was clear to Charman that something had gone terribly wrong. He also knew which skier had been racing.

As Charman began side-slipping down the icy course toward Bill, Burke, still alone with him, bent down and began talking.

"You're okay, Bill, you're a little banged up. I'm here to help you. More help is coming. We're taking good care of you," he said.

Burke had met Bill at a local bar a few days prior, although Burke jokes, "If I wasn't with a pretty girl he wouldn't have talked to me." With obvious admiration, Burke adopts an exaggerated lounge-lizard voice and imitates how Bill approached a female friend of his: "Heyyy, I'm Bill." Bill, "flirty and cocksure," was commanding a lot of attention in the bar. "People around here knew him," Burke says. "His comeback was a big deal."

Burke, with utmost respect, refers to Bill as "the worst accident victim I've ever seen that was still alive." Firmly believing that hearing is the last thing to go, he kept up a steady stream of encouragement to Bill as he attempted to stabilize him and prepare him for transport. There was no indication that Bill was hearing him, but then Burke had responded to accidents where he knew the person was dead but talked to them anyway. He is outraged by a press report that quoted him as believing that Bill "was a goner." He claims, with sincerity, that he would never be so unprofessional as to say such a thing and that in any event, in this case, "I did not, and would not, consider that." He viewed the statement as an implication that he and the medical personnel were giving up on Bill. When he met Bill's mother, Burke made a point of apologizing to her for the misquote and telling her that no one ever treated her son like a lost cause.

Charman, arriving at Bill's side within minutes of his crash, may well have been the least likely person in Whitefish to ever give up on him. Charman, it turns out, is a big fan.

A year later, when Bill returned to Big Mountain and skied with Charman on intermediate runs, Charman saw that skiing was a skill that never left Bill. When Bill, slurring his words, advised Charman that he was going to race again and told him, "When I'm ready to win I'll tell you," Charman saw that some of the brashness was back. That morning, however, Charman could see only one thing.

"A sports icon, nearly dead," he says. "I had a really overwhelming feeling of sadness. It was devastating."

Charman grew up in Norwich, Vermont, a town of 1,200 that has produced five Olympic ski jumpers. He taught English in a refuge camp in Thailand and did a stint as a bike messenger before attending Yale Medical School. An internal medical specialist at North Valley Hospital since 1998, Charman moved to Whitefish because he "lives to backcountry ski." Lanky, with an easy gracefulness that makes him a natural on the slopes, Charman, 42, regrets not pursuing ski racing and jumping as seriously as he might have. He followed Bill's career from the beginning, and he was watching his comeback with particular interest.

"Bill Johnson is a guy you never count out," he says. "I hoped he would do it. He came out of nowhere to win a gold medal—somebody who does that, you never know what they're capable of."

Over the course of his career, Charman had worked on injuries similar to Bill's in various emergency rooms, but treating Bill was different. "Other patients I see for a half -hour, I don't know their stories, I don't know why they were there or what had happened in their life," he says. "This was too much." Charman was depressed for weeks afterward, and years later, still seems a little shaken when discussing the experience.

At the time, however, Charman suppressed his emotions, kicked off his skis, and got to work. He assessed Bill from the neck down while Dr. McFadden, arriving at the scene with Charman, evaluated him from the neck up. Charman conducted a general trauma survey, examining Bill's heart and lungs, listening to his chest, feeling his pelvis. "His hands and arms were seizing, never good in the setting of head trauma," Charman says. "And he had gasping, obstructed breathing sounds—clearly not good."

It was apparent to the doctors, however, that Bill's immediate problem was his airway. He had nearly bit through his tongue in the crash, filleting it all the way to the back of his throat, and it was bleeding profusely into his mouth.

"That's what was going to kill him in the next two minutes," Charman says.

McFadden, a specialist in airway management, inserted a four-inch plastic airway into Bill's mouth to keep his tongue out of the way and prevent him from suffocating on his blood.

Nearby, a race official came up and began repairing the fencing on the course.

While the doctors worked on Bill, Mike Block, another ski patrol member, was waiting "in the horn," meaning that he was already strapped to an evacuation sled. The rescue helicopter obviously wasn't able to land on the steep slope, so the medics had to get Bill stabilized, on a backboard, on the sled, then to the bottom of the mountain. Block, anticipating his role, was like a horse straining at the gates, ready to ski Bill down to the helicopter.

"We knew time was…well, the faster the better," Burke says.

Then everyone heard the whir of the helicopter overhead, and their pace became frenzied. Once Charman heard the helicopter, he remembers feeling like he couldn't work fast enough. "We were trying to get him to the ship as fast as possible," he says, "and the ship was 800 vertical feet below us." Burke remembers the experience "moving rapid-time, like one big moment."

The helicopter landed—almost on the course, right past the finish line—seconds before the rescue workers finished securing Bill to the sled. Then Block, according to Charman, "just bombed" down the hill with Bill to reach the ALERT team.

ALERT received the call at 9:55, and the helicopter was in the air by 10:04. Sometimes the rescue helicopter is off responding to another call and not immediately available, often poor weather conditions prevent it from landing. Neither of those scenarios happened that day. The helicopter touched down at the base of Big Mountain at 10:15.

The plan in this type of rescue is to get the victim loaded onto the helicopter immediately, but in this case, Bill's pulse started to slow down outside the helicopter, a sign Charman carefully refers to as "ominous."

Bill was once again minutes from dying. He needed a breathing tube to survive, but the doctors were struggling, unable to see anything with all the blood and tissue filling his mouth. McFadden's attempts to insert a breathing tube the conventional way weren't working. In a final effort, he grabbed a combi-tube and blindly passed it through Bill's esophagus and trachea. Bill's breathing improved instantly and, for the moment, Charman says, "Everybody breathed a sigh of relief." At the scene for a total of 25 minutes, the helicopter took off for Kalispell Regional Medical Center at 10:40.

Looking back, Charman is struck by the luck involved in McFadden's presence on the mountain at that moment. He views it as another in a series of implausible events in Bill's charmed and tragic life. "He has had a life of incredible good fortune and incredible misfortune. The peaks and valleys are incredible. And now…there is the right guy at the right time…." Charman laughs and shakes his head. "It's Bill Johnson, man."

After the helicopter lifted off, Bill's situation was on the minds of nearly everyone on Big Mountain, and most had their doubts about his chances for survival. Selkowitz recalls one of the rescue workers saying, "He's gonna be lucky if he makes it to tomorrow.'"

But perhaps no one voiced these fears quite as succinctly—or as cruelly—as a local medical coordinator. While on the phone with the hospital, he relayed an update on Bill's condition to the ski patrol members gathered in the dispatch cabin by drawing his hand across his neck in a slashing motion and stating, "If he doesn't die, his family will wish he did."

Bill lost his balance on the course that day, but in truth, he had already gotten off balance years before. In a sense, Bill was wrecked long before he crashed.

From his position on the top of the mountain, Frizelle didn't see Bill's crash himself, but he has talked to other people that did, and he has watched the videotape of it. There could be no better analogy to the story of Bill's life than Frizelle recounting the details of his fall:

> "He high-sided that turn, got up too high, higher than he should have been, he went way out of line, so way out of the line he wanted to be on, he was trying to get back where he wanted to be, he tried to come back, he couldn't quite make it, there was no way to recover from it, he had no chance, and then he just went splat head-first."

Bill's friends and family would later recall doctors at the hospital telling them that Bill had anywhere from a 10 to 25 percent chance of survival, but Charman, based on Bill's appearance at the scene and "how he was acting," believed these odds to be slightly better than that. He had to monitor the remainder of the race, and in the afternoon he had to attend a meeting with Big Mountain officials about the accident, but he periodically checked on Bill's condition throughout the day. He went to sleep that night knowing that Bill was still alive.

CHAPTER SIXTEEN

"Quickly, boys, your dad has been in a terrible accident.
We just need to go see your dad."

– GINA JOHNSON, March 22nd, 2001

The bedside vigil was eerily surreal for Gina. A "flashback," she called it. The trach tube, the brain scans—she had lived it all before. It brought back another time, years ago, when she waited by a hospital bed for someone she loved to wake up. That time, like this one, the patient was in a coma for three weeks.

"I was familiar with all the equipment," she says. "I was familiar with all the processes. I was familiar with waiting for the doctors and the reports. It was all very familiar."

But this time, the result was different. When Gina held Ryan's hand in the hospital, he never squeezed back. By the time she left Bill's side in Montana, he had responded to her touch.

When Gina was first told about Bill's accident, in the midst of her grief she recalls hearing that Bill was "25 percent alive," not that he had a 25 percent chance of survival. Whatever the phraseology, her understanding was that Bill was essentially being sustained on life support until his family was able to see him one last time. The U.S. Ski Team had made immediate arrangements to fly Bill's entire family to Whitefish—a generous gesture, certainly, but as Blake Lewis (who drove 14 hours through the night to get to Bill) put it, "never a good sign."

There were not, in fact, so many good signs at first. The Glasgow Coma Scale is used to assess levels of brain injury, with ratings for eye opening, verbal response, and motor movement. A three means there is no brain activity and a 15 is fully cognitive. When Bill arrived at the hospital, his score was a five.

The helicopter flight from Big Mountain to Kalispell Regional Medical Center took eight minutes. En route, Bill suffered bradycardia, a slowing of the heart that prevents enough oxygen from getting to the brain. The helicopter team was directed by Dale Dallman, who later said that he wouldn't have bet money that Bill would have survived the first 12 hours. The ALERT team landed at the hospital at 10:48, just a few minutes shy of an hour after Bill's crash.

When Bill went through the emergency room doors, he had a heart rate, but it was rapidly deteriorating. His brain was also swelling inside his skull. His teeth were clenched and his mouth was so bloated that it wouldn't close. His tongue was flayed open and part of it was pressed tightly against the roof of his mouth. Dr. Keith Lara, the director of the emergency room, describes the rest of Bill's tongue as "sticking out like the Exorcist." Pieces of his teeth had been knocked backward into his throat. He also had a condition called raccoon eyes, caused by having cracked the base of his skull.

The ER became like an anthill as Bill's condition was evaluated. Hospital spokesperson Jim Oliverson says that Lara ran that emergency room like a general running an invasion. Lara had relocated to Montana from Tennessee, joining the hospital in 1979 (or, as Lara says, "like 150 years ago"). He refers to the area as "so outright, knockdown gorgeous I sometimes have to pinch myself."

When Bill entered the hospital, Lara had never seen a worse airway injury in his then 22 years in the ER. The combi-tube Dr. McFadden had inserted on the mountain was providing Bill with a small amount of air, but there was now so much blood and tissue in Bill's mouth that it had clogged his windpipe and entirely filled his left lung with blood. He was barely able to breathe. Once more he was seconds from death, and he again needed an immediate airway. It was impossible to intubate him—to force a tube past what was left of his tongue. Bill needed to have brain surgery the faster the better, but if his airway wasn't repaired that was going to kill him first, before he ever got to an operating room. Lara needed to make a decision, and he needed to make it fast.

It was anesthesiologist Mike Sugarman's first call to the emergency room after moving from a trauma center in New York City. He says that while it was clear that the patient was a skier because of the racing suit, at first no one was aware of Bill's identity, or even his nationality.

When Lara cut off Bill's racing suit, he noticed his Ski to Die tattoo. "Here he was skiing, and he was dead," he says. "That was spooky."

Lara quickly realized who his patient was, and he announced to his staff: "Ladies and gentlemen, we're working on a national treasure and we've got to beat the clock."

Relating the story now, Lara adds, "And that's when I cut his neck." Bill, who was sinking into a deep coma, gasped when Lara stuck his knife into his throat.

The procedure Lara performed was called an emergency cricothyroidotomy. He created a surgical airway below Bill's tongue, fed a wire through that up to his mouth, and then used the wire as a guide to insert a tube.

With Bill's airway again repaired and the blood sucked from his lung, Lara sent Bill for a CT scan to determine the extent of his brain injury.

Later, many people in the ski industry would comment that the rescue personnel on the mountain and the medical staff at the hospital were "so ready" for Bill's accident to happen. If Bill's wreck had happened anywhere else in the world, he almost certainly would have died before he even got to a hospital. And once Bill got to the Kalispell hospital, the advanced technology there, and the level of expertise among the staff, was way out of proportion to a valley of 80,000 people. There is probably not another ski resort in North America that has such a sophisticated facility so close to the mountain.

Dr. Rob Hollis was on duty when Bill came in, doing rounds in the clinic. The fact that Hollis, the hospital's only neurosurgeon, was present in the hospital in the first place, and moreover, was not already involved in another multi-hour brain surgery, was another aspect of that day that absolutely clicked into place. Not only were there incredible, brilliant doctors on staff in this remote mountain town in Montana, but they were also *available* at the moment Bill needed them.

Intending it as a compliment, Bill's brother Wally refers to Hollis as "a trip." Just about everyone else describes him as Doogie Howser. Hollis has a slight build and pretty much dresses like a teenager, even around the hospital—jeans and black utility boots that go a third of the way up his legs ($24 at Wal-Mart, he says). He wears the boots partially tied—with the tongues hanging out and the laces flying all over the place—so that he can kick them off easier. With round, wired-rimmed glasses, a scruffy growth of beard, and dark, almost cartoonishly quizzical eyebrows, Hollis looked about 17 when he operated on Bill. He was actually 34 at the time, nine years out of the University of Illinois medical school. After graduating he moved from Chicago to Montana, which he calls "the last, best place."

Hollis's dark hair sticks straight up in spikes, leading Oliverson to say, not unkindly, that he looks like a snowboarder. When the world press converged on Kalispell to speak to Hollis about Bill, Oliverson approached him and said, "I don't know how to say this, but…."

"It's okay," Hollis said. "I'll keep my hat on."

When Bill first entered the ER, Hollis noted that his pupils were equal. Just as Bill was about to get the CT scan, Hollis pulled Bill's eyelids open and realized that his right pupil had become hugely dilated. He says that the pupil was not even working, meaning that Bill's brain stem—"the center of consciousness, of inner connections"—was being crushed by a tremendous amount of pressure. Hollis refers to the situation as "a full-on emergency, a double critical period." He estimates that without removing the pressure in Bill's brain he would "suffer brain death" in about 30 minutes or so.

In terms of Bill suffering permanent brain damage, Hollis knew before he began the surgery that there was no way to entirely restore Bill's brain function to the way it had been earlier that morning. "The damage was done by the time we got to him," Hollis says. "What we got was what we got."

According to Hollis, after age 40, a body's ability to tolerate the type of head injury Bill suffered goes down dramatically. As with so many aspects of Bill's life, Hollis says that Bill was "right on the brink." At almost 41, Hollis makes it clear that in Bill's case it was "ethically right to be very aggressive" in his treatment.

After the CT scan, Hollis raced Bill straight into the operating room, where for the next three hours he performed an emergency left frontal parietal temporal craniotomy.

Bill had actually suffered three separate types of brain injuries—a hemorrhage on his brain, brain swelling, and shearing damage known as a diffuse anoxal injury. The bleeding in Bill's brain resulted in a subdural hematoma, a collection of blood that clotted and pooled on the left side of Bill's brain, causing pressure to build up there.

It is the shearing injury, however, in which Hollis says Bill's brain rotated and "sloshed back and forth," that produced widespread brain dysfunction and "kept [Bill] in need of care." When Bill's head hit the mountain at something like 70 mph, it resulted in rapid deceleration within his brain. The abrupt stop caused his brain to ricochet within his skull with the type of rotational force more often associated with high-speed car accidents. When a brain—which Hollis says has the consistency of jello in a baggie—swivels like that, it gets torn up, and the faster the deceleration, the more deadly the damage.

The purpose of Bill's surgery was to "evacuate the hematoma"—remove the blood surrounding his brain and ease the swelling by allowing room for his brain to expand. To access Bill's brain, Hollis first had to open his skull. He removed a section of bone roughly the size of a saucer from the left front of Bill's skull, then extricated a blood clot approximately seven inches long from his brain. Hollis left other, smaller clots, too risky to remove, to dissolve on their own. He also controlled the bleeding from two torn veins in Bill's brain.

Often in brain surgeries the surgeon does not reattach the removed section of skull right away—instead freezing it or even sewing it into the fat of the patient's stomach for safekeeping until swelling has reduced to a point that it can be safely put back. In Bill's case, the swelling in his brain improved somewhat during his surgery, so Hollis decided to put the piece of skull back where it belonged. He didn't want to firmly affix it, however, in case of additional swelling later. To give his brain more room to expand if it needed it, Hollis laid a sheet of plastic across Bill's brain and set the skull piece loosely on top of it, then closed Bill's scalp. The plastic sheet remains in Bill's head today.

Jill Zemke, a critical care nurse, said later that even though Bill was "so impressively injured," Hollis wouldn't give up on him. Lara says that Hollis "worked his butt off" saving Bill. Lara had to drive Hollis home that night. So totally focused on Bill that nothing else existed, the brain surgeon had lost his car keys.

Following Bill's brain surgery, Dr. Wilson Higgs was called in to repair Bill's tongue. He meticulously sewed the pieces back together in a separate, 90-minute operation. Higgs, who graduated from the Medical College of Virginia in 1964 and joined the hospital in 1973, says this was the worst tongue injury he'd ever seen. "It was as bad as it could be and still save the tongue," he says. Higgs removed a piece of Bill's tooth that was embedded in his tongue, then stitched several extensive, jagged lacerations. He also carefully sutured a massive gash at the base of Bill's tongue that had nearly detached it from the floor of his mouth. Looking back at the surgery now, Higgs rebuffs compliments about the quality of his work by responding simply, "I'm highly skilled."

In the end, the injury to Bill's tongue caused as much irreversible brain damage as the injury to his head. The blood from Bill's tongue that filled his throat and poured into his left lung prevented his brain from receiving sufficient oxygen in the few minutes it took to transport him from the mountain to the ER. The transfer could not have been smoother or faster—in fact, it was as perfect as a rescue could possibly be—but even so, those precious few minutes when Bill suffered that anoxic brain injury contributed to much of his memory loss and cognition problems. Hollis says that a combination of the two injuries—the airway obstruction and the shearing of his brain – was what caused Bill to lose some of his brain function. Since those two potentially deadly injuries rarely both occur in one patient, it is virtually impossible to determine the relative damage each of them caused.

After the surgeries, Bill was placed on a respirator. He was in a coma and remained in extremely critical condition, but his doctors considered him neurologically stable. Over the next few days especially, lethal risks to Bill included re-hemorrhaging, uncontrolled brain swelling, deep vein thrombosis (a blood clot in the leg), and pneumonia. As Hollis says, "There were several tigers floating about that we had pretty heavy concern for."

Back at Big Mountain, Daron Rahlves won the Kandahar Cup and dedicated his victory to Bill. Later, he says he wanted the win to be in Bill's honor, "Just to send him great thoughts. I thought any positive energy we can give, let's give it right now."

After the race, Paul Mahre and race administrators reviewed film from a local photographer to establish whether Bill's accident was caused by course fault or by what is referred to as pilot error. The official determination was that Bill's crash was not the fault of the course.

Picabo won the women's Kandahar Cup, run later in the day. She came to the hospital afterward to "feel Bill there." Saying that Bill couldn't have hit that spot on the mountain "any more right on," Picabo describes his accident as, "So meant to be. All destiny."

"Ski to Die is real eerie," she says. "I never used that as a motto. My mom always felt that's not a healthy one."

Handwritten notes supporting Bill were posted all around Big Mountain resort, with messages such as, "Our thoughts are with you, Bill."

"It shook everybody up on the mountain, big time," Daron says. "We were all just pulling for him. Bill Egan brought everyone together for a full-on football huddle and we said a prayer for him."

Daron was the one who first told Creel what had happened. As soon as Bill left the starting gate, Creel packed up and skied to the parking lot with about 200 pounds of extra equipment on his shoulders. He was waiting, as he had told Bill he would, by Bill's truck.

Creel saw Daron in the parking lot and mentioned that he was waiting for Bill but Bill wasn't showing up. Creel figured he must be hanging out in the finish area. He heard the helicopter, but he thought the crash involved the racer after Bill.

When Daron filled him in, Creel dropped the extra skis and raced to the landing zone. The doctors were working on Bill outside the helicopter at the time. A fireman for almost twenty years at that point, Creel was obviously an experienced rescue worker himself. He knew what he was looking at, and he assessed Bill's injuries clinically, as a paramedic.

As Creel puts it: "It's just like muffins—when you sell them, you get an idea when they're done."

He noted the oxygen stats and looked in Bill's eyes. Looking back now, Creel almost detaches himself from the situation when he describes it, viewing Bill as just another accident victim. He talks about the "golden hour" crucial to saving someone with a severe head injury, saying things like, "He maintained an oxygen saturation of 96. Below 90 you don't really have a viable patient."

Years after the fact, Creel talks tough about the crash as well, referring to the comeback as "positive," the accident "a bump in the road." Around the fire station he calls his friend "Hard-to-Kill Bill."

"We scared a lot of people, had a lot of fun," Creel says. "110 percent. Flat out go. Risking it all."

The night of Bill's accident, however, Creel let his true feelings show. He called his assistant chief back in Oregon and cried on the phone. "Shit, we fell," he said. "Billy hit his head. I think he'll be all right. This sucks."

Meanwhile, all around the country, phones were ringing with the news of Bill's accident. Everyone was essentially told what the doctors feared—that Bill might not make it through the night. Jo Jo, who heard about the crash on the radio in Chicago, phoned Sam Collins, then hopped on a plane. Sam, who was in Idaho at the time, commandeered a pizza delivery truck and drove immediately to Whitefish. Barry and Mark flew out from Tahoe. Tim Patterson came from Colorado.

Parke Frizelle got a call as well, at a bar in Whitefish. Andy Anderson phoned Frizelle to tell him Bill had died, and reminded Frizelle that he was the last person to talk to Bill. Anderson then called Frizelle back to let him know that Bill was holding on.

Word traveled quickly to Mt. Hood. Dave Ligatich, who knew Bill as a child, had reconnected with him just before his comeback. They had gotten together in a restaurant in Oregon a few months before, and Dave's son Justin, about ten at the time, kept coming over to the table bothering his dad for quarters to play games. Finally, Bill said, "You are so ugly. If I give you 25 cents will you leave the table?"

Justin was in awe of Bill from that moment on. The day of his accident, the boy actually got down on his knees and prayed for Bill. He stayed up way past his bedtime watching the news reports, then got up early to ask his dad if Bill had woken up yet. Not necessarily grasping the life and death aspect of the situation, Justin was mostly concerned about whether Bill would be able to ski again. "If he can walk, he can ski," Dave told him.

Gina was out when Bill's step-mom Mary called to tell her the news. When she got home, she picked up the phone message that Bill had been in a ski accident. While waiting for her boys to get back from baseball practice, Gina called Mary back and asked when she should bring the boys to see Bill.

"Don't wait," Mary said. "Come now."

Gina, along with her sons and her sister Rochelle, flew from Sonoma to southern California where they met up with Mary. From there they all flew to Montana together, arranged and paid for by the Ski Team.

When they arrived, Nick and Tyler were so eager to see Bill that they were jumping and running toward the hospital. As a sign of how desperate the situation was, Gina sent the boys—ages eight and six at the time—into the intensive care unit to say good-bye to their dad.

Bill was still attached to a respirator. There was a thick white collar around his neck and tubes—white and blue—running all over his head and body. His head was shaved and heavily wrapped in white gauze to hide the gruesome seven-inch scar on the left side of it. His head was swollen, as Jo Jo says, to the size of a basketball. There were constant squeaks and beeps from the assorted monitors and gages in the room.

"I don't think they got it," Gina says, "until they walked into that room and saw him. I never would have put them through that, let them see him like that, if I thought he was going to make it."

Mary claims that she was glad Bill's dad wasn't alive at the time because it would have broken his heart to see Bill in that condition. Referring to Bill now, after his recovery, Mary says nearly the same thing: "It would have been hard for his father to see him this way."

Although Gina had been told to prepare herself for Bill's death, she says that every minute they were there, Bill began to get a little better. There was more of a positive note in every test that was done. She felt the doctors were shocked by how much better he was doing, and as a result, she was hopeful.

"The boys had to walk in and see their dad, which was very bad," she says. "But by the time they left, they knew Daddy was getting better." While in Montana, the boys crayoned get-well drawings for their dad. They were plastered on the wall near him, a stark contrast to all the high-tech medical machinery.

The Ski Team also flew DB and Kathryn in from Portland and Wally from Seattle. When they first arrived at the hospital, there were a lot of reporters congregating in the hallway outside Bill's room. Before going in to see Bill, DB caught sight of the press, and several reporters and rescue personnel claim they heard her say "promotional opportunity." She then stopped to give an impromptu press conference outside Bill's hospital room. After the interviews concluded, she went inside to see her son.

Rochelle thought DB seemed cold when she saw her in Montana. "She never worked to make anybody like her, didn't care what anyone thought of her," Rochelle says. "Bill seems to have inherited that evil characteristic from her."

Bill's accident was on a Thursday. Preferring to leave the bedside waiting to Gina and Bill's friends, DB went back to Oregon after that first weekend. She recognized that Bill friends were talking and reading to him, but she says she was "not good at that stuff" and "uncomfortable doing those things." Unconvinced that Bill could hear her anyway, DB returned home and left the bedside duties, as she says, "to others."

Bill's friends stayed with him and talked to him for hours. They told him stories of their adventures together. They played music for him—Led Zeppelin, Stevie Ray Vaughn, Bob Marley. Gina gave him two body massages a day. Bill's old friend Tom Mahoney, who had witnessed the crash, held Bill's hand in the hospital every day for three weeks.

Both Jo Jo and Tim feel that Bill tried to respond to them at different points when they were in with him. Sometimes Bill made small movements with his arms and legs, almost like a newborn baby. Jo Jo recalls feeling that after all the "demons he had been haunted by," Bill finally looked at peace.

Bill's friends also read him his fan mail. On the day of his accident, Kalispell Regional Medical Center began to receive e-mails addressed to Bill. During the three weeks he was in a coma, and continuing for the next several months, Bill received e-mails (also to a website set up for him by the U.S. Ski Team) by the thousands, as well as faxes, cards, letters, flowers, plants, checks, CDs, and golf balls.

The letters were from skiers and non-skiers alike, from all over the world, some written in giant crayoned scrawl, some in the careful, spindly handwriting of the very old. Bill received mail from celebrities, prisoners, third-grade classes, longtime fans, and people who heard of him for the first time after his accident. Within one twenty-minute period, the hospital fielded calls from fans as diverse as Robbie Knieval and Ethel Kennedy.

Some people offered to donate blood. Others sent prayers, religious medals, and blessed rose petals. Many enclosed pictures of their babies. Bill received birthday cards, requests for autographs (some with the February 27th, 1984, *Sports Illustrated* enclosed), and offers to be his girlfriend.

The messages were always phrased in the present tense—"You *are* one hell of a champion," not "you were." Most people added that they hoped to see Bill on the slopes again one day. One e-mail stated, "The mountains are calling you back." Another one, from Juno, Alaska, said, "May the ski gods spare you to be returned to us."

Various people that connected with Bill during a single, chance encounter wrote to tell him what it meant to them. An overwhelming number of letters began, "You may not remember me but…." And it is clear that Bill made an impression on just about everyone he shared a chairlift with in the past 25 years.

There were letters from people who remember getting Bill's autograph in the '80s, including one from a man named Blake who kept, for 20 years, a ski poster Bill signed, "To Blake, no brakes, catch me if you can."

There was a letter from a mother recalling that Bill had loaned her youngest son skis at a recent race. There was an e-mail from a man who bought Bill's Yamaha Paramount 222 "boards" (with "Lefty" and "Righty" written between the front and back bindings) from the guy Bill sold them to in exchange for transportation home at that '82 race in Whistler.

There were letters calling Bill an American hero.

Several doctors sent articles about electrical stimulation for comas, and many fans mailed him information about new treatments for brain injuries. People who were in—or knew someone in—similar circumstances offered advice, shared stories, and sometimes, recounted terrible tragedies. One mother wrote of the death of her son in a ski accident. People at stressful times in their own lives reached out to Bill, empathizing with his suffering and relating their hopes for better days ahead for themselves and for him.

He received a letter from a man saying he "lived and died" waiting for the weather to clear in 1984 so Bill could run his race, and one from a man admitting that he cried when the national anthem was played.

Many people wanted to share their memories of the Olympic victory: *"I still scream No way!!! Incredible!! All right!!!! in my head when I picture the end of the Olympic downhill run."* –**Kenai, Alaska**

"Your gold medal will live in my mind forever – **Sugarloaf, Maine**

Many thanked him for the "exciting memories," for "everything you have done for American skiing," for "representing what is best in our country:" *"As one who followed your victory in 1984, I want you to know how proud you made us all feel."* – **Mount Holly, New Jersey**

He received letters from people who took up skiing in 1984 after watching him, and letters from people who began skiing in 2001, some at advanced ages, also after watching him. Some fans said Bill inspired them to ski, and some referred to his influence as greater than that: *"You were an inspiration to millions of Americans and you can be again."*– **e-mail sent on March 28th, 2001**

Several fans sent letters framing his medical recovery in the context of ski racing: *"Just keep gliding and you'll do it."* – **Boulder, Colorado**

"Everyone wants you to win this one. Point 'em down!" – **e-mail sent on March 29th, 2001**

He also received many letters from people who did not miss the parallels between his win in Sarajevo and his current fight to survive: *"If anyone can, you can."* – **San Diego, California**

Many of the letters showed that Bill did some impressive marketing for Atomic: *"The first pair of skis I owned were Atomics because those are what Bill skied on."* – **e-mail sent March 24th, 2001**

"I still remember buying a pair of "red sleds" right after your gold in 1984 because they looked so cool." – **Sugarloaf, Maine**

Some of the letters, mainly from young ski racers—containing expressions like "Crashing sucks!" and referring to Bill's accident as "a face plant," "a nasty-looking wreck," or "one of the most gnarly things"—were clearly heartfelt, if a bit irreverent: *"You are the original DH bad boy of the USA, you have been a total icon in the sport of ski racing."* – **Seattle, Washington**

"If the snow is good and the course is ready, Bill's going down it balls out. We wouldn't have it any other way. And so it is. Get better, dude." – **Burlington, Vermont**

Mixed in with the extreme messages sent from hardcore skiers, there was a note, handwritten on a sheet of stationery decorated with a picture of a covered bridge. It is dated April 12th, 2001, from a couple in Portland, Oregon, and it contains perhaps the most moving—and prescient—wish of all: *"We think of you as a winner, as someone who ignores the odds and goes on to win. That leads us to believe you will win this battle. Our hope is that you will eventually be able to enjoy recreational skiing with your children."*

And no hope for Bill's future was more concisely conveyed than in a fax from Steamboat Springs, Colorado, sent to Bill's hospital room on March 27th, 2001, that said simply: "Ski to Live."

Bill turned 41 while he was in the coma. Although he was obviously unaware of it, on March 30th Gina brought him a cake with candles and white and blue icing to celebrate. She and some of Bill's friends—Barry, Mark, and Tom—sang "Happy Birthday" to him. For a birthday present, Tyler gave his dad a hat to cover the scar on his head.

After a week, Rochelle took Nick and Tyler back to California so Gina could stay with Bill for another week. Before they left, Bill's sons brought him little stuffed bears. Tyler, who was turning seven a few days later and realized that his dad wouldn't be there with him, told him to be sure to make it to his next birthday.

"I couldn't leave," Gina says. "I said, 'I can't leave him, I'm not leaving.' I stayed. I just sat by Bill's side and I just talked with him. I told him you can't [die], your boys need you, we need you, you have to stay strong."

According to Barry, Mark, and Tom, in the hospital Gina appeared to be seriously thinking of reconciling with Bill. "She told him, 'I'm never gonna leave you, I'm gonna take care of you, help you through it,'" Tom says. "Then she said to us, 'But he better not come back the way he was.'"

Looking back now, she says, "I always held that fairy tale that Bill was going to wake up and be better and things were going to work out, he was going to start doing this, this was going to turn around. I always hoped it would be that way because I knew he could do it. He had it all once, he really did. He could do it [again] if he made the right choices. He just chose not to. I don't know why. That's the self-destructiveness that I don't understand."

Rochelle thinks Gina felt a lot of guilt, a lot of what-ifs, in connection with Bill's accident, and it definitely brought back feelings about Ryan for her. Gina told her sister that if she were still with Bill he wouldn't have gone out and gotten hurt. According to Rochelle, Gina felt like now Bill finally needed her.

"It made her question where her responsibility to her ex-husband lay," Rochelle says. "What other people would think of her and what she would think of herself. [She wondered] if she should quit the life she was building and take care of him. It was hard for her to know she was going to say 'no' to that."

Gina didn't leave Montana until Jimmy arrived from Oregon. Before she went home, Dr. Hollis assured her that the boys would have a relationship with their father. "But he said 'He won't be the same as he was,'" Gina says. "He straight-out said that." After Gina left, she called the hospital and had people hold the phone to Bill's ear while she talked to him.

From Oregon, DB had been e-mailing progress reports on Bill to friends and family based on information she received from people at the hospital. DB signed her e-mails, as she still does in matters pertaining to Bill, "Bill's MOM," all in capital letters.

At the end of March, she wrote: "Eyes open more, but not there."

As the weeks went on, Bill followed what was considered a normal progression of neurological improvement. He was still comatose, but he began to become agitated in bed. He grimaced and flinched in response to pain. He raised his eyebrows when his name was called. His eyes, although unfocused, did open occasionally. Hollis called it the process of Bill's brain repairing itself.

Throughout the three weeks Bill was at Kalispell Regional Medical Center, he was monitored relentlessly. Toward the end of his stay, he was given rudimentary physical therapy—positioned in a reclining chair and allowed to "dangle." Two physical therapists stood Bill up a couple times—he was slumped over and drooling, but he made an attempt to raise his head. By the time he was discharged and transferred to the hospital in Portland, a total of 21 physicians had signed off on Bill's chart.

Updates on Bill's condition were also provided on the Ski Team website, the sincerity of which was offset a bit by an article about Bill's life posted on the site on March 28, 2001, entitled "Johnson: Unlikely Hero."

The official word from the Ski Team about Bill's accident, as delivered by spokesperson Tom Kelly, was a bit defensive, and consisted mostly of platitudes: "The netting did its job but he did have a significant impact with the snow. He is a very capable downhiller. He had every right and ability to be on that downhill course."

Looking back now, Kelly discusses the specific emergency plans in place for that race and the confluence of events that led to Bill's survival. "He had no right to live through that," Kelly says. "No way he should have. Knowing where the problem spots [on the mountain] might be, the position of the doctors on the hill, a good [enough] day to get the helicopter in there, that neurosurgeon just happening to be there that day…. But mostly, it was just the planets lining up."

Like many people in the ski world, Kelly says that Bill's crash could have happened to anybody. As Daron Rahlves says, "We go down fast." Even so, most people see Bill's fall as something other than a freak accident.

"He pulled a 1988 move on 2001 skis," Jo Jo says.

Doug Lewis makes essentially the same comment, saying that Bill was trying to feather his skis at the time he lost control, and that old technique caused him to fall the way that he did.

"The natural touch that had worked for him [in the past] at any given moment was what crushed him in the end," Mike Brown says.

Tim Patterson says simply, "He didn't know how to ride the new skis. The thing bit and just catapulted him."

Bill Egan, who last saw Bill in the hospital in Montana, feels Bill's reaction time was as much of an issue as the equipment, saying, "A younger, quicker racer might not have had that problem."

Debbie Armstrong strongly feels that Bill's comeback was reckless, almost suicidally so. "Yes, it can happen to anybody, tragic things happen," she says. "But he was just starting his comeback—in prior races, the spotlight wasn't on him, the TV wasn't there. He had to step it up, perform. He couldn't do it. His first shot and he just about killed himself. It could have happened to anybody, but it hasn't."

Debbie's point is not that ski racing is not dangerous. No question it is a sport in which tragic things happen. The very day after Bill's accident, Canadian ski legend Dave Irwin, 46 at the time, suffered critical head injuries when he fell during a training run for an extreme skiing competition at the Sunshine Village resort, near Banff, Alberta. Irwin was in a coma on life-support at the same time as Bill. He has since recovered and is now living with a brain trauma.

Sometimes racers aren't so fortunate. In 2004 alone, two young American racers died on the slopes. Shelley Glover, a member of the U.S. Ski Team development squad, died on May 8th, 2004 at age 17, three days after suffering a major head injury in a training crash at Mt. Bachelor.

Ashley Stamp, who had won a Junior Olympic giant slalom title, died in December of 2004 as a result of a collision with a snowmobile while she was warming up before a race in Vail, Colorado. She was 13 years old.

Due to a twist of timing, Debbie Armstrong was one of the first people to come to the hospital after Bill's crash. She and Billy Kidd heard about Bill's accident in the airport after flying into Whitefish for a Return of the Champions event. Both Debbie and Billy (the silver medalist in the slalom in '64) have parlayed their experiences as Olympic medalists into positions as ski ambassadors—Debbie at Taos Ski Valley resort in New Mexico, and Billy, who still wears his infamous cowboy hat, at Steamboat Springs in Colorado. Phil Mahre, the other gold medalist in ski racing from 1984 (in addition to Debbie and Bill), retired that year and has worked in the ski industry ever since. In addition to corporate skiing/speaking events, Phil and his brother Steve run the Mahre Training Center in Deer Valley, Utah, the motto of which is, "To ski your best, learn from the best."

Debbie and Billy heard the news while they were getting their baggage. Despite how she had felt about Bill in the past, Debbie asked their shuttle driver to immediately take them to the hospital. "We were Bill's teammates," Debbie says. "I have a shared history with him. I respect the shared history." Leaving the shuttle full of their family and friends, they went into the hospital where they were briefed on Bill's condition.

Debbie recalls the discussion with the "hospital people" as very graphic, full of details like Bill's tongue exploding and his eyes popping out of his head, "horrifying things that I wouldn't wish on anyone." When she was told that the doctors did not expect Bill to pull through, Debbie says, "my tears were there."

Doug Lewis was also in town for the celebrity event. When he got off the bus at Big Mountain, someone initially told him Bill was dead. He found out shortly afterward that Bill had been revived, and he headed to the hospital with his wife Kelley.

"Our lives are tied together for some strange reason," Doug says. When he got back to Vermont, Doug found some old photos of Bill (with Doug on the Ski Team and also on the King of the Mountain tour) and mailed them to the hospital, where they were pinned up on the wall of Bill's room next to pictures of Nick and Tyler.

Asked the reason that he went to the hospital and sent the photos given his relationship with Bill, Doug makes nearly the same comment as Debbie: "We were teammates. It was the right thing to do."

Even while Bill's former teammates were supporting him, Doug says there was a fair amount of talk around the mountain about whether Bill would come out of the coma as the same person or not. The prevailing hope was, Doug says, "Maybe he'll come out nice."

These days Doug has less hair than he did in his Ski Team days, but he still has the same baby face. He lives in a gorgeous, rustic Vermont farm-house with views of Sugarbush resort. He and Kelley, who Doug met in Chile while she was ski racing, joke that they can check the weather conditions on the mountain by looking out their window. They share their home with a golden retriever named Maddy and a gray cat named Peanut. Doug's life is still heavily involved with skiing—he works as the ski ambassador and director of racing at Sugarbush, runs kids camps, participates in corporate speaking/ski events, and hosts two television ski shows with Kelley (one is Sugarbush Live, the other plays in ski resorts nationwide). He seems to know how lucky he is, how good he has it.

Bill's friend from Whitefish, Mike Maronick, came to the hospital as soon as he could. He had been out of town the day of the race, but he happened to catch a story about Bill's accident on a TV screen and immediately headed home. He went in to see Bill at about eight the morning after his crash. Creel was already there. After a little while, Creel turned to Mike and said, "There's nothing we can do here. Let's go finish his run."

Mike and Creel went up to the top of the downhill course, tucked, and skied down, following the turns Bill had made. They crossed the finish line together. "It was kind of a spiritual moment," Mike says.

There was a parade of past ski champions going through town that day, and Mike recalls the contrast as jarring. "There was a huge void," Mike says. "Bill was in a coma and there's a parade going on."

For the first few days after his accident, no one could find Bill's gold medal. Mike knew it had to be close. "Bill brought that thing everywhere," he says. Three days after his crash, Mike checked Bill's pick-up. There was about $5,000 worth of skis in the back of the truck bed with just a cover thrown over them. The car doors were all unlocked.

When Mike reached underneath the front seat, he found an old black goggle bag with Bill's medal inside. He gave it to Creel, who took it to the hospital and put it in Bill's hand. According to Creel, Bill moved his fingers around it.

CHAPTER SEVENTEEN

"There is no happy ending, and there never will be."
– KATHRYN PUNDT, May 2005

Bill lives on his own now, in a town called, fittingly enough, Zigzag, near Mt. Hood in Oregon, in a double-wide trailer where extreme skier Scotty Graham used to live. After Graham died in a car accident in 1995, his parents were unsure of what to do with the place, and Creel put them together with Bill. Bill rented it for a while, then bought it for $22,000.

The trailer is rather dark and very cluttered, with garbage cans strewn about for Bill to spit tobacco into. The huge fish tank Bill bought in 2004, with three little fish in it—two green and one orange—is against the front wall. The main room, one of the spare bedrooms, and part of the garage are all adorned with Bill's medals, trophies, and memorabilia, courtesy of his son Nick, who decorated his dad's place while spending five weeks of the summer with him in 2004 (Tyler visited that summer for a separate five- week span).

Bill doesn't clean himself or his place much—he and his trailer are similarly disheveled. He tends to put the same clothes on for a few days in a row. He almost always wears a jacket, even inside, and a baseball cap.

The fire station where Creel works is within a mile of Bill's place. DB's house in Gresham, which Bill moved out of in March of 2004, is about half an hour away.

Bill spends his time skiing, visiting friends. He sees Creel frequently, and also Petr Kakes, who once brought Bill exotic fish food when Bill called him to say that his fish would eat each other without it and he had no money to buy his own. "Billy is a total handful, always was," Creel says.

He also golfs, now at a 16 handicap, down from a 24 just after his crash. He still plays around with crossword puzzles, but he can no longer complete them.

"He is happy on the surface," Blake says, "but it's not a very deep crest."

Bill e-mails and calls his friends excessively, often at 4:30 in the morning to tell them he can't sleep. Erik Steinberg says that Bill just hits numbers on his speed dial and starts talking to whoever answers. During short bursts of conversation Bill sounds great—coherent, rational—but if he stays on the phone too long, he will frequently wander off on tangents or stop making sense entirely.

"It's hard to talk to him," Sam Collins says. "It's the same day for him every day."

Bill has upgraded his trailer, even built an addition on it. His small garden has tomatoes—three different sizes, he points out—as well as fruit and other vegetables, and he tends to that. He also sews racing bibs for his mom, recently receiving a raise from 50 to 60 cents a bib. When she has a big order, Bill has sewn as many as 600 bibs in a week. "He's just doing what he can the best way he knows how," DB says.

Ironically, Bill is more independent since his accident than he ever has been. At a time when he needs a structured environment, he is living by himself for the first time in his life. He lives in a fairly rural, isolated location, and he is alone much of the time.

"Think how much idle time he has," Andy Luhn says. "It's not good to be so isolated. He's still scrapping, still figuring it out."

Bill is drinking enough that his friends are concerned about the issue. During his visit to Tahoe last summer, Barry and Mark saw him "hittin' the hard stuff" first thing in the morning. Barry thinks there is probably more of Bill left inside, but that it is masked by alcohol. Kathryn recalls a morning when Bill literally searched in all of her cabinets until he found whiskey to put in his coffee.

Bill also can't seem to stop himself from spending, especially online. He has purchased nearly a thousand dollars of vitamins in one order, "free" trips he will never take, a crystal Santa and Mrs. Claus set that he had to have. He plays cards online as well, at various gambling sites.

"Some moms are good moms, some moms are bad moms," Tom Mahoney says. "I don't think his mom really has the motherly instinct that Billy needs. Now he's up at Zigzag without any supervision or friend to be with." DB realizes that Bill is lonely—"He makes my heart sad," she says—but she's not sure what type of living situation would be better.

Dr. Hoeflich has always maintained that Bill needs a supervised, structured environment. "I worry about judgment in day-to-day living," she says. "What he will do in an emergency, a fire, if a solicitor comes to the door…." Creel is all for Bill living in some sort of group home situation, but DB maintains that that isn't Bill, that he would hate it.

As Bill's legal guardian, DB remains responsible for him and manages his money. "He needs me and I need him," she says. Bill's high school teacher Peggy Hart, retired now and living in Colorado, explains the situation this way: "I don't know how it used to work—she took as much advantage of Bill's medal as she could. But I'm glad she's there for him now."

It's a fine line between sheltering Bill from harm and holding on too tight. "She is definitely controlling at the moment," Wally says. "Not then [childhood years], but she is now. She tells people what to do. She is who she is. I'm not approving of a lot of things that she says and does, controlling and manipulating Bill."

Bill lives now with constant frustration. His famous ability to concentrate, so strong in him in the past, is gone. Sometimes he will e-mail people to tell them he has their e-mail address but can't remember who they are. He continues to suffer enormous gaps of memory loss, and he is matter-of-fact about what he can and cannot recall --"I can't remember most of the '90s, so you're on your own." Then later, "I don't remember the '90s at all. Did they happen? I have some pictures of them here." As a way of explaining why the 1990s are lost, Bill will often ask people—frequently strangers—to feel the indentation in his head.

Surprisingly easygoing about his failure to remember names, even of people he has recently met, Bill does get upset by his inability to recall things many people wouldn't know in the first place, like the capital of Bolivia or which countries border the ocean in South America. He will immediately stop what he is doing until he has found a map or otherwise figured out what he has forgotten.

Bill is heavier than in his competitive days, with a bit of a paunch. He doesn't regularly work out, but he does have spurts of physical exertion. Tim Windell, a former world-class snowboarder, stopped by for a bike ride recently, and Bill challenged him to follow him on a vertical bike trail that Tim had never before attempted. Bill still favors his right side slightly but he is not aware that he does.

He briefly dated a girl named Adrienne, who was born with a brain injury, but he is currently unattached. DB says Bill hasn't had any real relationships since his accident, "not even close." Last year Bill told Mark, "Only ugly girls want me now."

Bill and Gina remain close. She lives with the boys in an attractive, well-kept townhouse in the midst of California wine country and works as a registered dental assistant. She remains as stunning as ever, and looks close to a decade younger than 40. She says that she wishes she could call Bill and really talk to him, ask him things about the boys, get help with decisions—but his brain trauma limits how helpful he can be. She tries to laugh it off by saying that she couldn't talk to him before the accident, either, so things haven't changed so much.

Gina obviously still cares deeply about Bill. When looking through old pictures of him, she refers to him as "my Bill." For a while she contemplated the idea of living with him again so they could both parent the boys, but she knows now that it would never work. "He's a 45-year-old child," she says. "He needs to be taken care of. He put himself in this place. I had to come to the conclusion that it's not my responsibility. I don't know whose responsibility it is."

There are also, of course, the reasons Gina and Bill broke up in the first place. "In the past, he put me through hell and the kids through hell," she says. "I told him, 'You don't remember but I do.'"

While Gina realizes that she can't be with him, she remains haunted by what might have been. While talking about friends in Tahoe—their beautiful house, their happy family—she breaks down in tears.

"That should have been me and Bill," she says. "That should have been us."

Bill seems to have accepted the idea that he and Gina will not get back together, but he still talks about it sometimes. His future plans change daily, but one of his recent ones involves building a truck stop/rest area near his place with an orthodontist's office attached so Gina would have a place to work.

Last Christmas, Bill bought remote-control cars for each of his sons, and also one for Gina. Tyler came up to Oregon for a visit the week before Christmas. Nick was supposed to visit for a few days after the holiday, but he didn't want to come. "Nicholas is not very happy about his dad's decision to ski race again, and he is angry about his accident," Gina says. "He thinks he made a poor choice."

The visitation situation has not been sorted out. Bill has recently asked Gina for custody of Tyler, "for all the things he needs from me, especially a mountain to ski on." The boys love their dad, and they defend him to other people, but they also feel an obligation to protect him, even to parent him.

The last time Tyler visited, Bill asked him if he wanted a steak dinner and then handed him the steak. Tyler, age 10 at the time, did not know how to cook a steak. Gina no longer wants the boys to visit Bill unsupervised, feeling that he is not capable of taking care of them by himself. She definitely, however, wants the boys to see their dad, to have a relationship with him.

Gina recently asked DB if the boys could be included in one of Bill's speaking engagements or special events. Explaining that they have rarely seen their dad in the spotlight, Gina told her that having Nick and Tyler see Bill in a positive role might go a long way toward helping them sort through their feelings toward him. DB turned her down. Missing Gina's point, DB suggested that perhaps when the boys are old enough to care for their father, they could accompany him as his support person.

DB says that she is not opposed to college funds for the boys, although she has not set any up yet. She is clear about what she does not want to do with any of Bill's income: "We don't want to support Gina. She just can't not spend her money."

Bill receives $1495 a month from Social Security, with $60 already taken out for Medicare. He lives on that, the money he makes sewing bibs for his mom, various appearance fees (often $5,000) for charity events, donations, and awards (in one case, $40,000 at a reunion of champions in Wengen).

The only child support Gina receives—or has ever received—is the $800 a month that Social Security has provided for the boys since Bill's accident. Kathryn recently sent Gina two big boxes of clothes that she bought for Nick and Tyler at a Nike outlet. "Gina should have gotten a bunch of the money Bill received from donations," Kathryn says. "In my opinion, Mom should have paid that as if it was a bill due. She is the conservator and has access to all funds. She has a responsibility to pay it."

Even though they were divorced, Gina was still responsible for sharing many of Bill's debts after his accident (she wasn't able, for example, to get her name off the RV when it was repossessed), and she came to DB for help. DB offered to pay Gina off—erase $100,000 in back child support and eliminate all future obligations—for $6,000. Gina rejected the offer. DB still can't understand why.

Gina was ultimately forced to declare bankruptcy. (Due to the additional income he receives, Bill himself has never filed for bankruptcy.) She is now suing Bill for child support, seeking a portion of the money he receives for appearance fees and donations. She does not think that Bill is the one holding money back from his sons. "It's his mom," she says. "It always has been."

DB explains her opposition to Gina's suit for child support by saying, "We did without. We did without, big time. I never asked anyone for a penny. I made my bed. I think this is appalling. I don't get it."

Bill seems largely immune to the financial chaos swirling around him. On a first impression, most people tend to believe that the accident has somehow made him nicer, kinder, even sweet. Newspaper articles mention that the crash slapped the badness out of Bill's bad-boy personality. That was a valid assessment closer in time to the accident, and superficially, it is still true now. Bill does, for example, frequently thank people these days. But those close to Bill know better. As Mark says, "The asshole portion of his brain was untouched."

"He's the same," Jo Jo says. "He still remembers how to be a jerk. He's still fighting for everything. He's so intense—small doses are recommended."

Bill's friends agree that his outlook remains unchanged. "He still sees things Bill's way," Blake says. "He's not able to balance it out."

Bill never had good impulse control prior to damaging his brain— now, that characteristic is amplified. He occasionally has volatile, irrational outbursts, much like a toddler's temper tantrums. Even Andy Luhn admits that he has a shorter temper now. Dr. Lovell says that with brain trauma, there is a "lack of dampening of propensities," meaning that the injury "makes worse what is already there."

Tom Mahoney stresses that Bill is "exactly the same but a little more pissed off, more violent, more aggressive." While Tom seems unconcerned about this in terms of the friendship, he is not unaware of the potential danger connected to the unpredictability of Bill's anger. When playing pool with Tom recently—another skill that Bill has retained post-accident—Bill told

Tom how to make a particular shot. Tom missed it. "I told you to do it this way," Bill screamed, then grabbed the cue ball and threw it at Tom, hitting him in the head.

Wally says that much of Bill's behavior now is similar to his actions in the past. "Bill before didn't shave, shower, use deodorant," he says. "But before he knew he needed to and now he needs to be told." Whether he is reminded or not, Bill's hygiene can be a little sporadic these days. One time Wally called Bill and asked about the background noise on the line. "I just spat," Bill says. "I was brushing my teeth." During another phone call with Wally, Bill blow-dried his hair during the conversation.

"It's like something broke inside, and something is not working right," Mark Schelde, who worked with Bill on the Jeep series, says. "But that spirit is there, whether he knows it or not."

And there are glimpses of Brash Billy still.

Perhaps Sam Collins sums it up best when he says, "Billy is still the same person with the same attitude. He's still there. And he's still in the same boat. Before the accident he was still looking for something to hang onto, and that's where he is now."

Although he bought a new truck, Bill still has his 1984 pickup—his first present to himself after he won the Olympics. It is in and out of the repair shop, and Bill himself is constantly tinkering with it, but he can't let it go.

Even though Bill's recent arrest did not result from, or involve, any type of moving violation, the court nonetheless released Bill on bail on the condition that he not drive. Bill, always the rule-breaker, continues to drive. And DB, always Bill's enabler, continues to let him. Bill said he wanted to work on his truck, so DB delivered his pickup to him with the keys and a full tank of gas.

Kathryn lives nearby in Portland and works as a paralegal at a law firm. She is concerned about Bill's driving and other safety issues, such as Bill building campfires in his backyard with gasoline. "We are just waiting for the accident to happen," she says.

"He was just such a bright light," Erik Pearson, Bill's high school class-mate, says. "But he was someone you wouldn't expect to live very long." Mary says that Bill himself never thought he would live to be an old person. Bill often tells Kathryn that he should have died on that mountain, that he's angry he's alive.

"If he could have made a decision between living and dying [in Montana]," Mary says, "he would have chosen to die."

Or maybe, Bill was right about that old beater helmet he insisted on wearing—perhaps it was lucky after all, and the luck it brought didn't have anything to do with winning a race.

In a way Bill has come full circle, back to his roots. Phil Mahre—who believes that much can be learned from Bill's mistakes—feels the situation is made more tragic because the accident never should have happened, that Bill never should have been in that race in the first place. Tommy Moe, the only other American gold medalist in the downhill, says Bill's life of lost opportunities has been a wake-up call for him. "Bill kinda showed me that there's a way to win a gold medal and do it right, and there's a way to win a gold medal and do it wrong," Tommy says.

"Bill is back to where he started, really," Phil says. "He lost everything. Disaster to greatness back to disaster."

Rags to riches, then down again. "Some people would look at it like poetic justice," Mike Brown says. "I just call it a tragedy."

Bill, looking back over his own life, simply says, "Well, it's a great story."

Bill has been called many things in the press over the years. An unrepentant speed demon. A redoubtable loudmouth and former juvenile delinquent. A brash, recalcitrant 23-year-old. A one-race wonder. A complicated athlete. A street-smart kid with more intelligence than God should have given him. A celebrity bad boy. An American hero. One reporter called him "too brash to love."

Through it all, the one constant has been his gold medal—the quest for it, the 1:45.59 it took him to win it, and the aftermath of living with it.

The winter of 1984 was Bill's season. By winning three World Cup races as well as the Olympics, he established himself as one of the greatest downhillers the sport has ever seen. But for Bill, it's always only been about the gold medal. His voice mail still says, "This is Bill Johnson, number one." He wants to put the winning time of his Olympic run on his license plate.

When he is at home, the medal is off by itself, in its original box on the table in his kitchen. When asked why he has it in there, not on the shelves with the other ones, he says, "It doesn't look like the other ones."

You could say it took less than two minutes for Bill to win the medal, or you could say it took a lifetime. It is, perhaps, the same difference in perspective that leads someone to think that he took all he could get from his sport and someone else to think that he gave so much to it. There are people who wonder when Bill will start giving back to skiing and others who believe that skiing owes something to Bill. No one sees it from both angles.

When he leaves the house, he takes the medal with him, just as he did during his comeback. He still brings it out to show people, the same as he did prior to his accident. Mostly he shows it to strangers who want to see it—kids, younger racers—but, sometimes, just like before he hurt himself, he takes it out to brandish it.

He brought it out recently, angrily flashed it at a policeman in connection with his latest arrest. "I bet you don't have one of these," he told him. The crash erased many of Bill's memories, but he remembers the medal. He remembers that he won.

After his accident, when Bill was asked if he knew what the medal was for, he said it meant that he was the best for one day. He was.

The world will remember.

ABOUT THE AUTHOR

JENNIFER WOODLIEF has worked as a reporter for *Sports Illustrated*, as well as an assistant district attorney and a case officer for the CIA. She lives in Tiburon, California, with her husband and children Tess, Griffin, and Owen.